W9-APY-957

MAN AND SOCIALISM IN CUBA

MAN AND SOCIALISM IN CUBA

THE GREAT DEBATE

EDITED AND
WITH AN INTRODUCTION BY

Bertram Silverman

NEW YORK

ATHENEUM

1971

Library of Congress catalog card number 71–139327
Published simultaneously in Canada by McClelland and Stewart Ltd.
Manufactured in the United States of America by
Kingsport Press, Inc., Kingsport, Tennessee
Designed by Kathleen Carey
First Edition

For Evie, Julie, and Devi

Preface

Some historic events bear the characteristics of farce, others of melodrama, while certain occurrences suggest absurdity—that is, irrationality. Marx, for example, stamped the image of farce on the advent of the second Bonaparte.* I think it appropriate to apply the drama metaphor to historic events that reflect the unfolding of complex social and economic forces that characterize an age. In this sense the Cuban revolution is true drama.** But are there elements of tragedy?

The scenario is all there: The heroic figures of Che and Fidel engulfed in a noble and uplifting purpose, yet confronting complex social forces which divert their intentions. Che's fate is known. But the struggle between revolutionary will and the power of circumstances is an ongoing dialectic of the Cuban revolution.

The drama is played over and over in the Cuban's daily experiences. I recall one Cuban friend in particular whose roots are deeply imbedded in the revolutionary process. Just ten years ago he would have thought absurd the suggestion that he would become a communist, yet today he is a *militante,* one of Cuba's new communists. His transformation was not without the emo-

* Karl Marx, *The Eighteenth Brumaire of Louis Bonaparte,* New World paperback, p. 15.

** A similar metaphor is used by James O'Connor, *The Origins of Socialism in Cuba,* Cornell University Press, p. 2.

tional scars that this process suggests. An extended family which formerly had been closely knit is now irrevocably divided.

I recall his passionate affirmation of the ethical principles of the revolution and the distinction he carefully drew between Cuban communism and the perverted varieties. He argued that Cuba's road to communism would leave behind the materialism and *egoismo* inherent in both Western capitalism and Soviet communism. It was this ethical commitment that had held him together psychologically and made his world reasonable and his sacrifices worthwhile. I am convinced that he was unconscious of the ideological nature of his argument. Yet he was uncertain. He knew too well the problems of bureaucracy, of *amigoismo,* and the inefficiency which was destroying confidence.

But ideology is no substitute for critical analysis. An understanding of the constraints on social policy and, therefore, the real possibilities for rational action can be found only in the real world that comes "from real active men on the basis of their real life process." * Unfortunately the revolutionary offensive that began in March 1968 has undermined such analysis. Self-serving ideology has too frequently been substituted for critical study. This relatively recent tendency is a break with the tradition of the Cuban revolution. Some of the tragic consequences are now more openly revealed.

It was precisely my interest in Cuban debates over social policy—what Ernest Mandel ** called "The Great Economic Debate"—that led me to the articles in this book. The controversy that unfolded during the period 1962–65 revealed the leadership's willingness to openly confront fundamental problems of Cuban socialism. But the issues raised in the debate transcend the Cuban context. The discussion provides an opportunity to examine the rationality of ethical goals, to explore the relationship between the goals of a communist society and the institutional problems of economic controls, planning, bureauc-

* Karl Marx and Frederick Engels, *The German Ideology,* Progress Publishers, Moscow, p. 37.

** Ernest Mandel, "Le grand débat économique," *Partisans,* April–June, 1967.

racy and incentives. Indeed, flashing throughout the argument is the vision of Marxist humanism . . . the creation of the authentic man. But creeping in are the images of Robert Michels' "iron law of oligarchy" and Max Weber's rational bureaucracy. The final outcome of the debate will be significant not only for Cuba but for the future of socialism.

Of particular current interest is the opportunity to see how Che Guevara, the leading spokesman for moral incentives, defended his position against his adversaries. Some readers may find to their surprise that Che linked moral incentives with a highly centralized form of economic organization. Moreover, when Che's defense is compared with his opponent's position, it becomes apparent that reason alone was not the major determinant that led Cuba down its current path.

The economic crisis through which Cuba is now passing has reopened the major issues of the debate. While the major journals that carried the articles in the debate have ceased publication and open polemics have ended, discussions have continued at the highest reaches of power. But this has little to do with real participation in decision-making and the constructive reevaluation of experience. The absence of such a dialogue in recent years is certainly one of the causes of serious policy errors. The comment of Alberto Mora [page 334], one of the participants in the debate, is becoming increasingly relevant: "we must at the same time assure that the superstructure is so organized as to prevent the substitution of the money motive by the power motive." Thus I hope the publication of the debate will prove useful inside Cuba as well as outside.

The reader unfamiliar with the Cuban experience should be forewarned about the style and language employed in many of the articles included here. The debate drew on the rhetoric and concepts of formal Marxist analysis. In this sense it drastically distorts the Cuban style which has strongly resisted developing a manualistic Marxism. For the student of contemporary communist movements this is one of the most refreshing and original aspects of the Cuban revolution. The reception that Professor Leontief, a well known Harvard economist, received while in

Cuba attests to their willingness to draw upon scientific analysis no matter where it originates.

How then can one account for the style of many of the articles in the debate? In the first place it was not the "new" communists such as Guevara who determined the format of the discussion. The initiative was taken by the leaders of the old communist party of Cuba (*Partido Popular Socialista*) as well as European, East European, and Soviet Marxists. Second, during the so-called phase of sectarianism, 1960–62, members of the old communist party assumed important administrative positions partly because of their organizational experience and more sophisticated ideology. As a result, a knowledge of the fundamentals of Marxism-Leninism became the litmus test for holding positions of responsibility. Finally, many of the "new" communists wished to show their own competence in Marxist theory in order to legitimize their own arguments. But, despite the stylistic difficulties, considerable rewards await the reader who is not deferred from digging deeply into the issues of the controversy.

Most of the published articles of the debate have been reproduced in this volume.* A few have been omitted because they did not add significantly to the arguments.** Fidel Castro's speech of July 26, 1968, is included as an epilogue to show his adoption of Che's position on moral incentives. My introductory chapter attempts to place the debate within an historical context and to explore its current relevance to Cuba.

I have incurred many debts while putting this book together. My Cuban friends first brought the debate to my attention and

* In addition to the sources noted here, many of the articles were reproduced in other Cuban journals as well.

** See for example: Mario Rodríguez Escalona, "La concepción general de las finanzas en la historia y el sistema presupuestario de financiamiento en el Periódo de Transición," *Nuestra Industria Revista Económica* (December 1964), 13–40; Marcelo Fernández Font, "Planificación y control de la circulación monetaria," *Cuba Socialista* (May 1964), 79–97; Luis Alvarez Rom, "El contenido político y económico del presupuesto estatal," *Trimestre Finanzas al Dia* (May–June, 1963), 31–39.

increased my awareness of the problems suggested. Stuart Borden, a former student, took on the burden of translating all but two of the articles.* Despite multiple pressures he performed his task with insight and empathy. Special thanks to Marcel Tenenbaum, a colleague and friend, for his general interest and critical concern for logical consistency. The Ford Foundation and Yale University provided the financial assistance that made the Cuban research possible. In particular, I wish to thank Nita Manitzas, Kalman Silvert, Anthony Maingot and Carlos Diaz-Alejandro for their commitment and understanding. Finally, my wife Evelyn and daughters Julie and Devorah intimately shared and will always remember our Cuban experience.

New York City
September 1970

* "Man and Socialism in Cuba," by Ernesto Che Guevara, and "To Create Wealth with Social Conscience," by Fidel Castro, are official Cuban translations.

Contents

MAN AND SOCIALISM IN CUBA

INTRODUCTION

The Great Debate in Retrospect: Economic Rationality and the Ethics of Revolution

BERTRAM SILVERMAN

DESPITE THE BEST INTENTIONS, all revolutions must confront the power of circumstances. In the unfolding drama of the Cuban revolution, Fidel Castro recognized this reality when he remarked how much simpler it was to destroy the old order than to create a new society. As Marx clearly recognized, "Men make their own history, but they do not make it just as they please; they do not make it under circumstances chosen by themselves, but under circumstances directly encountered, given, and transmitted from the past." [1] The Great Debate that developed during the period 1962–65 reflected this encounter with the "reality principle"; the advocates of "revolutionary ethics" confronted the supporters of economic rationality.

The "Economists" [2] argued that the level of economic and cultural development placed significant constraints on the transformation of economic and social institutions. They also felt that socialist morality could not be imposed through education, but was a product of economic necessity. Charles Bettelheim, the French Marxist supporter of the "Economists," wrote [page 32]:

> . . . in theory, the behavior of men—both as they relate to each other and as they function in their respective roles—should not be analyzed according to *appearances.* This would imply that altering such appearances, especially through education, would alter behavior itself; this is an idealistic outlook. Rather, behavior should be viewed as a consequence of the actual introduction of men into the technical and social division of labor and into a given process of production and reproduction (which also reproduces, progressively changing man's needs), the process itself being determined by the level of development of the productive forces. An analysis of this type brings one to understand, especially, that the decisive factor in changing man's behavior lies in the changes rendered to production and its organization. Education has as its principal mission the eradication of inherited attitudes and patterns of behavior, and the teaching of new standards of conduct imposed by the development of the productive forces.

Since the "Economists" were particularly concerned with the problem of inefficiency, they placed greater emphasis on economic constraints.

But what are the limits of socialist transformation? The revolutionary demands an answer. During the struggle that toppled the old order he had been constantly accused of naive romanticism. Had not the triumph of the revolutionary struggle demonstrated the tenuous nature of the "Economists'" argument? Revolutionary will had defeated the "superior forces" of the old order. If "real" socialism was not on the agenda in Cuba, this was tantamount to admitting that the Cuban revolution was at best an accident or at worst irrational.

Revolutionaries such as Che Guevara were more willing to risk the problems of economic inefficiency in order to create institutions more consistent with socialist conscience. The "Economists," on the other hand, argued that markets, mercantile and financial relationships, profit criteria, and material incentives were necessary if economic efficiency was to be fostered. Thus the underlying central theme of the Great Debate was: How rapidly can an underdeveloped nation implement communist institutions and values?

The Ideological Roots of the Ethics of Conscience

To Che Guevara, fostering a capitalist ethos raised doubts about the legitimacy of socialism in an underdeveloped country. His commitment to socialist humanism was expressed in an interview in 1963.

> I am not interested in dry economic socialism. We are fighting against misery, but we are also fighting against alienation. One of the fundamental objectives of Marxism is to remove interest, the factor of individual interest, and gain from men's psychological motivations. Marx was preoccupied both with economic factors and with their repercussions on the spirit. If communism isn't interested in this, too, it may be a method of distributing goods, but it will never be a revolutionary way of life.[3]

The "ethics of conscience"[4] reflected in Guevara's position have deep roots in the Cuban revolution.[5] Cuba's is the first socialist revolution whose leadership, party, and ideology were both noncommunist and non-Marxist. The social roots of the 26th of July Movement—the Cuban revolutionary party—lie in the breakdown of modern neocolonialism rather than in the socialist reaction to industrial capitalism in Europe. Virtually every Cuban leader stressed the nationalist element of the rebellion. Student leaders with whom I spoke expressed this roughly as follows:

> There were only a few communists who participated in the student movement during the last year. They were not significant. We did not spend any time arguing about Marxist ideology. Our position was very broad and in the long historical tradition of Latin American nationalism. We, of course, may have been less Marxist and thus less revolutionary in ideology, but we were more radical in action.[6]

The two central themes that held this broad movement together were *national independence* from the United States and *social justice*. Social justice was closely connected to national independence since national dependency had created the rural poverty and the corrupt political system. The Batista regime was just another recurrent characteristic since the War of Independence of 1895—political corruption and moral decay. Thus, unlike Lenin who turned to Marx for political insight, Fidel Castro looked to José Martí.

The leadership of the Movement, indeed most of the active rank and file who, incidentally, were mainly from the middle sector, shared a common revulsion against the economic, political, and social immorality that the position of national dependency had imposed. The leadership was young, almost all under thirty; many were university-educated and many had religious backgrounds. Fidel Castro was educated in a Jesuit school through high school, and he has spoken of his participation in politics as a "calling." The Cuban leaders were a counterpart to our New Left. But their rejection of middle-class politics was more deeply rooted in Cuban nationalism.

To this strong moral imperative must be added the importance of the guerrilla struggle. When the rebellion triumphed, the membership of the 26th of July Movement was approximately twenty-four thousand, whereas the guerrillas fighting in the mountains numbered only about one thousand. True, at the end they had the sympathy of the majority of the population. Yet, the leadership could proclaim: "Man can make history." The moral element in conjunction with the leadership's sense of making history has played an important role in the ethics of the Cuban revolution.

The Investment in Social Conscience

During the first two years of the revolution (1959–61), Cuba moved rapidly to implement its commitment to national independence and social justice, and the vigor with which it pursued these policies seemed to defy economic laws. Events appear to corroborate the leadership's perception that they could virtually make their own history. Between 1959 and 1961, Cuba had first, during the redistribution phase, nationalized the large privately owned landholdings through agrarian reforms; second, during the anti-imperialist period (1960–61), nationalized the major industries and financial institutions; third, in 1961, with the beginning of the socialist phase, established the following: (1) planning as the method of economic direction; (2) control over external and internal trade; (3) a policy of industrialization with the use of budgetary deficits; and (4) the creation of state farms (*granjas del pueblo*). Furthermore, this transformation was made with the support of the majority of the population.[7]

Cuba was able to mobilize support for its policies through a radical redistribution of income and because of strong nationalist feelings stimulated by the external threat of United States intervention. It has been estimated that real income during this period may have risen by 20 per cent.[8] Moreover, the symbols of privilege were destroyed: The private beaches and clubs were opened to the public; the integration of rural Cuba into the nation began; social services were opened in the country; a massive literacy campaign brought hundreds of thousands of city youths to remote regions of the island. These efforts fostered the commitment of the rural and urban working class to the Revolution.

How was this extraordinary growth of real income possible? The Revolution had available a large potential of unutilized or underutilized resources. The rate of unemployment in 1958 was officially estimated at 17 per cent of the labor force.[9] Prior to the Revolution, large tracts of land were kept idle—set aside for speculative purposes until the price of sugar rose. Furthermore, the Revolution had eliminated a great deal of waste and corruption in government, and it had inherited a large international reserve fund and domestic inventory that could be drawn upon.

Some observers have argued that the increased utilization of these resources for social-welfare purposes was irrational.[10] Resources that could have been used for economic development were "lost" as a result of the lofty idealism of the leadership. But investment in national commitment—in nation-building—is clearly an essential prerequisite for economic development. *Indeed, the development of social consciousness may be critical if economic development is to proceed without serious repression.* This phase, 1959–61, set the foundation for the development of what Carlos Rafael Rodriguez called the country's most precious resource—social conscience.[11]

Yet, this period of "euphoria" did create serious illusions about the process of economic development and fostered the idea that rapid social and economic development can be painless. In August 1961, Boti predicted that Cuban growth would be so rapid that in ten years Cuban living standards would be comparable to those of any European country.[12] Cuban economic development demonstrates that planning models do not ensure growth—nor is capital formation a sufficient condition. Economic development is more than economic engineering, and social organization is a limiting factor. This became increasingly evident as Cuba entered the phase of declining productivity.

Declining Productivity and Moral Incentives

Instead of increasing, Cuban national output declined between 1962 and 1963, and worker productivity may have declined by as much as 30 per cent between 1962 and 1965.[13] Man, after all, was still not omnipotent. Yet, declining productivity may be an inevitable phase of socialist development in an underdeveloped society. Cuba had rapidly transformed her important economic institutions; in human terms, this meant that individuals without previous experience, technical knowhow, or reliable information were directing an economic system. Also contributing to the decline in output was the shift in government policy away from agricultural production, particularly of sugar, and toward industrial development. This industrialization increased Cuba's dependence on imported raw materials and spare parts at a time when export earnings were sharply reduced. Production bottlenecks arose with greater frequency.

Problems soon emerged. First, a serious supply problem led to rationing in 1962. Second, shortages increased the political and economic resistance of the peasants, which in turn led to the Second Agrarian Reform that nationalized all landholdings above 165 acres in 1963. Third, labor shortages developed that required an increased reliance on voluntary work to meet agricultural manpower needs. Fourth, the growth of bureaucracy in the public sector led to the breakdown of responsibility. As a result, the economy seemed to be running *por la libre,* that is, without effective control.[14] The first response to these problems was an abrupt revision of Cuba's developmental strategy—a return to agriculture and sugar as the turnpike to development.[15]

I should stress that these problems were greatly exacerbated by the United States blockade and embargo that virtually required the country to depend on new sources of supply from communist countries at a time when virtually all of Cuba's capital equipment had been made in the United States. Moreover, counterrevolutionary activity and United States aggression meant that both scarce resources and talent had to be used for military purposes.[16]

While these external factors created serious difficulties, some Cuban leaders and foreign advisers began to argue that Cuba's economic difficulties were rooted in Cuban socialism. Out of this controversy, the Great Debate was born. The participants included most of the members of the Council of Ministers. Although formal polemics did not begin until 1963, many of the issues raised in the Debate can be found as early as 1960 in some of the critical observations of René Dumont, French agricultural economist. He attributed the breakdown of coordination, bureaucracy, and irrational resource utilization to overzealous nationalization and centralization. At this time, under Che Guevara's direction, the industrial sector moved rapidly toward central direction and control.[17] This system of central direction became officially known as central budgeting. Initially, as a result of nationalization, abandonment of enterprises and shortages of administrators, central control was a necessary expedient. However, a more decentralized form of organization developed in agriculture that became known as the "system of self-finance."[18] It was given official sanction in 1962 by the director of agriculture, Carlos Rafael Rodriguez, and was also adopted by the Foreign Trade Ministry directed by Alberto Mora.

In a more profound sense, these systems of economic organization represented alternative routes to communism. In order to understand the essential arguments that divided the "economist" and "revolutionary," it is necessary to understand the differences between the two systems.[19]

Theoretically, under the system of self-finance (decentralization), enterprises are legally (juridically) independent. They trade their products with different enterprises through a market; therefore, their output acquires the character of commodities.[20] Their success is determined by their profitability. Although each has considerable financial independence, they have to cover their current expenses through the banks that provide them with credit. (Interest is charged.) Thus, the banks play a critical role in evaluating and controlling the enterprise. (Interestingly, Marcelo Fernández Font, then the director of the Central Bank, supported the system of self-finance.) The central agencies (Treasury, Planning) set only aggregate limits under this system. Finally, labor income is based primarily on material incentives.

Under the system of central budgeting, enterprises are more seriously circumscribed and controlled by the national plan. Each firm is considered a part of a larger productive unit—the public sector as a whole. Therefore, the movement of products from one enterprise to another is considered an intermediary process. The products, then, acquire the characteristics of commodities only when they leave the socialized sector and are sold in the market. Profitability plays no role in the evaluation of the enterprise, and all net income is deposited with the Treasury, which centrally allocates funds to various enterprises. Each enterprise is directed by the central plan and, as its function, fulfills the targets set by the plan. Rigorous financial control is established through a central organization, Empresas Consolidades, which coordinates the accounts of enterprises in a particular sector (e.g., textiles). Finally, conscience rather than material incentives is emphasized as the prime form of motivation. Thus, in the system of central budgeting, the "administration of things" [21] provided greater possibility for eliminating mercantile and economic incentives. In 1963, when the argument reached the light of day, there existed in Cuba two systems of economic organization and ideology: one regulating agriculture and foreign trade, the other, industry. A confrontation was inevitable.[22]

Man and Socialism: Means and Ends

All the participants supported the proposition that economic institutions and economic goals must conform to the necessities of objective economic forces. As Ernest Mandel wrote, "For those who ignore this at times, Lady Dialectic continues to be the heartless *Bella Dama*" [page 92]. But the protagonists disagreed about the nature of the economic laws that regulated Cuban socialist development. Thus, the Great Debate began with a controversy over whether the law of value operated in the Cuban economy.

In June 1963, Alberto Mora criticized "some comrades" for suggesting that the law of value did not function in the public sector. For the uninitiated, in Marxian theory the law of value provided an explanation of the underlying forces that determined the relative prices of commodities. As long as social needs outstripped society's capacity to satisfy them, a system must be established to regulate the quantity of each of the goods produced—that is, the distribution of labor (socially necessary labor time) both present and past (capital) to various productive activities. Prior to the advent of capitalism, this problem was solved *primarily* by tradition and custom. With the development of the social division of labor and the private ownership of the means of production, economic needs were increasingly satisfied through exchange—the production of commodities. The stage of commodity production reached its highest form under the capitalist mode of production. During this period, the law of value regulated the distribution of labor time between the various branches of production necessary to satisfy the aggregate demand for goods and services.[23] This was accomplished by the capitalist's pursuit of profits—investing labor and capital in industries whose rates of return were greater than the average and disinvesting in those with less than average rates of return. Thus, the law of value revealed how the invisible hand of the market solved the problem of relative scarcity, as well as the role of class relations in the solution of this fundamental economic problem.

We are now in a better position to understand the significance of the law of value to the Great Debate. If the law of value operated extensively in Cuba, that is, if Cuba was still in the stage of commodity production, then the market and mercantile relationships would have to play an important role in the Cuban economy. Thus, the system of self-financing rather than central budgeting would be the more appropriate institutional form. Mora did not negate the importance of planning; he argued that the law of value must operate through the plan. Since commodity production did exist in the public sector, planners like engineers could not ignore its laws; they could only use them more rationally.

Guevara did not deny the existence of the law of value. However, he questioned its usefulness as a guide for policy and denied its existence in the public sector. If economic development is to be achieved and social justice pursued, isn't interference with the law of value necessary? Once the law of value is distorted through planning, how can you ever determine what it is? Indeed, the socialization of the means of production makes planning inevitable and thus eliminates both the inefficiency associated with the anarchy of production as well as the ethics of the marketplace. Moreover, Guevara argued that individual enterprises in the public sector were part of one big enterprise and therefore (as we have noted) did not produce commodities but merely intermediary inputs in the fabrication of a final product. This transaction is similar to the transfer of products from one plant to another within a large corporation such as General Motors. While strict cost accounting is necessary, this has nothing to do with the law of value. Therefore, commodity production exists only in the transfer of goods from the public to the consumers, in transactions between the public sector and the remaining private sector, and, most important, in international trade.

The rejection of the law of value meant that production must be regulated centrally through the planning system. Therefore, Guevara's approach implied a more complex and sophisticated level of administrative and organizational development than that suggested by the advocates of auto-finance. Guevara understood that the ethics of communism as opposed to the ethics of the market ("control by the peso") could only be realized under a highly organized system of administration. Yet he never fully analyzed the implication of such a system of direction on the development of communist morality. But the connection between the mode of control and social conscience cannot be neglected. I will return to this subject in another context [page 21].

The debate was broadened when Charles Bettelheim entered the discussion in April 1964 [page 31]. In opposition to Guevara, Bettelheim, a French Marxist and Cuban economic adviser, argued that economic organizations were aspects of man's relationship to production and could never be "higher" than society's level of technology and skills (the forces of production). Juridical (legal) organizational forms reflected the political and ideological structure of society. However, effective economic organization must conform to the economic structure of society. Thus, administrative inefficiency, bureaucracy, loss of control, erupted when "legal power" and "effective capacity" did not coincide because "the legal entity is not a true economic entity" [page 41]. Objectively, the law of value did operate in the public sector, and attempts to obscure this phenomenon through juridical means could only lead to inefficiency and to the breakdown of planning. Thus, Bettelheim's approach strongly supported the system of auto-finance and a more conservative policy regarding additional socialization.

Bettelheim's "orthodoxy" was subjected to a methodological criticism by Ernest Mandel [page 60], a well-known Belgian Marxist. First, Mandel contended Bettelheim's concepts were too abstract for an adequate interpretation of the richness and complexity of Cuban reality. The economic problems Cuba encountered during the transitional phase cannot be explained nor fruitfully interpreted by using general concepts such as forces of production and relations of production that apply only on a broad historical time scale. Indeed, during the transitional phase, the struggle of the new society with the old institutions and values will create innumerable problems. It is impossible to know during this period whether the productive forces correspond to the relationships to production. Second, Bettelheim neglected the qualitative changes brought about by a socialist revolution. Changes in property ownership do matter; the social revolution makes planning possible. Complete control of the means of production down to the last nail was not necessary. Any other conclusion places doubt on the success of every socialist revolution in an underdeveloped country. Third, the survival of mercantile categories (money, wages) is not due to the disparity between the forces and relationship to production, which would require greater decentralization of decision-making in the public sector. Knowing "to what degree minor decision-making must be centralized or decentralized . . . is merely a problem of organization and not 'proof' of the mercantile nature of the means of production during the period of transition" [page 80]. The survival of mercantile categories is due to the inadequate development of the forces of production "to ensure the distribution of consumer goods according to need" [page 71]. Thus, Mandel warned that abolishing the private ownership of labor power before these needs can be satisfied would only lead to forced labor.[24]

Mandel supported Guevara's position on the law of value. Using the law of value would subject the economy to anarchy of production and condemn Cuba to underdevelopment. In addition, Mandel argued that the law of value could not operate in the socialized producer-goods sector since overproduction could never occur. Unlike consumer goods, in the producer-goods sector, overproduction simply meant a higher rate of growth (expanded reproduction).[25]

Guevara's response to Bettelheim was more political [page 98]. Cuba had made a socialist revolution in a country where all the objective conditions did not exist. Did this mean the Cuban revolution was premature or irrational? On the contrary, a revolutionary vanguard was able to break through these limitations [page 102].

> The vanguard of the revolutionary movement, increasingly influenced by Marxist-Leninist ideology, is capable of consciously anticipating the steps to be taken in order to force the pace of events, but forcing it within what is objectively possible. We strongly stress this point because it is one of the principal defects in Bettelheim's argument.

The Cuban Revolution is an example that mechanical explanations of economic forces are false. The development of socialist consciousness viewed on a worldwide scale can transform the forces of production. Certainly contradictions will exist down to the level of the smallest unit of production, but revolutionary conscience can overcome them. But [page 107]:

> Why think that everything that happens in the period of transition is inevitable? Why think that the setbacks dealt by reality to certain bold acts stem exclusively from *boldness* rather than—perhaps entirely—from technical deficiencies in administration?

Thus, Guevara revealed his ultimate aim: to consciously use the process of socialist economic development as a force to create a new morality. As he argued, hidden behind the formal arguments was the issue of moral versus economic incentives [page 134].

For advocates of financial self-management, the use of direct material incentives throughout the various stages of building communism does not contradict the "development" of consciousness. But for us it does. It is for this reason that we struggle against the predominance of material incentives—because they would retard the development of socialist morality.

Yet, Guevara was realistic about the development of moral incentives. He did not deny the need for material incentives, but he rejected their use as the primary force. Guevara thus recognized the need for wage differentials, bonuses, and penalties for fulfillment and underfulfillment of norms. But he believed the development of socialist consciousness can help production more than a reliance on material stimulus. More fundamental, Guevara questioned the idea of basing socialist institutions mainly on material interest. To ensure the creation of the new society, the building of socialist consciousness must begin immediately.

Moral Incentives and Economic Necessity

The Great Debate officially ended in 1965. Our discussion has touched only briefly on some of the major issues. The reader may judge for himself the merits of the various positions. At the time of the Debate Fidel Castro's position was ambiguous. He was not committed to either position. Lack of interest in the abstract issues and political consideration probably kept him out of the Debate. Yet in 1965 he seemed to display impatience with the controversy when he argued, "Our obligations as revolutionaries are not to theorize in the field of philosophy." Moreover, in the same speech, his support of material incentives seemed to suggest opposition to Guevara.[26]

It is not clear why the formal debate ended abruptly in 1965. The crucial problems that were discussed remained unresolved. Perhaps Castro felt that the time was not opportune to air these questions publicly in the face of grave economic problems. Moreover, Guevara's radicalism—his willingness to direct the Debate into extremely sensitive subjects—may have also played a role.

In a speech in Algeria, he questioned the ethical implications of applying the law of value to trade relations between the Soviet Union and underdeveloped countries. The unbridled use of the law of value would simply reinforce underdevelopment. Furthermore, Figueras, a vice-minister in Guevara's Ministry of Industry, published two articles that raised questions about the renewed emphasis on agriculture.

There is evidence that before leaving Cuba Guevara felt that he had not been persuasive.[27] Nevertheless, in 1966 a decision to move more radically toward a system of moral incentives is taken. Castro not only adopts Guevara's ideas but carries them forward beyond what one would have predicted from the arguments of his former comrade. In July 1968, Castro stated:

> We should not use money or wealth to create political awareness. We must use political awareness to create wealth. To offer a man more to do more than his duty is to buy his conscience with money. To give a man participation in more collective wealth because he does his duty and produces more and creates more for society is to turn political awareness into wealth . . .
>
> The road is not easy. The task is difficult, and many will criticize us. They will call us petty bourgeois, idealists; they will say we are dreamers; they will say we are bound to fail. And yet, facts will speak for us, realities will speak for us, and our people will speak and act for us because we know our people have the capacity to comprehend these roads and to follow these roads.[28]

By 1968 Cuba had moved decisively toward developing an economy based on noneconomic incentives. The bureaucratic system of socialist emulation as well as competition between workers for material rewards were greatly modified. Instead, work centers began to set their own goals rather than complying with detailed standards established from above. Selection of vanguard workers was replaced by a new form of mass organization—The Advanced Workers Movement—whose aim was to create a more effective worker's organization at the plant level. In some work centers, this organization had already replaced the trade union*. The rewards were now flags representing significant events in Cuban history, thus linking achievement to national awareness. Moreover, economic penalties for infractions of labor discipline such as absenteeism were greatly modified. The growing importance of social consumption (in particular, social services and education as a percentage of income), rationing, the elimination of piece rates and bonuses, the trend toward narrowing wage differentials, all increased the movement to greater social and economic equality. Finally, Cuba had virtually eliminated all vestiges of the market as a mechanism for allocating factors of production as well as goods and services. All mercantile transactions, credit, and money between enterprises in the public sector had been eliminated, and profit was no longer the criterion for evaluating economic performance.

What caused this shift in policy? Economic necessities emerged that reinforced the revolutionary ethics of the leadership.

First, at the end of 1963, Cuba revised its economic-development strategy, reverting to agriculture and sugar production as its primary growth sector. Capital formation would be induced through the export sector. However, the initial income policy of the government had set in motion a large migration of labor from rural to urban employment, that is, from agriculture to the industrial and service sectors. Between 1962 and 1965 the percentage of the labor force employed in agriculture dropped from 38 to 32 per cent.[29] The reduction in the number and productivity of the traditional cane cutter—a seasonal worker—was particularly troublesome. Thus, the rural poor were either moving to the higher income centers of towns or taking part of their increased income and economic security in additional leisure.

As a result, Cuba was faced with a decline in agricultural labor at a time when extensive growth of this sector was planned. Reversing rural-urban migration through a program of resettlement made little sense because economic plans called for a

* The trade unions were reorganized in 1970, and given renewed emphasis.

technological revolution in agriculture that would shortly reduce agricultural labor requirements.[30] The leadership understood that technology was the ultimate solution to this problem.

Therefore, the short-run solution required the redeployment of urban labor to agriculture, particularly during planting and harvesting. The type of labor required was the most menial and unskilled. Material incentives would have had to be unusually high to induce urban labor into these occupations. Moreover, the use of wage differentials made little sense because the transfer was frequently of workers from more skilled and productive activities to less skilled, that is, from industry to agriculture.

Under such circumstances, reliance on unpaid voluntary labor is logical.[31] Since 1962 Cuba had increasingly relied on this method to mobilize labor for agriculture. In 1968 perhaps from 15 to 20 per cent of the agricultural labor force was made up of nonagricultural labor.[32] Such a transfer of labor could only make economic sense if it was based on moral rather than material incentives. Cuba's investment in social conscience could be tapped.

Coming now to the second factor, which explains the shift to moral incentives, the sharp decline in consumer goods and the system of rationing made the reliance on material incentives politically dangerous. An emphasis on material incentives during a period when workers were asked to increase hours worked and to reduce their consumption would merely heighten the sense of economic sacrifice. An emphasis on collective efforts toward social goals was more reasonable both politically and economically. Minister of Labor Risquet stressed this point in a conversation by saying:

> How can Cuba emphasize material incentives at a time of serious shortages and economic sacrifices when 90 miles away such goals can be more easily fulfilled? We simply would be creating conditions for the mass migration of Cubans to the United States.[33]

Moreover, like Che, he stressed the problem of United States aggression. A country faced with a constant threat of invasion must develop social commitment rather than a consumptionist orientation which is easily subverted.

A third factor in the shift to moral incentives, and perhaps the most important, is capital accumulation. Cuba's economic plans required a large increase in the rate of investment. In 1968 investment represented an unprecedented 31 per cent of national income.[34] What sources for capital accumulation exist when low consumption levels make impossible further reductions either through taxation or cuts in rations? Cuba seemed to be in a stage where a process of primitive accumulation—a phase of early capitalist development where force was used to create an economic surplus—could be applied. In the Soviet Union during a comparable period, the problem was ultimately resolved through the forced collectivization of agriculture. But such a policy made little sense in Cuba, where additional socialization would alienate the small peasant and would add little to the rate of investment.

Of course, the process of accumulation can be accelerated by increasing the amount of unpaid labor made available by the labor force. This may indeed, if it is voluntary, be a more consistent translation of Marx's idea of primitive accumulation when applied to a socialist society than the route used in the Soviet Union. In my opinion, this is the fundamental rationale behind the movement to increase the hours of overtime worked without pay, behind the creation of revolutionary work brigades and the great use of unpaid students and women in agriculture. Were moral incentives to fail, the ominous necessity of using coercion to produce the economic surplus would have to be faced. This is the reason for my earlier statement that the commitment of a large segment of the population to the Revolution had reduced the necessity for force to achieve its economic goals. But conscience is also a scarce resource, and failure to use it efficiently may be one of Cuba's fundamental problems.

Finally, the shift to moral incentives was also influenced by the unfolding of political and ideological problems that reflected the economic difficulties Cuba was experiencing. Economic scarcity of labor and goods placed the bureaucracy in a position of privilege. To leaders like Fidel, corruption in government represented the most serious violation of revolutionary ethics. Fidel Castro's own early involvement in politics can be traced to this issue. Yet, conditions of scarcity do create propensities toward using privilege for private advantage. In 1965 and 1966 exposure of corruption within the highest levels of government and the trade unions provided the initial stimulus for Fidel Castro's attacks on money incentives and vulgar materialism. Moreover, economic scarcity had created a thriving illegal trade within the private sector that seemed to subvert the regime's increasing emphasis on moral incentives. The private sector which still existed in retail trade and small-scale consumer industry gradually expanded so that it was not only supplying the growing black market but also illegally providing goods for the public sector and competing successfully for skilled labor. The nationalization of the remaining private enterprise in trade and industry in 1968 [35] clearly demonstrated Cuba's commitment to the goals of moral incentives. Yet, the spontaneous growth of the private sector merely reflected the existence of countervailing forces that subverted the policies of the government.

The Cost of Social Conscience: Lessons from the Debate

In the Great Debate, the supporters of material incentives had warned that policies cannot be fashioned under the illusion of free will. What are the social forces that undermined the development of social conscience? In a system based on material incentives, the relation of individual economic performance to the national goal of economic growth is clear to the individual worker: The greater his performance, the greater the national growth, and also the greater his material reward. But in a system of moral incentives which eliminates this direct connection between individual performance and reward, the individual's motivation for increasing his economic performance must come from a heightened identification with the goals of the nation (internalization of the social goals of the community).[36] Revolutionary commitment does not by itself ensure the rational and efficient utilization of resources. Economic controls through a system of planning must serve as a substitute for the market and economic incentives, for unless national output and efficiency increases, a cynical attitude may develop that undermines the worker's identification with the system—the essential ingredient of social conscience.

Yet, effective planning and economic controls are particularly weak in Cuba.[37] The virtual elimination of financial controls having increased reliance on record-keeping and centralized decision-making, planning depends heavily on accurate information and on managers capable of translating this information into rational decisions. But managers make little use of the data they collect and frequently know little about the financial operation of their enterprise. Success is frequently measured simply by fulfillment of gross-output targets expressed in physical terms and by the conservation of scarce raw materials. The fragile planning system is further undermined by "overcommitment" of resources and the uncertainty of foreign supplies. The inevitable has occurred: First, shortages and bottlenecks have reduced industrial capacity and worker productivity; second, the decision-making process has been plagued by bureaucracy, so much so that a parallel planning apparatus that bypasses the existing bureaucratic structure has been created to ensure the fulfillment of urgent strategic economic goals (this special apparatus is under Fidel's personal direction); third, there has been a large turnover of managerial and administrative personnel.

To meet their output targets in spite of the system's inefficiencies, managers have frequently relied on the worker's conscience, that is, labor's willingness to work overtime without pay. Managers often consider this type of labor costless, and some were perplexed when I asked them if they had wasted conscience in fulfilling their goals. The same attitude is prevalent in agriculture: since no production unit assumes the cost of voluntary work, party leaders frequently demand more labor than they can use in order to guarantee results.

The lack of effective economic control is the most significant force undermining moral incentives. Cuba must begin to calculate the cost of conscience.[38] Thus, one of the central issues of the Great Debate arises again. Are these problems simply due to a shortage of cadres and trained administrators, or do they reflect a more profound contradiction between the "forces of production" and the "relation to production" as Charles Bettelheim has argued? Some top Cuban economists have indicated that there is a sense of loss of control over the economy; Cuban leaders are becoming aware of the need for more effective controls. And once again the advocates of decentralization are raising their voices in the private councils of government.

But the relation of economic controls to moral incentives is more subtle than I have indicated. Moral incentives, if they are truly the individual's incentives, cannot be directed from above. That is why many Cubans ask: "How can you plan voluntary work? Is this not a contradiction in terms?" What types of economic controls are compatible with a system of moral incentives? Recognition of this issue has emerged in two forms. First, an understanding that moral incentives are directly related to the level of education and the nature of one's employment; [39] this is reflected in Cuba's intensive educational effort, particularly in technical training. Second, experimentation with a new worker organization and system of emulation whose aim in part is to stimulate greater participation and eliminate bureaucratic controls. But worker participation is an exceedingly difficult process that itself is related to the level of education, cultural development, and the pressures of economic development. Cuba will provide evidence as to whether moral incentives are compatible with the process of economic development in emerging countries.

Shortages of consumer goods and rationing are also important forces that frustrate the intentions of the government. The market cannot be willed away, as many of the participants in the economic debate noted. Rationing does provide a more equitable distribution of subsistence goods than would exist under the market system, and many basic services are virtually free. In periods of shortages, however, the covert market emerges with greater intensity. When consumer goods are scarce, small differences assume great importance and create attitudes that reinforce the desire for material goods. Cuba has developed a second market where goods are traded at nonofficial prices that reflect real preferences. Considerable time and energy are devoted to participation in this market. In addition, the black market exists of course, although I was rather surprised at its limited significance.

The impact of shortages on moral incentives cannot be ignored. Those naive conceptions that see the decreasing significance of money as a step toward communism are an ideological distortion of the very real existence of consumer shortages. If the decline of money reflects a decline in real income, that is, shortage of consumer goods, its consequences may be a reduction in worker-participation rates and productivity, an increase in absenteeism, and the movement of labor away from difficult and unpleasant tasks. Moral incentives need to be reinforced by eliminating anxiety over basic needs, and this is done by raising living standards. Shortages merely tend to undermine the effectiveness of moral incentives and, therefore, worker productivity.

In the face of the countervailing forces, there is a natural tendency on the part of the government to increase its use of ideological instruments to develop a greater expression of social commitment. I think that this is the basis of the revolutionary offensive that began in March 1968 and that has virtually declared a moratorium on public debate over economic and social policies and has increased the importance of the party bureaucracy in all spheres of Cuban life. At this critical juncture such efforts are quite understandable; for the Cubans this is the equivalent of a wartime situation. Yet, such an approach is not without dangers to the psychological and philosophical basis of the moral-incentives system. A system of incentives that relies on political directives from above becomes just another form of repression, a point very well recognized by the Cuban leaders. But the dialectical relationship between coercion and the success of the moral incentives must not be obscured.

Nevertheless, the reliance on social conscience has already had a dramatic impact on the quality of Cuban economic development. Moral incentives have meant intensive reliance on educational and ideological techniques to raise the population's awareness of economic goals. In a relatively small country of eight million, this is possible. The most striking aspect of Cuba is the extent to which all strata of society are involved in the problems of economic development. The differences between town and country, between student, intellectual, and worker, are being eliminated. In the long run, this transformation of the social structure, in combination with the involvement of a large proportion of the population in economic development, may be the most significant impact of the Cuban Revolution.

The Cuban experiment has put to the test many assumptions of our economic models. Therefore, we must be careful not to impose our traditional conceptions on new realities. Perhaps the orientation of the foremost historian of the Russian revolution, E. H. Carr, is relevant; he writes:

> Progress in human affairs whether in science or in history or in society has come mainly through the bold readiness of human beings not to confine themselves to seeking piecemeal improvements in the way things are done, but to present fundamental challenges in the name of reason to the current way of doing things and to the avowed or hidden assumption on which it rests. I look forward to a time when the historians and sociologists and political thinkers of the English-speaking world will regain their courage for that task.[40]

The conflict between revolutionary ethics and economic rationality continues to play an important role in Cuban socialism. A good deal of the commitment to revolutionary ethics can be explained by economic necessity. Thus, within the context of their developmental strategy, the "ethics of revolution" is rational. Yet there is much that is irrational which tends to contradict the policies of the leadership. A more detailed analysis of the dialectics of revolutionary ethics and economic development is necessary in order to understand the dynamics of Cuban socialism.[41] By focusing on these issues, the Great Debate not only contributes to an understanding of Cuban socialism but also provides greater insight into the "laws of motion" of socialism.

NOTES

1. Karl Marx, *The Eighteenth Brumaire of Louis Bonaparte* in Lewis Fuer (ed.), *Marx and Engels,* Anchor paperback, 1959, p. 320. See Fidel Castro's speech July 26, 1967, in which he said, "the most difficult task was not the overthrow of Batista . . . [but] the one we are engaged in today: the task of constructing a new country on the basis of an underdeveloped economy."
2. I have adopted Lenin's term used in his *What Is to Be Done?*
3. Cited in Sergio de Santis, "The Economic Debate in Cuba," *International Socialist Review* (August 1965), 254.
4. For modern use of this concept, see Daniel Bell, *The End of Ideology,* Collier Books, 1961, pp. 279–281. For classical version see Gerth and Mills, eds., *From Max Weber,* Oxford University Press, 1946, pp. 115–116, 127–128.
5. The importance of Cuba's ideological predisposition to moral incentives was stressed by Regino Boti, former minister of economics, in a conversation in Cuba.
6. Based on conversations with student leaders of the 26th of July Movement in Cuba and New York.
7. See Maurice Zeitlin, *Revolutionary Politics and the Cuban Working Class,* Princeton University Press, 1967. The absence of significant resistance from the national bourgeoisie was another reason the Revolution was able to move so rapidly.
8. Dudley Seers (ed.), *Cuba: The Economic and Social Revolution,* University of North Carolina Press, 1964, p. 34.
9. Juceplan, Dirección Central de Estadisticas, *Resumen de Estadisticas de Población No. 2,* Havana, 1966, p. 119.
10. This criticism was also expressed in retrospect by Cuban officials.
11. Interview in Cuba, February 1969.
12. *Obra Revolucionaria,* No. 30, 1961; see also Seers, *op. cit.,* p. 47.
13. Interview in Cuba.
14. For an insider's view, see Edward Boorstein, *The Economic Transformation of Cuba,* Monthly Review Press, 1968.
15. Unpublished paper by David Barkin, "Agriculture, the Turnpike to Development in Cuba," delivered at Seminar on Cuba, New York University.
16. Of course the military perform many economic tasks, but many Cuban administrators have indicated that some of the best executive talent goes to the military.
17. The development of central controls was probably influenced most significantly by shortages of cadres and reliable local administrators.
18. This system of self-finance is also called auto-finance and economic calculus.

19. For a good description of the two systems on which my account is based see Sergio de Santis, *op. cit.*

20. For a discussion of the Marxian concept of commodities, see Karl Marx, *Capital,* Vol. I, Part I. See also page 10 of this article.

21. In the Marxian model, nonmaterial incentives can only be fully realized when relative scarcity disappears and economic activity is simply an administrative matter.

22. The more orthodox position (economist) was not only defended by members of the "old" Communist Party. Mora and Fernandez were from the Directorio Revolucionario and the 26th of July Movement respectively.

23. For an excellent discussion of this subject, see Paul Sweezy, *The Theory of Capitalist Development,* Monthly Review Press, 1968, esp. Chaps. 2, 3.

24. Mandel was arguing that a premature use of moral incentives rather than economic incentives can lead to forced labor. The increased reliance upon the armed forces in Cuba today may be an early symptom of this problem.

25. In the consumer goods sector, consumer demand can make certain commodities socially unnecessary. But in the capital sector, unplanned increases can always be employed to increase total output. This assumes a high degree of liquidity of capital and neglects the indirect relationship between final demand and capital.

26. See Fidel Castro's speech "Criterios de Nuestra Revolución," *Cuba Socialista,* September 1965. In this speech Castro reveals a pronounced long-term commitment to moral incentives that probably accounts for Gerassi's suggestion that Castro supported Che's position (see *Venceremos,* Clarion, 1968, p. 20). But Castro's pragmatic approach strongly suggested the need to use material incentives. In the same speech, he argued that it would be idealistic to assume that the large majority of workers cut cane from a sense of duty. Therefore, it is logical to give incentives for work that is most important. Thus, Mesa-Lago in his book *The Labor Sector and Socialist Distribution in Cuba* (Praeger, 1968, p. 124) suggests that Castro rejected Guevara's thesis.

27. A number of Cubans have indicated to me that Guevara sent a letter to Luis Alvarez Rom that suggested he had not been successful in his advocacy.

28. Fidel Castro, speech, July 26, 1968.

29. Juceplan, *op. cit.,* p. 120.

30. There have been some attempts at resettlement through revolutionary youth brigades.

31. Of course, not all transfer of labor to agriculture is voluntary. However, the element of coercion is reduced to the extent to which agricultural work is accepted as part of one's employment. For a recent analysis of unpaid labor, see Carmelo Mesa-Lago, "Economic Significance of Unpaid Labor in Socialist Cuba", *Industrial and Labor Relations Review,* April 1969.

32. More than 50 per cent of the labor force was working in agriculture in 1969. See *Granma,* April 1, 1969.

33. Interview, January 1969, Cuba.

34. Thus the shortages of consumer goods were largely planned in 1968 in contrast to the problems that developed in 1962.

35. "La Nacionalización de los Establecimientos Privados en la Ofen-

siva," monograph, *El Militante Comunista,* June 1968.

36. For a discussion of the concept of identification, see John Kenneth Galbraith, *The New Industrial State,* Houghton-Mifflin, 1967, Chap. XI.

37. Many Cubans I spoke with did not realize that Guevara was a strong advocate of economic controls.

38. There seems to be an increased awareness of this problem among administrators.

39. Cf. Fidel Castro, speech, March 19, 1969.

40. E. H. Carr, *What Is History?,* Knopf, 1962, p. 207.

41. For a more detailed analysis of this problem, see my forthcoming book *Labor and Revolution in Cuba,* Atheneum.

PART I

The Problems of Socialist Development: The Transition to Communism

1

On Socialist Planning and the Level of Development of the Productive Forces

CHARLES BETTELHEIM

THE FOLLOWING HAS ITS ORIGIN in a theoretical reflection on some of the problems currently faced by the Cuban economy. Since these problems are among those that invariably arise in every country building socialism, I thought that the publication of this work in its original form (with some small changes) might be of interest. Clearly, I have ignored many important questions concerning the building of socialism which are not immediately pertinent to the Cuban economy. Perhaps I will return to these in subsequent articles.

As will be seen, the specific historical conditions characterizing Cuba and the U.S.S.R. have been abstracted here, as have problems which, though not economic, should nevertheless be considered when formulating specific solutions.

The work focuses, then, on economic theory, which is an in-

Charles Bettelheim is a French Marxist economist. He has written extensively on the problem of economic development and economic planning. He was an adviser to Cuba during the early years of the revolution.

SOURCE: "Formas y métodos de planificación socialista y nivel de desarrollo de las fuerzas productivas." *Cuba Socialista,* Año IV, Abril 1964, pp. 51–78.

dispensable instrument for formulating rational solutions to economic problems. Obviously, however, it cannot provide answers to all the problems which actually arise in planning and organizing the socialist economy.

To resolve, as well as possible, the problems presently confronting the Cuban economy, it is necessary to submit them to theoretical analysis. Solely on the basis of such analysis can one determine the economic strategy and tactics corresponding to the exigencies of the current stage, while at the same time taking into account the precise characteristics of that stage, including the level of development of the productive forces. Moreover, such analysis is the only means by which to define the forms of organization and methods of work that are consistent with the adopted economic strategy and tactics.

Theoretical analysis is necessary both objectively and subjectively. It alone can provide the correct scientific focus needed to guide the actions of the revolutionary leaders, the political cadres, and the working masses themselves. A scientific approach is also required to help implement the general lines to be followed.

Furthermore, it should help to:

a. overcome indecision about substituting new methods of work and forms of organization for those to which one is accustomed;

b. avoid the sensation that one is regressing in economic organization, when in truth he is but renouncing forms of organization that are outmoded, premature, or, at any rate, inappropriate;

c. resist the temptation to imitate methods or forms of organization that might have had positive results under different objective conditions, especially when it was necessary to heed priorities different from those of today's Cuban economy.

In theory, the fundamental problem is to deal with the productive forces in a manner consistent with their nature. Otherwise, it is impossible to control them and, therefore, to direct their development effectively.

Similarly, in theory, the behavior of men—both as they relate to each other and as they function in their respective roles—should not be analyzed according to *appearances*. This would imply that altering such appearances, especially through education, would alter behavior itself; this is an idealistic outlook. Rather, behavior should be viewed as a consequence of the actual introduction of men into the technical and social division of labor and into a given process of production and reproduction (which also reproduces, progressively changing man's needs), the process itself being determined by the level of development of the productive forces. An analysis of this type brings one to understand, especially, that the decisive factor in changing man's behavior lies in the changes rendered to production and its organization. Education has as its principal mission the eradication of inherited attitudes and patterns of behavior, and the teaching of new standards of conduct imposed by the development of the productive forces.

One must be guided by these general rules of analysis—those of historical materialism—in trying to resolve the theoretical problems posed by the evolution of the relationships of production (as a function of the progress of the productive forces), as well as those that arise in demarcating the different forms of property, the organization of the socialist sector, the organization of exchange, the distribution of income, and planning.

Demarcation of the Socialist and Private Sectors Under the Dictatorship of the Proletariat

Marx and Engels have shown that the development of the capitalist economy implies the appearance of increasingly social forms of production, and that it is the increasingly social nature of the productive forces that makes the *socialization* of the means of production *objectively necessary*.[1] They have also demonstrated that the social nature of the productive forces varies in degree with the type of economic activity and the kinds of techniques employed.

Based on such analyses, as well as his own contributions to

them, Lenin made certain practical observations with regard to the demarcation of the socialist and private sectors of the economy during the initial phase of the dictatorship of the proletariat; the conditions bringing about the decline of the private sector; and the integration into the socialist sector of those activities that, in the beginning, depended on the private sector.

Lenin especially stressed that the problems of the small and medium-sized peasant operation could not be solved unless the entire economy were reorganized, "by a transition from individual, disunited, petty-commodity production to large-scale social production." And he adds:

> This transition must of necessity be extremely protracted. It may only be delayed and complicated by hasty and incautious administrative and legislative measures. It can be accelerated only by affording such assistance to the peasant as will enable him to effect an immense improvement in his whole farming technique, to reform it radically.[2]

Lenin stresses, then, in 1919, the technical bases for the agricultural transformation, the very protracted character of the transitional period, and the aid that must be apportioned to the peasant during this period.

In 1921, in his well-known report regarding the replacement of surplus appropriation by the tax in kind, Lenin examines the above ideas more fully:

> Any Communist who thought the economic basis, the economic roots, of small farming could be reshaped in three years was, of course, a dreamer. . . . it will take generations to remould the small farmer, and recast his mentality and habits. The only way to solve this problem of the small farmer—to improve, so to speak, his mentality—is through the material basis, technical equipment, the extensive use of tractors and other farm machinery and electrification on a mass scale.[3]

As is known, Lenin draws all his practical conclusions from this analysis: As the individual peasant, poor and middle level, must subsist as such during a long period, "we must try to satisfy his demands. . . ."[4] And he goes on:

> How is the peasant to be satisfied and what does satisfying him mean? Where is the answer? . . . If we go into this, we shall see at once that it will take essentially two things to satisfy the small farmer. The first is a certain freedom of exchange, freedom for the small private proprietor, and the second is the need to obtain commodities and products. What indeed would free exchange amount to if there was nothing to exchange, and freedom of trade, if there was nothing to trade with![5]

Lenin finally had to insist on the need to maintain individualized agricultural production during the transition period[6] (that is, until the technical bases of social agricultural production were scaled to the needs of society as a whole) and on the need to offset it by restricting the degree of freedom of local exchange. The reason is that agriculture is the most difficult type of production to transform technically, both because of material conditions and because of traditional methods of production. It so happens that the peasantry is a particularly important class whose alliance with the working class is essential for the dictatorship of the proletariat. Even so, what is true for individualized agricultural production is also true for handicraft and small-scale industrial production so long as the underlying technologies are unable to support full-scale social production.

The Organization of the Socialist Sector

The distribution of productive forces between the private and socialist sectors has undergone a great deal of theoretical examination, but—astonishing as it may seem—the internal organization of the socialist sector has not received the same treatment. The principles governing such organization are therefore deserving of further study. This is particularly important for countries that have recently chosen the socialist path. The historical experience of other socialist countries must be subjected to theoretical analysis if it is to be used to full advantage.

Historically, until recent years, the internal organization of the socialist sector in the Soviet Union conformed to exigencies arising out of particularly difficult and complex conditions, and often situations of extreme urgency (war communism; reconstruction after the civil war; development and revision of the five-year plans; the rise of Fascism in Germany and the growing menace of a new world war; the war itself; the new reconstruction). Thus, it has sometimes been necessary to adapt pragmatically to rapidly changing circumstances rather than systematically adjust to the requirements of the level of development of the productive forces.

As a result, relatively frequent organizational changes have occurred with regard to production units, concerning such matters as their legal powers, their powers of decision, the nature of the jurisdictions under which they operate, and so forth. The solutions to these problems greatly affect the operation of the socialist sector with respect to economic efficiency, ability to adapt to technological progress, etc.

For a long time, organizational changes in the socialist sector of the Soviet economy were made primarily on the basis of immediate practical considerations rather than careful theoretical analysis. This remained true until a short time ago when the Soviets began to devote more attention—at the organizational level of the socialist sector—to the demands of the law of necessary correlation between the relationships of production and the nature of the productive forces.[7]

In *The Economic Problems of Socialism in the U.S.S.R.*, Joseph Stalin wrote:

> It would be a mistake to lull oneself into believing that no contradiction exists between our productive forces and our relationships of production. There are and will certainly continue to be contradictions, because the development of the relationships of production parallels—and will continue to parallel—the development of the productive forces. If administrative bodies pursue a rational policy, these con-

> tradictions cannot expand into a conflict between the society's relationships of production and its productive forces. It would be something else if we were to pursue an incorrect policy. . . . A conflict would then be inevitable, and our relationships of production might seriously obstruct the subsequent development of the productive forces.[8]

A suitable solution to organizational problems is of enormous importance for the building of socialism in Cuba or in any other country choosing the socialist path. To find a solution, we must refer to the experience of the more advanced socialist countries. We will therefore pause to consider at least a few of the reasons why such problems have not—even in the Soviet Union—received the kind of attention they merit.

Some of these reasons are purely practical. The most decisive would seem to be the essentially administrative nature of Soviet planning. This was due to the very strong priority assigned the development of the economic infrastructure, especially heavy industry. The Soviet Union was, in effect, an economically backward country that had to expedite the building of the material bases for expanded socialist reproduction. Thus, it was compelled to stress the development of Department I * of the economy, especially basic industry. Under such circumstances, the need for maximum economic efficiency, which is the purpose of organization, has frequently gone unattended, at least at the tactical level.

Other reasons, apart from the historical, are related to the theoretical formulation of decisive points of doctrine and require very careful attention.

Economic Laws and Socialism

One of the most important of these reasons appears to have been an inability on the part of some Marxists to appraise correctly the problem of economic laws and the contradictions existing in both the economy and the socialist society.

* In Marx's analysis, the producer (capital) goods sector.

An extreme example of this is offered by Rosa Luxemburg, who, in leftist perspective, thinks that economic laws do not exist in a socialist economy and that political economy no longer has a reason for being.[9] The same idea was expressed by Nikolai Bukharin in his book on the political economy of the period of transition.

> . . . once we examine the organized social economy, all the fundamental "problems" of the political economy disappear . . . : we have, then, on the one hand, a system of description, and, on the other hand, a system of norms. But there is no place here for a science which studies the "blind laws" of the market, because the market no longer exists. Therefore, the end of capitalist mercantile production means the end of political economy.[10]

Bukharin's opinion was refuted by Lenin.[11] (Bukharin then defended his ultraleftist positions.)

There are two points of note in Bukharin's errors:

a. The confusion between "economic law" and "law of the market" (which is the same as reducing political economy to a "science of exchange").

b. The confusion between the free play and the objective nature of these laws.

Clearly, errors of this order hinder an understanding of the conditions under which the law of value operates during the different phases of the socialist society's development. On the one hand, the strongest, most frequent, most systematic challenges to such misleading theoretical positions have arisen with regard to the operation of the law of value in the socialist society. On the other hand, with respect to the internal organization of the socialist sector, opposition has centered on only the consequences of such errors.

In *The Economic Problems of Socialism in the U.S.S.R.,* Stalin most emphatically stressed the existence of objective economic laws in the socialist economy.[12] He demonstrated particularly, though without clarifying all the consequences, that these laws also pertain to the organization of the socialist society as regards the forms to be given to the relationships of production, and to the social and technical organization of the productive sector. Such forms must be continuously changed in accordance with the evolution of the productive forces themselves, for otherwise they obstruct rather than aid the progress of these forces.

So the notion of a "possible" contradiction between forces of production and forms of organization in the socialist sector is placed in evidence. Moreover, it is apparent that this contradiction brings about no open opposition, because there is no social group in the socialist society that possesses sufficient means to oppose the necessary changes.[13]

Mao Tse-tung has also stressed the need to resolve the contradictions arising in the socialist society.

> Many [he says] refuse to admit that contradictions still exist in the socialist society. . . . They fail to understand that the socialist society is in fact brought into ever closer union through the never-ending process of confronting and resolving such contradictions. . . . The fundamental contradictions in the socialist society continue to be between the relationships of production and the productive forces, as well as between the superstructure and the base. . . .[14]

The theory that objective economic laws are absent under socialism was rejected only ten years ago. And we must continually stress the existence of contradictions between the relationships of production and the productive forces. This should suffice to indicate the backwardness of theoretical thought in this field and to explain why the problem of organizing the socialist sector has undergone so little scientific analysis.

Ownership and the Relationships of Production

The situation described above has an even deeper theoretical root in the inadequate and sometimes misleading nature of analyses regarding the notions of "relationships of production" and "ownership."

Marx realizes that the relationships of production are made up of the relationships that men form among themselves in the process of social production, and that these relationships change in accordance with the development of the material productive forces.[15]

The nature of the relationships of production is, then, determined by the productive forces themselves and by their level of development. The ownership of the means of production is the legal and abstract expression of certain relationships of production. It must change when the productive forces and the relationships of production that correspond to them change.[16]

The connection among productive forces, relationships of production, and forms of ownership has not been very well understood. For this reason, especially in his *Treatise on Political Economy,* Professor Oskar Lange, like many economists, considers ownership of the means of production to be the "basis" of the relationships of production.[17]

It is actually the level of development of the productive forces that determines the nature of these relationships. The form of ownership of the means of production is merely their legal expression. Marx pointed this out several times.[18]

If one starts with the idea that the "basis" of the relationships of production is merely their legal expression and form, his conclusions are likely to be wrong. Such a concept in effect obscures the real meaning of socialist ownership and its forms. It is also contrary to clear, concrete analysis of socialist appropriation, of the origins of mercantile exchange, and of the law of value during the first historical stage of socialist society. Thus, we must pause to clarify several points.

Although Lenin himself denounced this mistake, legal form of ownership and *effective appropriation* are still frequently confused.

In his well-known " 'Left-wing' Childishness and the Petty-Bourgeois Mentality," Lenin distinguishes between *nationalization,* which is merely a legal measure, and *socialization,* which implies in particular the society's ability to calculate and distribute.[19] This ability is in turn linked to a certain development of the productive forces (which encompass not only men themselves but their levels of knowledge as well).

Lenin differentiates between legal form and concrete relationships of production. He points out that legal form is devoid of content when the relationships are such as to prevent it from being fulfilled (because the *effective capacity to control the means of production and products* need not coincide with formal ownership).

This brings us back, after an apparent circle, to the problem of the internal organization of the socialist sector.

Such organization is effective only if the legal power to employ certain means of production or products coincides with the effective capacity to control them efficiently. What social stratum possesses this ability at a particular time obviously does not depend on the "good will" of men, but rather on the evolution of the productive forces.

When legal power and effective capacity do not coincide, when the legal entity is not a true economic entity, there is a divorce between, on the one hand, *the real process of production and distribution* and, on the other hand, *the process sought* by those possessing legal power without effective capacity. This implies that those who are supposedly in charge of economic administration have failed to do their job, and on the whole engenders the proliferation of regulatory measures and the growth of bureaucracy. These harmful phenomena are linked to the hopeless effort to close the gap separating the legal structure from the real relationships of production. Because of this discrepancy, the legal structure lacks sufficient content.

Thus analyzed, the problems of the internal organization of the socialist sector and the diverse forms of socialist ownership become well defined.

For example, in the Soviet Union the *kolkhoz* * form of socialist property is better adapted to the level of development of the productive forces than the State form. In other words, the socialization of the production process is greater under the

* Collective farm as distinguished from State farm.

kolkhoz system than if the ownership of these productive forces were formally transferred to the State. If this were done, the State would be compelled, in effect, to attempt to centralize the administration of a production process that, in the present state of affairs, can be managed and controlled only at the local level. That is to say, it would have to delegate the powers of decision to an administrator dependent on the State who would thus assume the functions that today pertain to the *kolkhoz* collective and its organs. In fact, such a transference would be a step backward for socialism (that is, for collective control of the production process) rather than an advance. When one speaks of "superior" forms of socialist property, meaning State property, he is speaking (as respects those production processes that are still not mature enough for this form of ownership) in a strictly *historical* sense as provisionally viewed. But such forms are not relevant at the current level of development of the productive forces. Precisely for this reason, it is necessary to preserve the so-called "inferior forms." The latter's existence is justified not by "the conservative spirit" of the peasants, as at times is believed, but rather by the concrete relationships of production.

The sale to the *kolkhozy* of agricultural machinery once controlled by the Machine Tractor Stations provides us with an example of the transference of State property to the *kolkhozy,* which would normally imply a "retrocession" in the level of socialization of these means of production. More realistically, however, this "retrocession" may mean progress in the socialization process if in practice it increases the economic efficiency with which the society utilizes the means of production so transferred.[20]

With regard to progress in the socialization and administration of the production process, there must be the strictest possible correlation between the legal entities that have the right to employ certain means of production and products, and the economic entities that have the actual ability to employ them efficiently because, as a matter of practice, they have them. This helps to explain why the Chinese State's transfer to the popular communes of a great number of industrial establishments whose administration was either centralized or located at the provincial or regional level constitutes progress in the socialization of production rather than a step backward.

The goal is always, from the standpoint of assuring a closer correlation between legal power and effective capacity, to determine and decide what type of collective has the right to control and manage particular production processes. This cannot be done correctly except by taking into account the nature of the productive forces that such production processes set in motion.

The distribution of legal powers over means of production and products among the various socialist state agencies, or economic jurisdictions of those agencies, must be determined in the same way. (Thus, in the Soviet Union, the *Sovnarkhozy* [regional economic councils] are regional jurisdictions of State power, and the Soviet enterprise is an economic jurisdiction of State power.)

The attribution of legal powers to certain social sectors is expressed by the existence of diverse forms and levels of State socialist ownership.

Therefore, just as the Soviet State owns certain enterprises, so these enterprises may own their means of production and products, provided they enjoy both the legal power and the effective capacity to employ them.

Individual right of ownership, which is a characteristic of bourgeois law, is thus eliminated. Understanding that this can and must be so during a phase of development of the socialist society is important not only from the standpoint of the organization of the socialist sector but also in order to comprehend the meaning of socialist commerce and the role of the law of value. But we will return to this.

From what has already been said, one gathers that if legal power to employ means of production is granted to a jurisdiction that does not, at the given stage of evolution of the productive forces, have the effective capacity to control them, then social control over the productive forces is attenuated. This is what has happened in Cuba in those branches of industry in which legal power to control the means of production has been entrusted to the *Consolidados,* while in truth the production units themselves are the true economic entities with the effective capacity to control these means of production. What may be called a "unit of production" (and what constitutes a true economic entity) obviously varies according to the level of development of the productive forces. In certain branches of production in which integration of activities is sufficiently advanced, a branch itself can constitute a "unit of production." For example, in the electrical industry, interconnection permits single centralized management of the whole branch.

It should be pointed out, moreover, that, according to the kind of use to which certain means of production are put, the effective capacity to control such means of production may correspond to several jurisdictions. This gives rise to the possibility that legal powers may be superposed over the means of production themselves.

These are the diverse considerations that must be borne in mind in defining the place of the different forms of socialist ownership, the regulations governing enterprises, the relationships of those enterprises to central economic agencies, the ways in which the economy is managed, the forms and rules of economic planning, etc.

The Organization of Exchange

The organization of exchange and, it follows, product distribution, may appear to be dominated by the technical organization of production. But the organization of exchange is in fact an integral part of the organization of the social reproduction process, a process that is, at one and the same time, production, consumption, distribution, and exchange of products and services.

In a socialist economy encompassing both individualized and social production, the form assumed by the organization of exchange necessarily coincides with the type of production. Theoretical analysis is necessary here as well. What form of exchange organization is best suited according to this fixed relationship between the development of the productive forces and the satisfaction of socially recognized needs?

Individualized Production and Exchange

It is universally accepted that under the dictatorship of the proletariat individualized production necessarily implies the maintenance of the "commodity" and "money" categories. But that the existence of such categories also requires the existence of a market and some freedom of exchange is sometimes doubted. This is now the case in Cuba, and it was also the case in the Soviet Union toward the end of war communism, a period during which circumstances compelled the Soviet power to suppress freedom of exchange and to reduce the functions of money to a minimum. During this period, there were many communists in the Soviet Union who believed that the suppression of freedom of exchange was reconcilable with the maintenance, then inevitable, of individualized production and that it would not obstruct the development of the productive forces, or, therefore, the consolidation of the dictatorship of the proletariat.

Lenin responded to such ideas by asserting the need for some freedom of exchange as a counterpart to the existence of individualized production, but controlled and limited freedom so that such production would serve the interests of the dictatorship of the proletariat rather than turn against it.

Lenin also declared that, on the basis of "individualized production," it is impossible to do without freedom of local exchange.[21] He adds, "We can allow free local exchange to an appreciable extent, without destroying, but actually strengthening the political power of the proletariat." [22]

That some freedom of local exchange is necessary, not merely as a temporary measure but for an entire historical period, is proved by the retention of the *kolkhoz* market in the Soviet Union even today. This verifies the need for a local agricultural market as a corollary to the existence of private agricultural production. The latter, in certain important food products, even now provides an appreciable part of Soviet consumption.

Similarly, the recent experience of People's China has demonstrated that the reestablishment of some individualized agricultural production has perforce been accompanied by the reestablishment of local markets; this has significantly improved the urban supply situation and has helped to bring about a new high in industrial production.[23]

Thus, both theory and practice confirm the need for some freedom of exchange as a corollary to the existence of individualized production.

The substantive questions that must be answered here are what degree of freedom should be permitted and what conditions are necessary to assure that exchange is subordinated to the interests of the socialist society's development. These questions can only be answered by studying the international experience of the socialist countries and by analyzing current experience along the lines of the theory of dialectical materialism.[24]

The observations and examples given above suggest, in any case, that the problem regarding the reestablishment of a local agricultural product market in Cuba derives, in historical perspective, from the nature of the existing agricultural productive forces.

The transition of private agriculture to socialist forms of production, primarily by means of the cooperative organization of the countryside, must also be viewed in this perspective.

The organization of private exchange presents, in the main, concrete problems. But the same is not true with regard to organization of exchange within the socialist sector. This raises important theoretical issues.

Socialist Production and Exchange

Here, in effect, the very nature of the problems has often been obscured by an analytical focus on abstract legal categories—such as the notion of the "single state trust" or the general idea of "social ownership"—rather than on the actual relationships of production.

If the concrete relationships of production corresponding to such categories were of a kind such that a single social jurisdiction, that is, a single legal entity, were actually able to employ all the means of production in an efficient manner, to determine how they were used and how their output was distributed, then products would lose their commodity nature and mercantile categories (money, price, etc.) as a whole would disappear. In this case, there would be no harm in using the notion of social ownership to indicate society's total control over its products and the correlative disappearance of mercantile categories.

In fact, the disappearance of mercantile categories would imply a more advanced socialization of the social reproduction process than is true today. Such advanced socialization is the only basis on which the different forms of ownership that exist today in the socialist countries will give way to complete social ownership. And complete social ownership is the only form that will permit the mercantile categories to be undermined and attenuated.

Stalin analyzed the process by which the mercantile categories are weakened in terms of elevating *kolkhoz* ownership to the status of national ownership and gradually replacing commodity distribution by a "system of product exchange," so that the central power, or any social economic center, could employ all the goods produced by the social sector in benefit of society.[25] The notion that the effective capacity to control all products in society's benefit should reside in a social economic center seems to be decisive here. Nevertheless, the society's evolution toward communism prohibits such a future role to the State, or, with greater reason, to an economic entity such as Bukharin's single State trust. The center would be the society itself, through a central administrative body, which obviously does not exclude the possibility that this center may have "reliefs" in order to make a great number of decisions. Once this has been achieved—i.e., once the social reproduction process has been integrated and internal coordination of its various phases has been achieved—the categories will have disappeared. This does not imply the disappearance of objective economic laws, however, but rather the disappearance of the laws of the mercantile economy.

For the moment, at any rate, even in the more advanced socialist countries, expanded social production and reproduction is not yet a fully integrated and internally coordinated process whose various phases are mutually dependent and, as such, able to be completely controlled by society.

The development of the productive forces has led to growing interdependence among the various economic activities, among many basic processes of production. It is precisely this interdependence, this *beginning of integration,* that has made socialist economic planning necessary. Socialist planning gives meaning to social ownership of the means of production (without which effective economic planning would be impossible).

But the process of integrating the various basic production processes has only begun. Each of these processes must still develop fairly autonomously. As a result, man's appropriation of nature is effected in separate and distinct centers (units of production). Many complex and more or less standard relationships are established among these centers. Each unit of production is therefore a separate and unique appropriation of nature.

The interdependence of these centers corresponds to the social character of production and, to repeat, gives meaning to social ownership of the means of production. Thus, the separate, distinct character of such centers determines the legal form of ownership of the means of production assigned to them.

Under these conditions, the line of reasoning that bases itself solely on the general notion of "state ownership" in an attempt to embrace the various higher forms of socialist ownership under one designation, reducing the latter to a single reality, encounters insuperable difficulties—above all when it tries to analyze the distribution of commodities within the socialist sector of the State, socialist commerce, the role of money, etc.

An example of such difficulties is supplied by certain of Stalin's analyses in *The Economic Problems of Socialism in the U.S.S.R.,* cited above.

In this work, Stalin attempts to explain the existence of commercial relationships in the midst of Soviet socialist society, beginning with the existence of two forms of socialist ownership:

ownership by the people (that is, the State) and ownership by more limited social groups (especially the *kolkhozy*).[26]

This legal point of departure and the analyses derived from it tend to deny the currently necessary mercantile character of exchange among State socialist enterprises, as well as to obscure, at the theoretical level, the nature of purchases and sales effected among State enterprises, the nature of money, prices, economic accounting, financial autonomy, etc. These categories are thus deprived of all real social content. They appear to be abstract forms or more or less arbitrary technical procedures rather than the expression of objective economic laws, the need for which was brought out by Stalin himself.[27]

We see here, again, that one can get into deep theoretical waters when his analysis of a social process starts from the wrong point, that is, from an abstracted legal notion rather than the concrete relationships of production. This is especially true when he believes this notion to be the "basis" of the relationships of production.

The method based on dialectical materialism requires, in fact, that such an analysis begin with the social relationships which constitute the reverse of the process of man's appropriation of nature (that is, with the relationships of production and the actual modes of appropriation). By following this trail, we find that at the present stage of evolution of the productive forces, even in the most advanced socialist society, the appropriation process *is not yet* a single process entirely controlled by society, but instead a multiform process, fragmented, divided into a number of centers of activity, into a number of elementary appropriation processes that have only begun to be coordinated on a social scale (by socialist planning). This brings us to comprehend the need for exchange among these centers of activity and the real social and economic meaning of the different forms of socialist property, socialist mercantile exchange, the role of money within the socialist sector, and so on.

From the vantage point of such analysis, the various forms of socialist property no longer appear to be the reason "explaining" the existence of mercantile relationships within the socialist sector (which would be equivalent to explaining economic categories by a particular legal superstructure). It is, on the contrary, the existence of particular relationships of production that explains mercantile relationships and the legal forms they assume.[28]

Therefore, to the degree that the development of the productive forces conduces to *effective integration* of the production processes, to their internal coordination, the area of mercantile relationships and the operational sphere of the mercantile categories are reduced. Once this evolutionary process reaches its end, the planning and management of the economy may fall under a single social jurisdiction (which does not necessarily mean a single legal entity).

Until then, however, socialist planning assumes the conscious supervision of all the increasing number of social reproduction processes. These processes begin to be coordinated (as they are objectively interdependent) when socialist economic management assumes the conscious supervision of the diverse processes performed by the various economic entities. These processes, then, are linked together by both the plan—to the extent that they are objectively interdependent—and by the mercantile relationships—to the extent that they are still relatively independent.

During the course of the past several years, the increasingly complex nature of the Soviet economy—and the other socialist economies as well—is evidence that the idea of rapidly undermining the mercantile categories and Socialist mercantile exchange was premature. For this reason, it was necessary to make greater allowance for these categories, for the relative autonomy of the socialist enterprise, and so forth. Concomitantly, the growing integration of the production process *in the most technically developed branches* has provided new possibilities for managing such branches by electronic means. Thus, one is better able to perceive *a priori* the development paths that lead to the definitive disappearance of the mercantile categories.[29]

The consequences or implications of the foregoing analysis are multiple. We will only concern ourselves with those that appear most important from the vantage point of the planning and organization of the socialist economy.

a. Relative to the above, it is understood that at the current level of development of the productive forces and integration of the basic production processes, the labor expended on production is not yet completely *direct social* labor.

In other words, although the plan fixes the amounts of labor that should be expended in the different branches of production, it can do so only approximately. One can know only *ex post* what portion of the labor expended on different products is *socially necessary labor.*

The existence of mercantile categories and money in the midst of the socialist sector means, in effect, that the *socialization of labor* takes place partly through the market.

On the other hand, the operation of the socialist market, which serves as mediator and medium for the socialization of labor, has already been very profoundly changed by the development of the socialist relationships of production. Thanks to these socialist relationships, producers no longer relate to each other *solely* through their products (this, in the pure mercantile society, led to domination of producers by products, the fetishism of commodities, etc.) but, rather, also maintain direct relations with associated producers. They strive to coordinate their efforts *a priori* and (to a degree) to achieve this coordination through the economic plan. The latter sets the basic goals of economic and social development and leaves only a subordinate role to the market. This is possible because beyond the elementary processes of the appropriation of nature—processes that are still separate and continue as such to hinder producers to some degree—there is evidence that the integration of the social production process has begun. Moreover, because private ownership of the means of production has been eliminated and because planning has been started up, this social process, now on the way to integration, is not destroyed or fragmentized as it is under capitalism. For capitalism retains relationships of production and ownership that are surpassed by the development of the productive forces.

b. The above means, too, that at the current state of development of the productive forces, even in the more advanced socialist countries, society cannot yet clearly define the state of *social needs* (including the needs that arise in the sphere of material production itself). Nor can it determine in policy—well enough—the needs that will come about in the future.

This leads to the impossibility of satisfactorily, that is, efficiently, carrying out an integral *a priori* distribution of the means of production and products in general, and to the need for *socialist commerce* and commercial State agencies. Here lies the reason for the role of money within the very heart of the socialist sector. The role of the law of value and a price system must reflect not *only* the social cost of the different products but must *also* express the relationship between supply and demand for these products. It must assure, eventually, a balance between supply and demand when the plan has not been able to do so *a priori* and when the implementation of administrative measures to bring about this balance would compromise the development of the productive forces.

c. Likewise, the above implies the need to endow each production unit (that is, each social rung at which a basic production process develops) with a certain *freedom of action.* This would enable the unit to deal with contingencies and to make maximum use of society's resources in benefit of the society. These resources cannot be properly used except in function of social needs—which are not necessarily those that the plan has tried to anticipate. This freedom of action should, at the present level of development of the productive forces, operate on certain parts of each production unit's program of activity as well as on the means of production employed to carry out the program.

The practical problem consists in fixing limits for this freedom of action that would be appropriate to the plan's real objectives (the building of socialism, the harmonious development of the productive forces, and the satisfaction of the growing needs of society). The problem can be rationally resolved by interpreting experience through theory.

It is important to point out here that if each production unit is not given sufficient freedom of action, if its activities as well as the conditions under which it would carry them out are predetermined in minute detail, then, in the present state of affairs, there would be an enormous waste of labor power and material.

As a matter of fact, in planned economies where the units of production are not given such freedom, very often waste is reduced in part through exchange operations that take place among units in formal violation of the plan, but usually with a view toward achieving the plan's real objectives. Thus, economic laws —which are objectively necessary—open their own road. The bad thing is that they are not used consciously (which is the idea of the plan), but instead are allowed to operate spontaneously.

d. The survival of mercantile categories in the very heart of the socialist sector during an historical period, combined with the limited freedom of action that must be granted to each unit of production, makes the principle of accounting autonomy meaningful. Economic calculus should be performed at the production unit level, and each unit should be allowed to make use of its potential for auto-financing. These categories, these rules, this potential, hinge on the level of development of the productive forces. They translate the objective conditions and requirements for the operation of the socialist economy at the current state of development. Failure to heed them can only hinder the economy's performance and obstruct planning.

Organization of Distribution

It is commonplace in Marxist analysis to recognize that relationships and modes of distribution are determined by the organization of production.[30] It can be concluded, therefore, that if mercantile relationships survive within the socialist sector at the current level of development of the productive forces, then these relationships must continue to affect the relationships of distribution. This is one of the reasons for which distribution, too, currently takes place through the mercantile categories (money and wages) in all socialist economies.

Such a phenomenon was unforeseen by Marx as demonstrated by, among others, his analyses in the *Critique of the Gotha Program*. There Marx contemplated the distribution of products by means of "labor bonds" rather than through the medium of true money. If Marx considered such a solution to the distribution problem in the first phase of the socialist society, it was because at the time he wrote there seemed to be a definite possibility that the society would control the entire process of social production and reproduction. But the possibility appeared greater than it really was or, for that matter, is now.

Nevertheless, Marx's realism was on target when he foresaw that products would be distributed primarily according to labor rather than to need during the initial phase of socialism. Still, what seemed to him at the time to be a requirement stemming essentially from the "survival" of certain elements of bourgeois law can today be seen, in the light of experience, to be the result of the survival of mercantile categories. The producers of the socialist society do not, however, relate to each other *solely* through their products but also directly, personally, in their quality as associated producers who seek to coordinate their efforts *a priori,* and can do so successfully thanks to the socialization of the productive forces. Thus, the mercantile categories no longer dominate either the society or the individuals that compose it, so their meaning is profoundly changed. Wages in the socialist society are, therefore, no longer the "price of labor power" (because producers are no longer separated from their means of production, they are, to the contrary, collective proprietors) but *rather* the form of distribution of a part of the social product. At the same time, distribution takes place through the "wages" category because the labor contributed by each worker is still not direct social labor. But society's increasing control over its productive forces permits it to distribute an ever greater part of the social product according to need instead of labor, and in commodities rather than through categories. The standards of bourgeois law have already begun to disappear from the sphere of distribution and will continue to do so at an accelerating rate as men increase their control over social reproduction and as mercantile relationships and categories move toward extinction.

The survival of mercantile relationships and categories, as well as the superstructures related to them, explain the need to base each worker's remuneration on the quantity and quality of his labor (this is what is called the "system of material incentives"). Thus, the progressive elimination of these relationships and categories—and corresponding changes in the superstructures—which has already begun, suggests that a growing place can be given to behavior based on noneconomic motivations.

Which of the various categories of incentives should be used cannot, therefore, be determined arbitrarily, in the name of this or that moral outlook, or of this or that idealistic conception of socialist society, but rather on the basis of the level of development of the productive forces. For men themselves, including their knowledge, their skills, and more generally, their culture, are a part of these forces.

NOTES

1. In a broad sense, the link uniting the level of development of the productive forces with the nature of the relationships of production and the property relationships that correspond to them is currently described as the "law of necessary correlation between the relationships of production and the nature of the productive forces." This phrase was first coined by Joseph Stalin and used in his book *The Economic Problems of Socialism in the U.S.S.R.*, page 9 of the French translation published in Paris in 1952 by the F.C.P.
2. V. I. Lenin, "Economics and Politics in the Era of the Dictatorship of the Proletariat." [Translator's source: *Selected Works* (New York, International Publishers, 1967), Vol. III, p. 279.]
3. V. I. Lenin, "Report on the Substitution of a Tax in Kind for the Surplus-Grain Appropriation System," delivered at the Tenth Congress of the R.C.P. (B.), March 15, 1921. [Translator's source: *Selected Works, op. cit.*, Vol. III, pp. 564–565.]
4. *Ibid.*, p. 565.
5. *Ibid.*
6. As is now known, Lenin recognized this need not only in the case

of Russia's backward economy in 1921, but also in the "advanced capitalist countries." V. I. Lenin, *Complete Works* (Havana, Editora Politica, 1963), Vol. XXXI, pp. 152–154.

7. It is important to understand the evolution of Stalin's thinking in this regard. Speaking of the socialist society, he wrote: "The relationships of production are in consonance with the state of the productive forces, because the social nature of the production process is validated by the social ownership of the means of production." J. Stalin, *On Dialectical Materialism and Historical Materialism* (Havana, Editorial Paginas, 1945), p. 34.

8. *Ibid.*, pp. 56–57.

9. Thus, Rosa Luxemburg writes: ". . . as a science, the role of political economy came to an end when the anarchy of the capitalist economy was replaced by a planned economy consciously organized and directed by the working society as a whole. The victory of the contemporary working classes and the arrival of socialism signify, therefore, the end of political economy as a science." *Einführung in die National Oekonomie, Ausgewahlte Reden und Schriften* (Berlin, 1951), Vol. I, p. 491.

10. Nikolai Bukharin, *Oekonomik der Transformationperiode* (Hamburg, 1922), p. 2.

11. In a marginal note on Bukharin's book, Lenin points out that Bukharin's definition of political economy ("the Science of social economy based on the production of goods—that is, the science of an *unorganized* social economy . . .") causes us "to take one step backward in relation to Engels," who, as is known, broadly defined political economy ". . . as the science of the conditions and forms under which the various human societies have produced and exchanged and on this basis have distributed their products. . . ." *Anti-Duhring.* [Translator's source: *Anti-Duhring* (New York, International Publishers, 1966), p. 166.]

For the purposes of this paper, the issue raised in Bukharin's book is evidently very important. Lenin's opinions on this book were not always as negative as claimed by various commentators some years later. These commentaries may be found in "Zamechaniye na knigu N. Bujarin," *Ekonomika Perekhodnova Perioda,* 2nd ed. (Moscow, 1932); and in V. I. Lenin's *Complete Works,* Vol. XI, 1928 ed. Similarly, a commentary on this discussion and its ramifications (with numerous side references) appears in A. Kaufman's "The Origin of the Political Economy of Socialism," *Soviet Studies,* January 1953, p. 243; and in Ronald L. Meek's *Studies in the Labour Theory of Value* (London, 1956), particularly pp. 256–267.

12. ". . . The laws of political economy under socialism are objective laws." J. Stalin, *op. cit.,* p. 10.

13. This does not mean that certain social strata (a bureaucratic structure, for example) may not be interested in opposing certain changes, however necessary.

14. Mao Tse-tung, "Sobre el tratamiento correcto de las contradicciones en el seno del pueblo" (On the Correct Treatment of the Contradictions in the Midst of the People), Havana, Editorial Politica, 1963, pp. 18–19.

15. Marx put it this way: "In the social production which men carry on they enter into definite relations that are indispensable and independ-

ent of their will; these relations of production correspond to a definite stage of development of their material powers of production." Karl Marx, "A Contribution to the Critique of Political Economy," *Marxism and Communism,* ed. Robert V. Daniels (New York, Random House, 1967), p. 29.

16. Thus, immediately following the paragraph quoted above, Marx writes: "The sum total of these relations of production constitutes the economic structure of society—the real foundation on which rise legal and political superstructures and to which correspond definite forms of social consciousness. . . . At a certain stage of their development the material forces of production in society come into conflict with the existing relations of production, or—what is but a legal expression for the same thing—with the property relations within which they had been at work before." *Ibid.,* pp. 29–30.

17. Oskar Lange, Economie Politique, *Problèmes Generaux* (Paris, 1962), Vol. I, p. 18.

18. See, particularly, *Introduction à une critique de l'économie politique,* pp. 326–330 of the Laura Lafargue translation (French). See also the draft of the letter from Marx to Vera Tasuluch in which Marx points out that it is the need of collective labor in the primitive community that constitutes the basis of common ownership of land, rather than the reverse. Vol. XXVII of the works of Karl Marx and F. Engels, in Russian, p. 681.)

19. V. I. Lenin, " 'Left-Wing' Childishness and the Petty-Bourgeois Mentality." [Translator's source: *Selected Works, op. cit.,* Vol. II, pp. 692–693.]

20. One should not, of course, jump to the conclusion that the manner in which the means of production and the corresponding forms of ownership are distributed should, during the period of the building of socialism, be determined *solely* on the basis of considerations regarding the efficient utilization of the various means of production. Clearly, in order to safeguard the building of socialism, immediate economic efficiency is not the only thing to consider. Far from it: "Politics must take precedence over economics. To argue otherwise is to forget the ABC of Marxism"—V. I. Lenin, "Once Again the Trade Unions, the Current Situation and the Mistakes of Trotsky and Bukharin." [Translator's source: *Selected Works, op. cit.,* Vol. III, p. 527.]

Under the dictatorship of the proletariat, it is because nationalization signifies the end of the control exerted by the capitalists over the means of production that, under certain conditions, an imperfect utilization of certain means of production by the proletarian powers (lack of sufficient correlation between legal power and the actual capabilities of the worker's state) may be preferable (even essential) from the standpoint of the building of socialism, to temporarily more efficient utilization of such means of production by a different social class.

Similarly, relatively inefficient utilization (from the immediate standpoint of the means of production available to the Machine Tractor Stations) might have been preferable to the concession of these means of production to the *kolkhozy* during the first years of collectivization. In a general sense, it could be that the degree of social development of the productive forces of this or that industry, or this or that industrial enterprise, may not *warrant,* from the standpoint of immediate economic efficiency, its nationalization. But it may be perfectly justified from the standpoint of strengthening the dictatorship of the proletariat in that it requires the destruction of the economic power bases of the hostile classes.

Conversely, when the dictatorship of the proletariat is sufficiently solid to forgo the nationalization of productive forces that are still barely socialized, there may be no justification to proceed with any such nationalization because the proletariat has sufficient leverage to put such means of production at the service of the building of socialism, preserving what still constitutes, for the time being, the best conditions for efficient utilization of these means of production.

21. V. I. Lenin, "Report on the Substitution of a Tax in Kind, etc.," *op. cit.,* pp. 566–567.

22. *Ibid.,* p. 567.

23. *Peking Informations,* Feb. 9, 1963, pp. 16–17.

24. Lenin, in his report to the Tenth Congress, refused to define where the limits to the freedom of exchange should be placed. He asserted the need to establish this principle, but beyond that said: "Try one thing and another, study things in practice, through experience, then share your experience with us, and let us know what you have managed to do. . . ." V. I. Lenin, *op. cit.,* p. 569.

25. J. Stalin, *Les problèmes économiques du socialisme en U.S.S.R.,* p. 56.

26. This explanation is developed extensively in Point II of the *Observations on the Economic Questions Relative to the Discussion of November 1951,* entitled "On Mercantile Production in the Socialist Regime." The attempt at an explanation presented here is essentially in reference to the attitudes of the *kolkhozy*. In this respect, Stalin wrote: "The *kolkhozy* are unwilling to sell their products other than in the form of commodities, in exchange for which they want to acquire other goods that they need. Today, those of the *kolkhozy* do not accept economic relations with the city other than those arising through the exchange of commodities. Therefore, mercantile production and commodity circulation are today, among us, a necessity similar to the one of thirty years ago, for example, when Lenin proclaimed the need to develop commodity circulation to its fullest extent." Stalin, *op. cit.,* p. 16.

27. The difficulties inherent in this approach to the problem appear very clearly in that section of *Problèmes économiques du socialisme en U.S.S.R.,* entitled: "In response to comrade Alexandre Ilich Notkin." Here, Stalin raises particularly the question: "Why . . . do they talk about the value of the means of production, of its cost price, of its selling price, and so on?" And he answers: "For two reasons: First, because it is necessary for the purpose of calculus, for the settling of accounts, to establish whether the enterprises are operating at a profit or a loss, to control and verify these enterprises. But this is only the formal side of the question. Second: it is necessary in order to be able, in the interest of foreign trade, to sell means of production to foreign powers. Here, in the area of foreign trade, *but only in this area,* our means of production are in fact commodities, and are in fact sold." Stalin, *op. cit.,* pp. 44–45. It is evident that the second part of the answer in no way explains why one speaks of the value of the means of production inside the Soviet Union, and no explanation may be expected from the first part of the answer because it is precisely a matter of knowing why "it is necessary for the purpose of calculus."

28. This analysis is somewhat similar to that of O. Sik in his book *Economie, Interêts, Politique* (Prague, 1962), in Czech.

29. Soviet economists, in increasing numbers, think that the step toward more detailed planning based on the use of electronic equipment will become feasible through progressive integration of the activities of the different branches. Such integration creates the possibility of using mathematical methods of management and electronic equipment at the level of production units and branches. Only later can they be employed at the level of the national economy as a whole. It should be understood that this does not in any way exclude the use of mathematical and electronic methods right now in national economic planning. But this use cannot be, for the time being, anything but very partial and limited to repetitive processes. For further information on this point, see the works of J. Kornal and Th. Liptak, *Planning at Two Levels,* a series of studies on programing prepared at the Center for Calculus of the Hungarian Academy of Science, Budapest, 1963. In English. It cannot be the only, or even the principal, basis of current planning.

30. "The organization of distribution is determined entirely by the organization of production. Distribution is itself a product of production, not merely as an object, since only the results of production may be distributed, but rather in regard to the particular form of distribution, the form of participation in distribution." Karl Marx, "Contribution to the Critique of Political Economy," *Selected Works* (Havana, Editorial Politica, 1963), Vol. I, p. 325.

2

Mercantile Categories in the Period of Transition

ERNEST MANDEL

Economic Categories and Historical Reality

ECONOMIC CATEGORIES are the result of the study and understanding of an economic system as a whole. The mercantile categories come about from the unfolding of the system of commodity production and distribution that attains its greatest development under the capitalist mode of production. In this sense, economic categories are indisputably products of historical evolution. Marx stressed that the nature of commodities is not permissive of thorough investigation except in the period during which the commodities have already manifested all their contradictions—that is, during the era of capitalist production.[1]

But even though economic categories are products of the historical process, they are also the result of a thought process that has been synthesized from an infinitely complex and diverse historical reality. In order to understand this thought process in its dialectical development, in order to comprehend its law of

---

Ernest Mandel is a Belgian Marxist economist and author of the two-volume *Traite d'Economic Marxiste*.

SOURCE: "Las categorías mercantiles en el periódo de transición," *Nuestra Industrial Revista Economica,* Año 2, Junio 1964, pp. 9–36.

development and the internal contradictions from which it derives, one must begin by abstracting all that is secondary or nonessential in such reality, all that confuses surviving elements of the past with things to come. He may thereby reconstruct the historical reality as a "grand total of diverse determinations and relationships." [2]

The relationships between economic categories and historical reality are, then, much more complex than they appear to be at first sight. Categories emerge from reality, but reality cannot be reduced to categories. Reality is always richer, more complex, more ambiguous than categories. On the other hand, reality cannot be incorporated into theory without the aid of those same categories. In fact, it is the whole dialectical relationship between the abstract and the concrete that reappears in the relationships between economic categories and historical reality.

The best-known example used to illustrate this proposition is the capitalist mode of production itself. All students of *Capital* know that Marx does not analyze capitalism as it actually develops *historically* in a number of countries—fused with precapitalist forms of production (semi-feudal, even slave forms, as in the United States until the end of the Civil War). Nor does he consider it as it has developed *concretely,* enmeshed in the interrelationships of the world market. Rather, he speaks of "pure" and "abstract" capitalism, which permits him to conceptualize the internal contradictions of commodities, capital, and capitalism developed to their extremes.

In view of the dialectical relationship between historical reality and economic categories, one must avoid two basic methodological errors. He must not *confuse* complex reality with its simplified reproduction in theoretical thought. In other words, he must not close his eyes to all the intricacies of reality, which is always infinitely richer than theory. He must avoid, however, *falling again into eclecticism.* He must not refuse to apply abstract categories to concrete reality under the pretext that reality is much richer and more intricate than those categories. *Despite* its complexity, reality cannot be understood as a whole, in the development of its contradictions, except through abstract categories. Anything else is to substitute understanding of reality with chaotic description, with a juxtaposition of a great number of details that merely prevent one from grasping the internal logic of a phenomenon.

These initial reflections are necessary in order to fathom the methodological error committed by comrade Bettelheim in his article "On Socialist Planning and the Level of Development of the Productive Forces," appearing in number 32 of the journal *Cuba Socialista.* Although we agree with many of the ideas the author advocates in this article, several of his conclusions are basically invalidated by his failure to apply certain categories to a particular historical reality with the excuse that such categories are not "purely" manifest in that reality.

Thus, comrade Bettelheim contends that one cannot really speak of social ownership of the means of production unless [page 47]:

> . . . a single legal entity were actually able to employ all the means of production in an efficient manner, to determine how they were used and how their output was distributed.

Moreover, further on he stresses that today, even in the more advanced socialist countries [page 48],

> . . . expanded social production and reproduction is not yet a fully integrated and internally coordinated process whose various phases are mutually dependent and, as such, able to be completely controlled by society.

Based on this statement, comrade Bettelheim concludes that social ownership of the means of production in the socialist sector is simply a legal phenomenon; that the relationships of production are not entirely consistent with this legal form; that enterprises have some degree of control over the ownership of the means of production; and that the means of production are actually commodities because they change ownership when transferred from one socialist enterprise to another.

A bit further on we will return to the *substance* of comrade

Bettelheim's argument, to wit, the nature of the means of production in the socialist sector during the period of the dictatorship of the proletariat. But first we would like to examine the *method* of reasoning that led the author to the above conclusions.

Forms of Ownership and Mode of Production

The step from private to collective ownership of the means of production goes from the anarchy of capitalist production to the objective possibility of socialist planning. Private ownership of the means of production implies multiple-investment decision-making centers and also suggests that investment and economic growth will be directed according to the imperatives of profit (more precisely, according to deviations from average profit). It implies, therefore, competition, the possibility of overproduction, crisis, etc.

Many non-Marxist economists, including those in the midst of the labor movement in the capitalist countries, argue that this thesis is "dogmatic." They assert that in the age of stock-based organizations, in the era of the *corporation,* it is not so much private *ownership* that is important but rather the "actual right to control" that is in the hands of the *managers.* They state that trusts have been largely successful in doing away with competition, and that they can put into practice "forms of planning" or "economic programming" that practically eliminate the anarchy of production. They say, in other words, that the real content of the relationships of production under modern capitalism—the age of monopolies and "neocapitalism"—no longer corresponds "completely" to the "legal form" of private ownership.

Thus, they revert to eclectic optimism, forgetting that the *capitalist mode of production constitutes an economic infrastructure that has its own laws of development* and that these laws remain in force whatever the quantitative changes—however important at times—that may occur within this mode of production. If these laws are to be taken out of force, a *qualitative rather than a quantitative* change is necessary. In other words, both the capitalist mode of production and private ownership of the means of production must be eliminated.

Just as the relationships of production corresponding to private ownership of the means of production (monopolized in the hands of a single class) are *qualitatively* different from those that precede or follow the capitalist mode of production, likewise the relationships of production corresponding to collective ownership of the means of production are qualitatively determined and distinct from those of any other social structure. To confuse a new quality with a quantitative change can only hinder one's understanding of economic and social reality.

In today's capitalist regime, private ownership of the means of production does not actually exist in "pure" form. The owners of the means of production by no means "completely" control "all" the means of production. Some of them—particularly the small stockholders of the large trusts—control practically nothing. The large stockholders and directors of financial groups, of the large monopolies, are the ones who willfully take control of another's property and extract State subsidies—profit guarantees hidden beneath thousands of forms. In exchange, they yield some of their "control" over the means of production to the bureaucracy of their own enterprises as well as that of the State. Nevertheless, the mode of production corresponds, in effect, to the "legal form" of ownership. We are dealing with the same old capitalism, which determines its own laws of development.

During the period of transition, the State, the society, does not really "control" all the means of production in the socialist sector—at least not completely. But this is not the problem. Actually, the relationships of production correspond to the legal form of socialist ownership of the means of production from the moment that socialist planning by means of a single economic plan becomes really possible, once investments cease to be made according to the imperatives of gain and begin to be made according to the priorities of the plan. This is to say, once regular economic growth is possible, it overcomes the contradictions and laws of development of the capitalist mode of production.[3]

Comrade Bettelheim quotes a passage from Lenin describing the conditions for real socialist planning: the society's actual ability to calculate and distribute the productive forces (Lenin takes great care not to add "completely"). This definition obviously is correct. In other of his writings, Lenin also defines the source of this ability: large-scale industry, industrial centralization brought about by banks and bank concentration, a large-scale transport system, etc. The problem must be posed in light of this definition: In a country such as Cuba, is it possible to "calculate and distribute efficiently"—that is, to plan the use of machinery, raw materials, and labor in the country's few thousand industrial enterprises? The answer is obviously affirmative. Doubtless, it is at first done in an imperfect, partial, inadequate manner. The problem then, however, is not the level of development of the productive forces but organizational deficiencies and lack of experience. These can and must be corrected gradually, through practical experience, through development of cadres, through control, and through the creative initiative of the masses, etc. In fact, any other conclusion places doubt on the success of every socialist revolution in an underdeveloped country.

The passage quoted by Bettelheim in which Lenin distinguishes between nationalization and socialization really concerns the *bourgeois or petty bourgeois sectors of the economy*. We agree entirely with his point of view: The "nationalization" of tens or even hundreds of thousands of small, mutually independent peasant, handicraft, or commercial enterprises *whose technique has not yet effectively socialized labor,* and whose technological base (for example, agricultural mechanization) is inadequate to permit such socialization, is evidence of harmful voluntarism.[4]

But Lenin never denied that large-scale modern industry was "mature" for socialization in Russia or in a country like Cuba. To argue otherwise is to condemn the October Revolution as a utopian, voluntaristic undertaking.

We should add as well that the idea that society will some day "completely" control "all" the socialized means of production as well as "all" products is disputable. Here, comrade Bettelheim emphasizes the importance of industrial integration to arrive at some semblance of "complete control." But he seems to forget that the growth of the productive forces produces a contradictory result: the integration of one part and the growing diversification of another. At the risk of provoking the anger of the admirers of electronic machines, we frankly doubt the possibility of achieving "complete control" over all the nails produced in an industrial country as highly developed as the United States or the U.S.S.R. (This is not to speak of a completely developed communist society.) We cannot support the thesis that the "effective distribution" of the means of production "by a single economic entity" is easier when there are 250,000 enterprises than when there are no more than 3,000. The Soviet experience has proved this in any case. It is precisely the colossal development of the productive forces that would today make rigid central planning much less operable, much less efficient, and much more detrimental to the optimum development of the productive forces than in the period of the first five-year plans. This was why changes were made in the Soviet industrial-administration system during the 1950s.

The important thing to understand is that we are actually dealing with artificial planning. "Complete control of the means of production" down to the last nail is a somewhat mechanical and technocratic approach and in no way the end goal of socialism. The nature of social ownership of the means of production does not reside, in the last analysis, in making such "complete control" possible, but in sufficient "control" *to eliminate the action of the motive forces of capitalism and to assure economic growth according to other economic laws, those of a socialized and planned economy.*

Relationships of Production and Level of Development of the Productive Forces

Comrade Bettelheim makes a similar mistake in method when he deduces from the famous central passage of the "Prologue" to *A Contribution to the Critique of Political Economy* that the development of the productive forces determines the nature and transformation of the relationships of production in a *direct, mechanical,* and almost quantitative fashion. But here is the entire passage:

> In the social production which men carry on they enter into definite relations that are indispensable and independent of their will; these relations of production correspond to a definite stage of development of their material powers of production. The sum total of these relations of production constitutes the economic structure of society—the real foundation, on which rise legal and political superstructures and to which correspond definite forms of social consciousness. The mode of production in material life determines the general characters of the social, political, and spiritual processes of life. It is not the consciousness of men that determines their existence, but, on the contrary, their social existence determines their consciousness. At a certain stage of their development the material forces of production in society come into conflict with the existing relations of production, or—what is but a legal expression for the same thing—with the property relations within which they had been at work before. From forms of development of the forces of production these relations turn into their fetters. Then comes the period of social revolution. With the change of the economic foundation the entire immense superstructure is more or less rapidly transformed.[5]

We may draw the following conclusions from this quotation:

1. Marx is using the notion of relationships of production in a very broad sense, practically identical to the notion of mode of production and economic structure, because he requires that "the sum total of these relations of production constitutes the economic structure of society." The phrase that follows, "mode of production in material life," is used as a synonym of "the sum total of these relations of production."

2. Marx establishes no direct correlation except between the

relationships of production *taken in this sense as economic structure* (mode of production) and a certain phase of development of the productive forces; or, to put it another way, between a certain phase of development of the productive forces and the *qualitative* nature of the relationships of production, rather than a stricter and more mechanical correlation between *every quantitative* increase in the productive forces and quantitative changes in the relationships of production (that is, changes that do not conduce to the advent of a new mode of production).

3. Comrade Bettelheim has deduced from this passage, for no reason, that a mechanical correlation exists between the evolution of the productive forces during the transition period and the successive forms of production relationships that remain qualitatively undifferentiated. He assumes, at any rate, that once capitalism has crumbled there are no different modes of production and different economic structures that succeed one another in the march toward socialism.

4. Even the most determinant correlation between a specific phase of development of the productive forces and a specific quality of the relationships of production would not be valid *except on a broad historical scale* inappropriate to the short run and would become even more unrealistic for the "periods of social revolution" because such periods *are obviously supported on two different economic structures,* on two "sum totals of relations of production"—the old, which does not die easily, and the new, which clears the path to victory with a varying number of difficulties.

Now, we are living precisely in this "period of social revolution" today, or, more succinctly, since the victory of the October Socialist Revolution. The struggle between capitalism and socialism—between a dying system that will not give up easily and a system that is just emerging and experiencing thousands of difficulties, imperfections, partial defects, and temporary setbacks—is a worldwide struggle embracing an entire historical epoch. It is impossible during this period to determine at a specific moment, or for the short run, whether the level of development of the productive forces "corresponds" or "does not correspond" to the relationships of production brought about by the socialization of the means of production. And it is even more inconceivable to do so on a world scale rather than within the sphere of the particular country.

One of the characteristics of this period as a whole is, in fact, that the level of development of the productive forces "corresponds" to the struggle between capitalism and socialism. Capitalism may still survive even though it now obstructs the development of the productive forces. Even though the socialist revolution has not yet triumphed on a world scale, it can come to victory in several countries and in these introduce new relationships of production that are qualitatively different from those of capitalism. There is practically no specific correlation in any country between the precise level of development of its productive forces and the feasibility of introducing such new relationships of production.

This is so true that, as Lenin sensed so clearly, the imperialist chain breaks first at its weakest links. The series of victorious socialist revolutions from 1917 to 1959, from Czarist Russia to semi-colonial Cuba, has affected almost exclusively those countries in which the level of development of the productive forces is grossly inferior to that of the more developed capitalist countries.

This in no way contradicts the general laws of historical materialism formulated by Marx in the "Prologue" to *A Contribution to the Critique of Political Economy*. It simply means that the "certain stage of their development [when] the material forces of production come into conflict with" the old capitalist mode of production, with the antiquated capitalist economic structure, should be understood *as the worldwide development of productive forces achieved since the First World War.* Its concrete configuration explains particularly why imperialism is such an enormous obstacle to the continued development of the productive forces in colonial and semi-colonial countries. Thus, the victory of the socialist revolution is objectively possible even in those countries called "underdeveloped." Socialized relationships of production may be introduced into these countries, especially because such countries already possess or can rapidly acquire industrial sectors based on the highest level of contemporary technology, which implies a high degree of effective labor socialization.[6]

It is true that new contradictions between the level of development of the productive forces and the relationships of production may arise after the victory of the socialist revolution and that these contradictions will finally be resolved by changes in the relationships of production. But there neither is nor will be a *mechanical correlation* between each important phase of development of the productive forces and changes required in the relationships of production. And most important, such changes will be *quantitative*. They will affect neither the nature of the already socialized relationships of production nor the social nature of the large-scale means of production that evolve out of the changes themselves. The only qualitative change in the relationships of production will be determined by the extinction of the mercantile categories and the broad social automation of industry.

The Historical Conditions Leading to the Extinction of the Mercantile Categories

Although we have criticized several of comrade Bettelheim's positions, we agree with him completely in rejecting Stalin's theory that the basic reason for the survival of the mercantile categories in the Soviet economy is "the existence of two forms of socialist ownership: ownership by the people (that is, the State) and ownership by more limited social groups (essentially the *kolkhozy*)." Bettelheim rejects this reasoning because it "would be equivalent to explaining economic categories by a particular legal superstructure." In the final analysis, the survival of mercantile categories corresponds *to the inadequate development of the productive forces*. This prohibits the distribution of consumer goods according to the maxim "from each according to his ability, to each according to his needs." Thus, the portion of consumer goods produced that go back to each worker should be measured exactly, which implies its exchange for a given quantity of labor (according to the Marxist theory of value, different qualitative types of labor can be quantified).[7]

It follows that the historical reason for the survival of the mercantile categories during the period of transition is to be found in the level of development of the productive forces that is still inadequate to ensure the distribution of consumer goods according to need.

The above implies that the historical factors conducive to the process by which the mercantile categories are extinguished—following the victory of the socialist revolution—have to do mainly with the development of the productive forces. Such development assures the *abundance of consumer goods.*

The new program of the CPSU, approved by the XXII Congress, incorporated this idea as set forth in our *Traité d'Economie Marxiste.*[8]

By the same token, the CPSU implicitly rejected Stalin's thesis regarding the "ever-growing needs of the people" under socialism—unless the thesis is limited to the phase during which the mercantile categories still survive. A moment of reflection will lead one to realize that to assume the "limitless" expansion of "needs" and individual consumption is actually to deny the feasibility of communism. Material abundance would be impossible, and the mercantile categories, which in fact correspond to a state of semi-scarcity of goods and economic resources, would survive.

In our *Traité d'Economie Marxiste,* we described in detail the concrete mechanism through which the mercantile categories will be extinguished. The development of the productive forces will enable the society to satisfy progressively a number of needs for goods and services. The elasticity of demand for these goods and services will evolve toward zero and may even become negative. This means that distribution according to need without the medium of money will engender only insignificant risks of waste,[9] that can be eliminated by means of education, propaganda, social control, etc.

It also implies significant economies in means of circulation and costs of distribution. The higher the level of development of the productive forces, the greater the number of goods and services that can be distributed in this way and the greater the portion of each citizen's consumption that is provided free by the society rather than attained as a result of individual reward. We mean free to the individual, of course. The society must always expend a certain amount of labor—that is, some fraction of available labor power and economic resources—on satisfying these needs. Thus, it "charges" the satisfaction of such needs to its general budget.

Clearly, at a certain point in this evolutionary process, it will become irrational to increase individual money income because such income can then be used to buy only a small and declining portion of available goods and services. Society will recognize that there is a growing possibility of eliminating the mercantile categories and will drastically cut back money income. Money will be "cornered" in increasingly marginal areas of economic and social life, becoming more and more removed from the consciousness and habits of the people. It will eventually become a mere unit of account and will then finally be replaced by direct calculus in units of labor (which is facilitated by the development of electronic calculating machines).

Obviously, it would be a mistake to believe that the process by which the mercantile categories are extinguished is conditioned solely by the progress of the productive forces. Indeed, the productive forces play the principal role in this evolutionary process, which is actually the most significant revolution ever witnessed by man. But the process itself is dialectical in nature and is conditioned as much by changes in society's productive forces as by changes in man's conscience and current behavior.

Man has lived under the system of the "struggle for individual survival" for millennia. To paraphrase Lenin, *social practice* had proved that a man's choice was between being the thief and being robbed. The antisocial habits of individual behavior engendered by such experience cannot be eliminated immediately after the revolution. A long and difficult job of education must be done to overcome such behavior. Here, voluntary work plays a particularly preponderant role.[10]

But all the revolutionary drive and all the socialist enthusiasm will not be enough to purge the masses of the old ideas handed down by "the man of the past who has not yet completely emerged from the animal kingdom." This is true so long as *daily life* contradicts and neutralizes in part the effects of socialist education; so long as the productive forces are not sufficiently developed to satisfy the basic needs of all the people; so long as equality is not total; so long as greater individual effort may still result in appreciable individual advantages; and so long as those who obtain such advantages may live better and better satisfy their needs than those who lack them.

Only when "free" distribution of goods and services makes it possible to completely satisfy the people's basic needs; only when the first generations of socialist man come of age, man who has never known thirst or hunger or cold or lack of shelter because society has guaranteed him the automatic satisfaction of all his needs; only when man has actually been liberated from the slavery of "material need" and become fully conscious of the "miracle" he has just lived, and when this consciousness creates a second habit, a second nature. . . . Only then will it become normal for man to contribute his labor to society in complete accordance with his ability and with no expectation of a greater or precisely measured reward because he has received from society beforehand all that he needs. And only then will the communist consciousness have definitively triumphed in the masses (although it is essential to begin communist education and practice immediately following the socialist revolution's victory).

Concrete Mechanisms of Survival of the Mercantile Categories

We already know that the survival of the mercantile categories into the period of transition manifests, in the last analysis, the low level of development of the productive forces existing at the time the socialist revolution comes to victory. We must now determine through what mechanisms the deficiency enables these categories to survive and define *the exact sphere within which they operate during the period of the dictatorship of the proletariat.*

A *first category of commodities,* which undeniably exists during the period of transition, relates to the whole of private peasant and handicraft production, which is by definition *small mercantile production.* Everything not consumed by the producer in this sector is commodity production. The same is true with regard to production and sales cooperatives insofar as there is a clear *change of ownership* when the cooperative sells goods to the people or to the State.

A *second category of commodities* derives automatically from the existence of the first: It relates to all the means of production and *exchange* sold by the state sector to the private or cooperative sector: machines, fertilizers, agricultural tools, transportation equipment, commercial devices, handicraft tools and equipment, etc. Here, again, the commodity nature of the goods cannot be doubted because they are clearly exchanged, that is, they change ownership. Obviously, the same is true of all means of production that are exported.

A *third category of commodities* poses more theoretical than practical questions. All consumer goods sold by the socialist sector to private consumers (including imported consumer goods) constitute commodities, because there is an evident change of ownership. Idle enough discussions are possible as to whether the exchange of wages for commodities (consumer goods) is an actual act of exchange depending on the degree to which wages are no longer classic "wages," that is, the price of *labor power.* Such arguments have root in another regarding whether the "sale of labor power" still takes place during the period of transition (Bettelheim, following Soviet authors, says no).

We contend that these discussions are fruitless because, in fact, nobody denies that consumer goods sold to individual consumers are commodities, nor that the "distribution of a portion of the social product" to the worker: (a) is effected by a precise and strictly calculated method (the "social wage" does not, up to this point, play more than a marginal role in socialist countries); (b) is effected solely in exchange for labor (social security payments, as in the advanced capitalist countries, can be considered an integral part of the "price of labor power" that extends over the life of the worker, and must, in particular, guarantee the reproduction of the proletariat); and (c) continues to be an *economic obligation* rather than an expression of consciousness and habit deriving from the fact that work has been transformed into a natural and social need.

If these three characteristics are admitted—and we do not see how they can be denied—it is useless to argue whether labor power is sold, because the *real economic content* of the sale is already admitted. The objection that one cannot refer to the sale of labor power "because producers are no longer separated from their means of production and . . . are, to the contrary, collective proprietors" appears to us to stem from a simple misunderstanding: Why cannot a member of a *collective* enterprise, a co-proprietor of the enterprise, sell individually owned property to that enterprise? The crux of the matter is that labor power is still private property, while the means of production are already (in essence) collective property. To abolish private ownership of labor power before the society can assure the satisfaction of all its people's basic needs would actually be to introduce forced labor.

But the essence of the debate hinges on still a *fourth category of commodities:* the means of production within the socialist sector. In our opinion, these are not commodities because there is neither exchange nor substitution of ownership. The transfer of means of production from one State enterprise to another is at bottom no more than the transfer of a product from one factory to another within a large capitalist trust. Certainly, it presents the *appearance of a mercantile operation* because it occasions a "price" for the purpose of economic calculus and control. But this apparent form does not imply real mercantile content: Means of production that are not removed from the socialist sector are not true commodities.

Comrade Bettelheim's attempt to refute this thesis constitutes the central nerve of his article. He bases himself chiefly on two arguments, which are discussed below.

Are the Means of Production of the Socialist Sector Commodities?

Comrade Bettelheim's first argument (and by far the most important): If in determining whether there is commodity production one bases himself on the legal form of ownership alone, he is committing a serious methodological error, in fact determining phenomena of the economic structure by those of the superstructure rather than the contrary. For Marx, the production and exchange of commodities merely manifest a fundamental phenomenon of the economic structure, that is, that labor contributed by commodity producers is not yet direct social labor. Producers do not agree on a plan of production; rather, they find themselves in an anarchic market. Only after exchange operations have been established, regulated by the "invisible hand" of the law of value, can one ascertain whether labor expended on the production of commodities has been *socially necessary labor.*

Marx expressed this difference succinctly in a letter to Kugelmann on July 11, 1868:

> . . . that the mass of products corresponding to the different needs require different and quantitatively determined masses of the total labour of society. That this necessity of distributing social labour in definite proportions cannot be done away with by the *particular form* of social production, but can only change the *form it assumes,* is self evident. No natural laws can be done away with. What can change, in changing historical circumstances, is the *form* in which these laws operate. And the form in which this proportional division of labour operates, in a state of so-

> ciety where the interconnection of social labour is manifested in the *private exchange* of the individual products of labour, is precisely the *exchange value* of these products.[11]

Let us now pose the following question: Are the society's labor power and material resources divided among the different socialized factories that manufacture the means of production during the period of transition according to "private exchange among these factories" (that is, according to the law of value)? Or are they divided, on the contrary, according to a plan pre-established by the society? Obviously, they are divided according to the plan; were it otherwise the anarchy of capitalist production would be in full reign. There is not, therefore, true *exchange* among these factories, nor production of commodities in this sector.

Now, as regards consumer goods, the situation is completely different. A *production plan* exists; but as consumers are free proprietors of their wages, and as they *actually exchange* their wages for the consumer goods they choose to buy (within their possibilities), there is doubtless an important element of anarchy present in this sector. In the final analysis, the market (and consequently "the law of value") determines the "interconnection" among individuals. Brusque changes in preferences, tastes, and priorities on the part of millions of consumers, even a "consumer strike" (to protest high prices, poor quality, or inadequate product mix), may completely change the "provisions of the plan."

In this concrete way, the nonmercantile nature of the socialized means of production (in which no "private exchange" intervenes because there is no private ownership) becomes apparent in practice, as does the mercantile nature of consumer goods (which concern consumers who clearly are "private owners" of their wages, and in this sense engaged in "private exchange" operations).

How does comrade Bettelheim define the nature of direct or indirect social labor under the regime of the dictatorship of the proletariat? He writes [page 51]:

> . . . although the plan fixes the amounts of labor that should be expended in the different branches of production, it can do so only approximately. One can know only *ex post* what portion of the labor expended on different products is *socially necessary labor.*
>
> The existence of mercantile categories and money in the midst of the socialist sector means, in effect, that the *socialization of labor* takes place partly through the market.

This analysis, which on the whole is correct relative to consumer goods, is wrong with regard to the means of production. In order to demonstrate this difference, we will state a practical problem: One can determine only on an *a posteriori* basis (that is, as respects the market) whether commodities contain more labor than is socially necessary. But how does this fact become concretely apparent? Clearly, by the possibility of *overproduction.* Commodities may remain unsalable, and this unique quality is what demonstrates in practice that the labor time expended on their production has been, from society's viewpoint, wasted.

Can consumer goods produced by socialist industry remain unsalable? Without any doubt, and one can ennumerate many cases in which this has actually taken place.[12] Can the means of production of the socialist sector remain unsalable? Can there be "overproduction" of the means of production in the socialist sector? Obviously not. If, by "accident," production of machinery and equipment exceeds the figures of the plan or surpasses its technological provisions, there is nothing to stop socialist industry from using the surplus to go on to a succeeding stage of expanded reproduction, either at once or in the future.[13] Thus, the means of socialist production, never being "unsalable," cannot contain "socially unnecessary labor." The means of production, then, *immediately and automatically crystallize social labor;* it is unnecessary for them to go through the medium of exchange to determine that condition. The means of production, therefore, are not commodities.

This does not mean that they cannot have been produced at a cost greater than the measure of the social productivity of labor or greater than the cost provided for in the plan, etc. The crux of the question is that even in this case they are not "unsalable" or lost to the society, because their division is effected according to the needs of the society as established by the plan, and not according to their "mercantile value." There are successive degrees of efficiency in socialist planning; but even the lowest degree of planning implies a greater degree of economy in the use of society's labor time than is possible in the capitalist economy.

As the interdependence among the various "units of production" corresponds to a certain level of development of the productive forces, the lack of integration among these units reduces the real economic content of social ownership of the means of production, and the means of production, therefore, may belong to the enterprise. Thus, the circulation of the means of production among State enterprises clearly constitutes a process of exchange because to a degree there is transfer of ownership.

Here comrade Bettelheim confuses two notions—that of *technical* integration of the production process and that of *social* integration, which does not automatically derive from the first, but rather, in essence, from the levels at which "strategic" decisions regarding the enterprise are made: investment and price policies.

Let us take an example from today's monopoly capitalism. In the 1920s the *Lever Bros. Unilever* trust came (for reasons we need not enter into here) into simultaneous control—that is, to *possess* in the sense of actually controlling the means of production—of soap factories, plantations producing raw materials for the factories, paper, fishing, engineering and construction enterprises, etc.[14]

No one could seriously claim that there was then—or could be today—any degree of actual *technical* integration among these different enterprises. But their *financial* integration—including numerous "compensatory operations"—was a very real phenomenon, bound together with ready money. And if the manager of a factory belonging to the trust had dared to consider the factory's means of production as belonging "to a degree" to the factory rather than to the trust, he would have found himself not only unemployed but possibly imprisoned.

Under the capitalist regime, such "integration" does not eliminate the mercantile nature of the means of production produced under these conditions, because it is only partial. In other words, "integration" encompasses only a small sector of the economy that is still regulated by the anarchy of production. During the period of transition to socialism, financial integration—including the possibility of "compensatory operations"—encompasses industry as a whole. Under these conditions, to allege the absence of *technical* integration in order to characterize production as mercantile, to deny that labor expended on the production of machinery and equipment is direct social labor, makes no sense. Simply knowing the complexity of the decision-making process—to what degree minor decision-making must be centralized or decentralized in relations among the various enterprises—is merely a problem of organization and not "proof" of the mercantile nature of the means of production during the period of transition.

The Law of Value During the Period of Transition

We have come to the heart of the debate and to the point at which the relationships between theoretical analysis and the political economy of the State during the transitional period become clear.

Because mercantile production continues to exist, the law of value will continue to operate to some extent. Mercantile production precedes and follows the capitalist mode of production. It precedes it during the whole period of small mercantile production and follows it up to the point at which the distribution of consumer goods can be effected according to the needs of the people under conditions of abundance. *In a sense,* then, the law of value plays a role before the advent of capitalism, during capitalism, and after capitalism. But such a statement is empty until the law's sphere of operation is defined relative to each successive form of social organization.

Under petty mercantile production as, for example, in classic feudal society, the law of value actually regulates nothing except commodity exchange. Moreover, it regulates exchange in a direct way, because the quantity of social labor necessary to produce most commodities is known and is unchangeable over a long period of time. The law of value does not essentially regulate the division of available labor power among the various sectors of the economy. This still depends on the feudal structure, especially the serf's bondage to the soil.

In capitalist society, the law of value regulates commodity exchange as well as the division of labor power and economic resources among the various sectors of the economy. But it now regulates indirectly rather than directly through capital competition and deviations from average profit. Capital flows into sectors where profits are above average and out of sectors where profits are below average. Enterprises whose technology enables labor productivity to rise above the average, which economize on socially necessary labor time, are rewarded in the market by above average profits. Enterprises whose technology holds productivity to below the average waste social labor and are "penalized" by below average profits, etc., etc.

Let us now return to the main problem. *What is the function of the law of value during the period of transition?* We know that production retains a monetary form during this stage (for the reasons already indicated) even though the form varies in content according to the product categories under study. This monetary form itself implies, however, the strategic nature of economic decisions in the areas of *investment* and *prices.*

Can the "law of value" guide socialist investment? This would not only put an end to all real planning, but, even more, would condemn the underdeveloped countries—and all countries engaged in the process of building socialism that until now have been underdeveloped, with the exception of Czechoslovakia and the GDR—to remain underdeveloped for a long time, if not indefinitely. Clearly, in an underdeveloped country, agriculture is more "profitable" than industry, light industry is more "profitable" than heavy industry, small-scale industry is more "profitable" than large-scale industry, and, above all, the importation of industrial goods from the world market is more profitable than their manufacture domestically. To permit investment to be governed by the law of value would actually be to preserve the imbalance of the economic structure handed down from capitalism.[15]

The same is true relative to a whole system of prices. If the means of production are priced according to their inherent values during the initial phase of industrialization, they will, of course, be dearer than the same products manufactured abroad. Were enterprises left "free" to select their own suppliers so as to maximize profits, they would provision themselves from abroad. But if this is not the objective, if one recognizes that foreign trade is monopolized and that control over imports and exports is in the hands of the State, then he must realize for the same reason that the law of value's sphere of operation is restricted by the State foreign-trade monopoly.

Does this mean that one can "negate the law of value?" Obviously, this is an absurd way to state the problem. We are concerned with a *tough, long-term struggle between the principle of conscious planning and the blind operation of the law of value. During this struggle, the planner can and must consciously use the law of value to an extent so as to deal with it more effectively in an overall way.* In particular, this suggests:

1. The need for objective, serious, and controlled cost calculus in all socialized enterprises, beginning with the *producer's goods sector.*

2. The need for a new awareness of what constitutes an overall price policy. Basically, there are only two possible methods: *"subsidization"* (the sale of a commodity at a price below production cost) and *"indirect taxation"* (sale at production cost plus an arbitrary tax). Once the funds retained for socialist accumulation and other budgetary costs have been taken into account, avoiding double entries caused by use of gross indices, the sums of these two operations must balance out. (Only the

"accountable value" that has been created can be distributed.)

3. The need to avoid price distortions, particularly with regard to consumer goods. In other words, commodities should be priced according to the amounts of labor expended on their production. One commodity should not be priced higher than another that has required more labor to produce—unless there is a conscious desire to reduce consumption of the item.

4. The need to constantly compare production costs with average world-market prices. This enables one to make the most propitious changes in import/export plans, as well as to calculate the actual net revenues that exports can add to the country's accumulation fund. Such comparison also allows one to establish a number of medium and long-term labor productivity goals: to obtain per-unit costs equal to or below world-market prices.

5. The need to stimulate production by small proprietors (especially in the agricultural sector) by offering them industrial commodities in exchange for their products under conditions that do not appear too unfavorable (avoiding the "scissors" formed between agricultural and industrial prices that could "cut" the worker-peasant alliance in two).

6. The need to design a policy whereby prices would revolve around values in the consumer-goods sector (within the limits set by resource availability and accumulation policy). Raising the producer's standard of living is a major way to stimulate output and raise labor productivity. Under certain conditions, when consumer goods of industrial manufacture are costly and in short supply on the domestic market, it may be advisable to import them on a large scale in order to bring about an increase in domestic output. A scarcity of consumer goods severly restricts the use of "material incentives," as workers have no long-run interest in merely accumulating paper money.

Consumer goods acquired by producers could, moreover, be considered as "indirect means of production," above all in the underdeveloped countries. Their stimulating effect on current production has been proved.[16]

In light of the above, let us examine the following passage from comrade Bettelheim's article [page 52]:

> This leads to the impossibility of satisfactorily, that is, efficiently, carrying out an integral *a priori* distribution of the means of production and products in general, and to the need for *socialist commerce* and commercial State agencies. Here lies the reason for the role of money within the very heart of the socialist sector. The role of the law of value and a price system must reflect not *only* the social cost of the different products but must *also* express the relationship between supply and demand for these products. It must assure, eventually, a balance between supply and demand when the plan has not been able to do so *a priori* and when the implementation of administrative measures to bring about this balance would compromise the development of the productive forces.

We will ignore the "integral *a priori* distribution of the means of production and products" through planning. This was treated above. We will also ignore the "need" for socialist commerce, which in no way results from the so-called impossibility of "integral distribution." (During the communist phase, abundant production will by definition be consistent with "integral *a priori* distribution." Though only because of the existence of considerable stocks and a degree of free fluctuation of the people's needs, the "need for socialist commerce" will have disappeared a long time ago.) Rather, it results from an inadequate supply of consumer goods, that is, relative scarcity. The crux of the problem is *price policy and the law of value's influence on investment policy,* which cannot be based on comrade Bettelheim's general formulae.

What exactly does he mean by saying that prices should reflect not only the social costs of the different products but also the relationships between supply and demand? Are we perhaps dealing with all prices, all consumer goods, and all producer's goods? If the answer is yes, then, in an underdeveloped country engaged in industrialization, would not this imply that the entire price structure would systematically rise to extremely high levels, which would in turn compel the country to heavily subsidize imports (frequently in disproportion to actual production costs)? What would be gained by such a "bookkeeping operation"? The law of value would be "respected" in one area and openly violated in another.

Clearly, comrade Bettelheim is not suggesting that the overall price structure be determined "by market forces." This would mean abandoning socialist planning in favor of investment determined by "effective demand" as indicated by a scale of "market prices" for the means of production. Comrade Bettelheim appears instead to be concerned with balancing *excess* demand (relative to the plan) with additional *supply* induced (through hidden reserves) by the incentive of "market prices." In a sense, this would be to legalize and institutionalize the "parallel market."

We will not deny that some increase in production can be obtained this way. But one should be aware that:

a. This method could lead to major social injustices to which workers would not easily submit. Under conditions of privation, even rationing would ensure greater equity.

b. The prices formed by this "free" market would not coincide with average costs of production, and they would inevitably cause distortions as well as an enormous amount of speculation, which could well disrupt the plan in the area of production. For example, in some world agricultural-product markets, prices are formed according to changes in supply and demand caused by national production surpluses in the large exporting countries; in other words, by an insignificant fraction of world production. This leads periodically to drastic price shifts. Even bourgeois economists see the need to control this chaotic state of affairs in the capitalist economy. Is it really worth considering its introduction into *a socialized economy?*

c. This method may create additional disturbances rather than bring about the more harmonious operation of socialized industry, because the face-to-face existence of two systems of prices, some low, some high, is a permanent temptation for enterprises to shift some part of the production intended for the regulated market to the "free market." This is especially true if such enterprises operate under the auto-finance system. The logic of a system of "free" prices determined by equilibrium between excess demand and additions to supply would exert a growing pressure to *have investment priorities determined* by the size of unsatisfied effective demand. It is useless to recall that this would mean building luxury apartments before investing in public housing. In other words, it would be to recreate an economic logic nearer capitalism (where investment is determined essentially on the basis of the profit to be derived from effective demand) than socialism (where investment is determined by priorities *consciously* established in accordance with socialist socioeconomic criteria).[17]

Socialist Organization and Financial Economy of Enterprises

As a whole, the theoretical problems put forward by comrade Bettelheim suggest, in short, some practical options in the area of economic organization. Thus, comrade Bettelheim advocates "limited freedom of action" to each unit of production. According to him [page 53], this freedom of action, with means of production within the socialist sector defined as commodities:

> . . . makes the principle of accounting autonomy meaningful. Economic calculus should be performed at the production unit level, and each unit should be allowed to make use of its potential for auto-financing.

Again, this conclusion does more to raise problems than it does to answer questions concerning the organization of the socialist sector during the period of transition.

Comrade Bettelheim will certainly admit that the idea of *financial autonomy of enterprises* [18] can by no means be used as a general and absolute rule for organizing socialist industry. To argue the contrary would actually be *to propose a step backward* in relation to monopoly capitalism, for the latter already employs a far greater degree of autonomy in the form of compensatory operations practiced by large holdings, trusts, and financial groups. In fact, the economic progress made possible by socialist planning, as compared to the capitalist economy during the monopoly period, is due largely to the fact that the former goes beyond *estimating profits for individual financial units* (each capitalist trust already groups together a number of production units) to *calculus of the return to the national economy as a whole.* The best national return is *never* the sum of the best returns to the various financial units.[19]

Consequently, if one is to avoid extremes that would erode all socialist planning (extremes leading to, for example, refusal to finance the payroll obligations of an enterprise operating at a loss, which would assist the birth of phenomena such as "socialist bankruptcy," "socialist layoffs," and "socialist unemployment"), he cannot really speak of financial autonomy except within certain limits. Rather than argue this question in the abstract, we should examine such limitations empirically and determine the potential for autonomy that they permit.

Now, one comes up against a problem of method when he approaches the problem in this way. A criterion of "return" (in common language: "profit") is advantageous in that the return comes about, in a sense, from *all* commercial and economic activities carried out within the sphere of the entity under study (the national economy, industry as a whole, an industrial branch, a group of enterprises, an individual enterprise). But this advantage also implies a prerequisite: that those who make the decisions on the part of the entity in question are actually able to manipulate all the levers of economic activity. Once a number of levers are obstructed because they are *remote controlled,* economic return loses its efficacy as an optimal criterion for guiding that *partial* economic activity. This is the reason why a giant capitalist enterprise employing tens of thousands of workers does not always use it as a basis for regulating the interrelations among the different shops or factories that compose the trust.[20]

In the socialist sector during the period of transition, however, at least some of each enterprise's essential decisions must be made at long distance. For example, in Yugoslavia, the most decentralized of the socialist economies, large national investment projects, as well as machinery and raw-material prices, are still determined strictly by the central authorities. One may conclude from this that the economic efficiency of the individual profit criterion is quite limited, to say the least.

The discussion should center on the methods and factors of organization that argue for or against "centralization" or "decentralization" of this or that concrete decision. The more underdeveloped a country's economy, the fewer able, experienced, and truly socialist technical cadres it will have, and the wiser it is, in our opinon, to reserve decision-making power over the more important investments and financial matters to the central authorities. As the economy progresses and becomes more sophisticated and diversified, the number of able technical cadres grows, and successive moves toward decentralization become appropriate as risks are lowered. But this should take place within the frame of reference described above. In any case, the decentralization of executive functions is advisable when organizational conditions so permit.

The central issue of comrade Bettelheim's argument is, it appears to us, the struggle for increased labor productivity, for higher returns, and the selection of a system of economic administration that most favors such growth. With regard to a system under which prices, basic wages, large investments, and broad planning lines are determined centrally, the issue is reduced to two questions: the enterprise's internal work organization and material and moral, individual and collective incentives.

As to the enterprise's internal organization of work and production, we believe it is essential *to pursue the goal* of placing administrative responsibility in the hands of the workers themselves (laborers and employees). One cannot conceive of socialism, much less communism, without this "performance of administrative functions by each worker in turn." [21] Once such a goal has been decided on, the steps leading to it must be determined, considering the worker's level of consciousness and technical training, the deficiencies present in organization, the technical imperatives, and so forth. It turns out, then, that in practice the *mobilization of the creative and organizational ability of the working class* is an excellent way to increase labor productivity, provided the working class is closely associated, through *ad hoc* committees, with enterprise management, and that the same methods of explanation, discussion, persuasion, and mobilization of the masses that have had such success in other areas of the Revolution should also be employed in the area of production.

As to incentives, we have previously expressed the reasons why we believe it is impossible to base oneself entirely on moral incentives, on socialist education of producers. Such education must be supported by an economic and *social* reality that does not largely neutralize its effects.

But this does not justify a preponderant role for *any* material incentive. A system of such incentives creates, in effect, an economic and social reality that conflicts with the raising of the worker's socialist consciousness. For example, there are incentives that cause division among workers within an enterprise (piecework, stakhanovism); and there are incentives that bring about competition among enterprises, thus bringing the material interests of enterprise administrators (or members of a collective) into conflict with the interests of the economy as a whole.[22] Clearly, such incentives help to rapidly increase labor productivity. But they also have unhealthy effects, both in the long and the short run, on socialist attitudes toward work and society as a whole, effects that could neutralize any immediate advantages, including economic.

In fact, we must start with a *dialectic of ends and means.* Some means will not conduce to the intended ends, whatever may be the honorable intentions of those who propose them. The objective results obtained from using such methods tend to put off the proposed goals rather than bring them nearer. From this point of view, it would be advisable to choose material incentives that at the moment are of an *educational nature,* which would contribute to, rather than detract from, the growth of the worker's socialist consciousness. In this regard, we would suggest an incentive based on progressive levels of training (which stimulates effort toward study) and a collective material incentive based on distributing a portion of additional resources obtained through improved organization and labor productivity (which stimulates, in particular, collective interest in work organization and enterprise management).

Mercantile Categories and Mode of Distribution

On the premise that the mercantile categories of distribution survive in all socialist countries, comrade Bettelheim concludes his article by attempting to prove that they also survive in the relationships of production of the socialist sector. Because, he says [page 53]:

> It is commonplace in Marxist analysis to recognize that relationships and modes of distribution are determined by the organization of production.

Once more, he applies dialectical method superficially. The correlation between the mode of distribution and the mode of production is obviously a "law" of historical materialism. But we are dealing with a "structural" law, that is, with a correlation that is real only on an historical scale at the level of an economic structure taken as a whole (for example, its progress as a whole). To apply such a "structural" law to a transition period is like trying to understand the transition through the categories of formal logic. It can only lead to error.

The classic Marxist theorists unanimously agree that during the period of transition from capitalism to socialism there is no *integral correlation* among the mode of production, the relationships of production, the mode of exchange, and the mode of distribution; on the contrary, there is a *combination of contradictory elements.*

Lenin wrote:

> Theoretically, there can be no doubt that between capitalism and communism there lies a definite transition period which must combine the features and properties of both these forms of social economy.[23]

Engels stated the matter even more succinctly (i.e., regarding the relations between the mode of production and the mode of distribution *during the phases of transition* from one economic structure to another):

> Distribution, however, is not a merely passive result of production and exchange; it has an equally important reaction on both of these. Each new mode of production or form of exchange is at first retarded not only by the old forms and the political institutions which correspond to these, but also by the old mode of distribution; it can only secure the distribution which is essential to it in the course of a long struggle.[24]

And Karl Marx was still more incisive in speaking of the mode of distribution that would exist during the first phase of socialist society. In the *Critique of the Gotha Program,* he refers to the "survival of bourgeois law" and bourgeois standards of distribution.

Comrade Bettelheim, of course, believes that Marx lacked perspective on the matter [page 54]:

> . . . because at the time he wrote there seemed to be a definite possibility that the society would control the entire process of social production and reproduction. But the possibility appeared greater than it really was or, for that matter, is now.

Marx made no mistake in denying the feasibility of socialist planning (which eliminates the mercantile categories in the socialist sector) so long as these categories (bourgeois law) survived within the sphere of distribution. The replacement of money by "labor bonds" does not imply the replacement of the capitalist mode of distribution by a socialist mode, but simply the substitution of one form of bourgeois distribution by another. Marx specifically states that there is only one possible socialist or communist mode of distribution—that is, which does not correspond to bourgeois standards of distribution: distribution according to need. He even says that the development of the productive forces at the time capitalism is overthrown would be inadequate to support the immediate introduction of the communist mode of distribution. He does not, then, explain the existence of these bourgeois standards of distribution on the basis of phenomena related to the legal superstructure ("a dilemma linked essentially to the 'survival' of certain norms of bourgeois law"), as Bettelheim contends, but rather based on the inadequate development of the productive forces.[25]

In other words, Marx confirms our analysis that the principal contradiction during the transition period is between the non-capitalist mode of production and the bourgeois standards of distribution. Thus, there is no need to search further for the origin and meaning of the survival of the mercantile categories during this period. For those who ignore this at times, Lady Dialectic continues to be the heartless *Bella Dama.*

NOTES

1. Karl Marx, "Introduction to a Critique of Political Economy," *Critique of Political Economy* (Havana, Editorial de Trabajadores Graficos), pp. 164, 165.

2. *Ibid.*, p. 162.

3. "A look at Germany will bring out the dimensions and value of GOELRO's effort. Over there, the scientist Ballod produced a similar work; he compiled a scientific plan for the socialist reconstruction of the whole national economy of Germany. But his being a capitalist country, the plan never got off the ground. It remains a lone-wolf effort, and an exercise in literary composition. With us over here it was a state assignment, mobilising hundreds of specialists and producing an integrated economic plan on scientific lines within 10 months (and not two, of course, as we had originally planned)." V. I. Lenin, "Integrated Economic Plan. [Translator's source: *Selected Works* (New York, International Publishers, 1967), Vol. III, p. 552.]

4. "Socialism means the abolition of classes.

"In order to abolish classes it is necessary, first, to overthrow the landowners and capitalists. This part of our task has been accomplished, but it is only a part, and moreover, *not* the most difficult part. In order to abolish classes it is necessary, second, to abolish the difference between factory worker and peasant, to make *workers of all of them.* This cannot be done all at once. This task is incomparably more difficult and will of necessity take a long time. It is not a problem that can be solved by overthrowing a class. It can be solved only by the organisational reconstruction of the whole social economy, by a transition from individual, disunited, petty commodity production to large-scale social production. This transition must of necessity be extremely protracted. It may only be delayed and complicated by hasty and incautious administrative and legislative measures. It can be accelerated only by affording such assistance to the peasant as will enable him to effect an immense improvement in his whole farming technique, to reform it radically." V. I. Lenin, "Economics and Politics in the Era of the Dictatorship of the Proletariat." [Translator's source: *Selected Works, op. cit.,* Vol. III, pp. 278–279.]

5. Karl Marx, "A Contribution to the Critique of Political Economy," *Marxism and Communism,* ed. Robert V. Daniels (New York, Random House, 1967), pp. 29–30.

6. "The extraordinary degree of development of world capitalism as a whole; the replacement of free competition by monopolistic capitalism; the preparation by banks and capitalist groups of the system needed to regulate the social production and distribution process; increased scarcity and increased oppression of the working class by the consortiums as a result of the increase in capitalist monopolies; the enormous obstacles before the economic and political struggle of the working class; the horrors, the calamities, the ruin and despair engendered by the imperialist war, all this makes the stage that capitalist development has now reached the era of proletarian, socialist revolution.

"This era has begun." V. I. Lenin, "Draft of the Program of the R.C.P.," *Complete Works,* Vol. 29, p. 97.

7. "We stated, on a previous page, that in the creation of surplus value it does not in the least matter whether the labour appropriated by the capitalist be simple unskilled labour of average quality or more complicated skilled labour. All labour of a higher or more complicated character than average labour is expenditure of labour power of a more costly kind, labour power whose production has cost more time and labour, and which therefore has a higher value, than unskilled or simple labour power. This power being of higher value, its consumption is labour of a higher class, labour that creates in equal times proportionally higher values than unskilled labour does. Whatever difference in skill there may be between the labour of a spinner and that of a jeweller, the portion of his labour by which the jeweller merely replaces the value of his own labour power does not in any way differ in quality from the additional portion by which he creates surplus value. In the making of jewellery, just as in spinning, the surplus value results only from a quantitative excess of labour, from a lengthening-out of one and the same labour process in the one case, of the process of making jewels, in the other, of the process of making yarn.

"But on the other hand, in every process of creating value, the reduction of skilled labour to average social labour, e.g., one day of skilled to six days of unskilled labour, is unavoidable." Karl Marx, *Capital* (Vol.

I). [Translator's source: *Great Books of the Western World* (Chicago, Encyclopedia Britannica, c. 1952), Vol. L, pp. 95–96.]

8. "The step to communist distribution will be taken when the possibilities of the principle of distribution according to labor have been exhausted; in other words, *when there is an abundance of material and cultural goods* and work is the prime need of all the members of society." Emphasis is ours. "Program of the Communist Party of the Soviet Union," *The Road to Communism: Documents of the XXII Congress of the CPSU* (Moscow, *Edicićnes* en Lenguas Extranjeras, 1961), p. 58.

Of course, on page 548, the same program speaks of the "growing demands of the members of the society."

". . . The end goal of all production is abundance. And abundance means not only plethora, but also a variety of use-values, which implies that man must develop considerably as a producer, develop his productive abilities in general." Karl Marx, *Critical History of the Theory of Surplus Value* (Mexico, Fondo de Cultura Económica, 1945), Vol. III, p. 48.

In our *Traité d'Economie Marxiste* (Paris, Editions Julliard, 1962, 2 vols.), we thoroughly examined all the economic and psychological aspects which argue against the idea that human needs can increase indefinitely (Vol. II, pp. 339–361). And we scored the fact that in capitalist society, among the social classes that enjoy the highest incomes, a pattern of *more rational consumption* has already begun to win out over a pattern of *consumption which is always quantitatively on the rise.*

9. Example: urban public transportation. It would not look good for a communist man to take his time to travel needlessly on a train or a bus simply because the service were free. . . .

10. See especially Lenin on the "communist Saturdays": "The heroism of the workers in the rear is no less worthy of attention. In this connection, the *communist subotniks* organised by the workers on their own initiative are really of enormous significance. Evidently, this is only a beginning, but it is a beginning of exceptionally great importance. It is the beginning of a revolution that is more difficult, more tangible, more radical and more decisive than the overthrow of the bourgeoisie, for it is a victory over our own conservatism, indiscipline, petty-bourgeois egoism, a victory over the habits left as a heritage to the worker and peasant by accursed capitalism. Only when *this* victory is consolidated will the new social discipline, socialist discipline, be created; then and only then will a reversion to capitalism become impossible, will communism become really invincible." V. I. Lenin, "A Great Beginning." [Translator's source: *Selected Works, op. cit.,* Vol. III, p. 205.]

11. Karl Marx, *Letters to Kugelmann.* [Translator's source: *Letters to Kugelmann* (New York, International Publishers, 1934), pp. 73–74.]

12. Here is what the Soviet author A. G. Kalikov contends: "Practice has convinced us that . . . when commodities remain warehoused in the distribution network and cannot be sold, the labor crystallized in such commodities has not been socially recognized" (*Voprossi Ekonomiki,* No. 2, 1957).

13. We do not take account here of varied production, mistakes in planning, etc., which can take place even in a communist society, and which have nothing to do with varied production of a mercantile nature.

14. Charles Wilson, *The History of Unilever* (London, Cassel and Co.), Vol. I, p. 260).

15. For this reason, it is particularly impossible in an underdeveloped country to make all industrial enterprises "profitable." The same difficulty does not necessarily exist in the agricultural sector.

16. We need to score here the strange contradiction between recognizing, even proposing the use of "material incentives" in the *micro-economic* sphere, and resolutely refusing to use the same "incentives" in the *macro-economic* sphere. This defines the approach of many economists in the socialist countries, particularly with regard to the thesis that the development of Department I has "permanent priority" over the development of Department II. We treated this thesis at depth in our *Traité d'Economie Marxiste* (Vol. II, pp. 296–311). We derive from this the rule that the maximum rate of accumulation never leads to the highest rate of growth because of the interrelation between the worker's level of consumption and the productivity of labor.

17. Comrade Bettelheim strongly emphasized this in his notable article "International Trade and Regional Development," which just appeared in the journal *Nuestra Industria Revista Económica* (No. 6, April 1964, pp. 22–43). It should be assured, then, that the formation of "market prices" does not affect investment. But this obviously implies that this "play" of "market forces" is more strict.

18. We prefer the term "financial autonomy" over "accounting autonomy," which is ambiguous because it can imply simply the need for precise cost calculus at the enterprise level (which is completely justified it seems to us) or the need to balance costs and revenues within each enterprise in addition to the calculus. Financial autonomy is obviously impossible without accounting autonomy; but accounting autonomy need not imply financial autonomy.

19. It should be added that, to be precise, such calculus must take the following factors into account: socialized costs under the capitalist system, which to a large extent determine the profitability of certain industrial branches (example: highway construction paid for collectively, without which the automobile industry could not have achieved such great development); the *harmful social effects* of some economic activities that are not "accounted for" because the future of the collective is irresponsibly sacrificed for the immediate benefit of a small minority (example: the poisoning of air and water by several chemical industries, etc.); and the *factors that cannot be counted* in dollars and cents but that are no less important from the socialist viewpoint (example: consideration of human dignity that argues against unemployment, even when the unemployed worker who is given work produces less utility than he receives).

20. Here are a few examples out of many of bourgeois writers who frankly admit this: "With rising cost curves and/or other cost functions for the various enterprises and/or product differentiation, the industry's profits could only reach a maximum if the enterprises forming the industry pool resources and markets. Coordination must be complete enough to bring about the pooling of resources, products and direct payments among enterprises." William Fellner, *Oligopoly* (Fondo de Cultura Económica, 1953), pp. 121–22.

"The integrated firm may deliberately 'manipulate its margins' so as to put pressure on nonintegrated rivals greater than they can cope with, even though the rivals' efficiency in the area in which they alone operate may be superior to that of the integrated unit. In fact, the margins of the integrated firm will be 'manipulated,' like it or not, by the force of varying competitive pressures in its several spheres of operation. Thus, operations having the greater profitability inevitably 'subsidize' those in fields where there is greater competition. The 'subsidy' allows a competitive 'squeeze,' the most dramatic examples of which come out of vertical integration." Alfred E. Kahn, "Standards for Anti-Trust Policy," *Readings in Industrial Organization and Public Policy* (published for the American Economics Association by Richard D. Irwin, Inc., Homewood, Ill., 1958).

See also "Vertical Integration: Impact of Anti-monopoly Laws on the Combinations of Successive Stages of Production and Distribution," *Columbia Law Review,* Vol. XIX.

21. ". . . on the other hand, trusts must become more and more educational bodies, where all the working masses may engage in socialist labor so that the practical experience of participation in administrative functions will extend, under the control of the working vanguard, to the most backward working strata." V. I. Lenin, "Draft of the Program of the Russian Communist Party," *Complete Works,* Vol. XXIX, p. 106.

"*We,* the workers, shall organise large-scale production on the basis of what capitalism has already created, relying on our own experience as workers, establishing strict, iron discipline backed up by the state power of the armed workers. We shall reduce the role of state officials to that of simply carrying out our instructions as responsible, revocable, modestly paid 'foremen and accountants' (of course, with the aid of technicians of all sorts, types and degrees). This is *our* proletarian task, this is what we can and must *start* with in accomplishing the proletarian revolution. Such a beginning, on the basis of large-scale production, will of itself lead to the gradual 'withering away' of all bureaucracy, to the gradual creation of an order—an order without inverted commas, an order bearing no similarity to wage slavery—an order under which the functions of control and accounting, becoming more and more simple, will be performed by each in turn, will then become a habit and will finally die out as the *special* functions of a special section of the population." V. I. Lenin, "The State and Revolution." [Translator's source: *Selected Works, op. cit.,* Vol. II, pp. 303–304.]

22. The Soviet economist Liberman (whose conclusions we do not share) has shown how the system of premiums for surpassing the plan systematically impels administrators to underestimate production capacity, to create "hidden" reserves of raw materials and machinery, thus entering into conflict with the general interests of the society, etc. We pointed out this malady before Liberman did, in our *Traité d'Economie Marxiste.*

23. V. I. Lenin, "Economics and Politics in the Era of the Dictatorship of the Proletariat." [Translator's source: *Selected Works, op. cit.,* Vol. III, p. 274.]

24. Friedrich Engels, *Herr Eugen Duhring's Revolution in Science* (*Anti-Duhring*), trans. Emile Burns, ed. C. P. Dutt (New York, International Publishers, 1966), p. 165. [Translator's source.]

25. "Here obviously the same principle prevails as that which regulates the exchange of commodities, as far as this is exchange of equal values. Content and form are changed, because under the altered circumstances no one can give anything except his labour, and because, on the other hand, nothing can pass into the ownership of individuals except individual

means of consumption. But, as far as the distribution of the latter among the individual producers is concerned, the same principle prevails as in the exchange of commodity-equivalents, so much labour in one form is exchanged for an equal amount of labour in another form. . . .

In a higher phase of communist society, after the enslaving subordination of individuals under division of labour, and therewith also the antithesis between mental and physical labour, has vanished; after labour, from a mere means of life, has itself become the prime necessity of life; after the productive forces have also increased with the all-round development of the individual, and all the springs of cooperative wealth flow more abundantly—only then can the narrow horizon of bourgeois right be fully left behind and society inscribe on its banners: from each according to his ability, to each according to his needs!" Karl Marx, *Critique of the Gotha Program.* [Translator's source: *Critique of the Gotha Program* (New York, International Publishers, 1934), pp. 8–10.]

3

The Meaning of Socialist Planning

ERNESTO CHE GUEVARA

NUMBER 32 OF THE JOURNAL *Cuba Socialista* contained an article by comrade Charles Bettelheim entitled "On Socialist Planning and the Level of Development of the Productive Forces" [page 31]. The article touches on points of considerable interest and has, for us, the added importance of being written in defense of so-called economic calculus and the categories such a system implies exist within the socialist sector—credit, commodity, money as a function of means of payment, etc.

We believe that two fundamental errors have been committed in this article.

The first is one of interpretation, and regards the necessary correlation between the productive forces and the relationship of production. Comrade Bettelheim illustrates this point by drawing examples from the Marxist classics.

Productive forces and relationships of production are two mechanisms that advance together, indivisibly, in all the intermediate processes of society's development. At what times might the relationship of production not faithfully reflect the development of the productive forces? In times of a society's ascent, as it advances on the previous society in order to break it asunder;

Ernesto Che Guevara was Minister of Industry during the period of debate.

SOURCE: "La planificación socialista, su significado," *Cuba Socialista,* Año IV, Junio 1964, pp. 13–24.

and in times of the old society's breakdown, when the new one, whose relationships of production are yet to be introduced, struggles to consolidate itself and bring down the old superstructure. Thus, analyzed realistically, the productive forces and the relationships of production may not, at a given moment in history, so precisely correspond to one another. This is, in fact, the theory that allowed Lenin to say the October Revolution was a socialist revolution and at another time to propose the need for State capitalism and recommended caution in dealing with the peasantry. The reason for Lenin's proposal is to be found in his momentous discovery of the development of the world capitalist system.

Bettelheim says [page 33]:

> . . . the decisive factor in changing man's behavior lies in the changes rendered to production and its organization. Education has as its principal mission the eradication of inherited attitudes and patterns of behavior, and the teaching of new standards of conduct imposed by the development of the productive forces.

Lenin says:

> "The development of the productive forces of Russia has not attained the level that makes socialism possible." All the heroes of the Second International, including, of course, Sukhanov, beat the drums about this proposition. They keep harping on this incontrovertible proposition in a thousand different keys, and think that it is the decisive criterion of our revolution.
>
> But what if the situation, which drew Russia into the imperialist world war that involved every more or less influential West-European country and made her a witness of the eve of the revolutions maturing or partly already begun in the East, gave rise to circumstances that put Russia and her development in a position which enabled us to achieve precisely that combination of a "peasant war" with the working-class movement suggested in 1856 by no less a

> Marxist than Marx himself as a possible prospect for Prussia?
>
> What if the complete hopelessness of the situation, by stimulating the efforts of the workers and peasants tenfold, offered us the opportunity to create the fundamental requisites of civilisation in a different way from that of the West-European countries? Has that altered the general line of development of world history? Has that altered the basic relations between the basic classes of all the countries that are being, or have been, drawn into the general course of world history?
>
> If a definite level of culture is required for the building of socialism (although nobody can say just what that definite "level of culture" is, for it differs in every West-European country), why cannot we begin by first achieving the prerequisites for that definite level of culture in a revolutionary way, and *then,* with the aid of the workers' and peasants' government and the Soviet system, proceed to overtake the other nations? [1]

As capitalism expands into a world system and as the relationships of exploitation develop not only among individual members of a people but even among entire peoples, the world capitalist system—which has become imperialism—comes into conflict and can break at its weakest link. This was czarist Russia after the First World War and the beginning of the Revolution, when Lenin's economic types coexisted: the most primitive form, patriarchal agriculture; small mercantile production—including most peasants who sold their wheat; private capitalism; State capitalism; and socialism.

Lenin pointed out that all these types spring up in Russia immediately after the Revolution; but what provides him with a general classification is the socialist aspect of the system, even though the productive forces at certain points had not yet reached maturity. Apparently, when the backwardness is very great, the correct Marxist action should be to accommodate the spirit of the new epoch, which tends to suppress man's exploitation of man, to the country's concrete situations. This is what Lenin did in a Russia recently freed from czarism, and it was applied as a norm in the Soviet Union.

We hold that this entire argument, absolutely valid and extraordinarily perspicacious at the time, is applicable in concrete situations at given historical junctures. But since these events, things of transcendental significance have occurred: establishment of a world socialist system, with nearly a thousand million inhabitants, a third of the world's population. The steady advance of this system influences the consciousness of peoples at all levels. Therefore, in Cuba, at one moment in its history, a definition of socialist revolution was born that did not in any way precede the existence of economic bases for such a proposition.

How, in a country colonized by imperialism, its basic industries underdeveloped, a mono-producer dependent on a single market, can the transition to socialism be made?

The following answers might be given: to declare, as did the theorists of the Second International, that Cuba has broken all the laws of the dialectic, of historical materialism, of Marxism, and that, therefore, it is not a socialist country or must revert to its former status.

One can be more realistic, on the other hand, and try to find in Cuba's relationships of production the internal motors that brought about the Revolution. But, of course, this would lead to the discovery that there are many countries in the Americas, and in other parts of the world, where revolution is much more feasible than it was in Cuba.

There remains a third explanation, which in our judgment is correct: that within the huge framework of the world capitalist system, struggling against socialism, one of its weakest links, in this particular case Cuba, can be broken. Taking advantage of special historical circumstances under the astute leadership of its vanguard, the revolutionary forces, at the proper moment, take power and, assuming the existence of sufficient objective conditions for the socialization of labor, they eliminate stages, declare the revolution's socialist nature, and begin the building of socialism.

This is the dynamic, dialectical way in which we see and analyze the problem of necessary correlation between the relationships of production and the development of the productive forces. After the Cuban Revolution, a fact that cannot escape analysis or be ignored when our history is studied, we conclude that a socialist revolution did take place in Cuba and that, therefore, conditions for it did exist. Because to carry out a revolution without the necessary conditions, to attain power and declare socialism by magic, is something unforeseen by any theory and something I do not believe comrade Bettelheim would support.

If socialism can come about under such conditions, it is because the development of the productive forces has clashed with the relationships of production before what might rationally be expected in an isolated capitalist country. What happens? The vanguard of the revolutionary movement, increasingly influenced by Marxist-Leninist ideology, is capable of consciously anticipating the steps to be taken in order to force the pace of events, but forcing it within what is objectively possible. We strongly stress this point because it is one of the principal defects in Bettelheim's argument.

If we start with the fact that revolution can take place only when there are fundamental contradictions between the development of the productive forces and the relationships of production, then we must also admit that this phenomenon has occurred in Cuba and that it imparts to the Revolution socialist characteristics, even though, when objectively analyzed, there is a whole system of forces still in an embryonic state. But if under such conditions a revolution succeeds, how afterward can one use the argument of the necessary and imperative concordance, that is made mechanical and rigid, between the productive forces and the relationships of production in order to defend, for example, economic calculus and to attack the system of consolidated enterprises practiced in Cuba?

To say that the consolidated enterprise is an aberration is just about equivalent to saying that the Cuban Revolution is an aberration. The concepts are much alike and could be based on the same analysis. Comrade Bettelheim has never said that the Cuban Socialist Revolution is not authentic, but he does say that our present relationships of production do not correspond to the development of the productive forces, for which reason he anticipates significant setbacks.

Comrade Bettelheim fails to apply dialectical thought in these two categories of different magnitudes but similar orientation, wherein lies his error. The consolidated enterprises saw light, developed, and continue to develop because they are able to do so; it is the truth of practice. Whether or not the administrative method is the most suitable is of little importance in the end, because the differences between one method and the other are primarily quantitative. Our system looks toward the future, to a more accelerated growth of consciousness and, through consciousness, of the productive forces.

Comrade Bettelheim denies this particular action of consciousness, basing himself on Marx's arguments that this is a product of the social milieu rather than the reverse. We may utilize Marxist analysis in order to join Marx against Bettelheim, telling him that this is completely true, but that, in today's age of imperialism, consciousness acquires world dimensions. Today's consciousness has come about through the development of all the world's productive forces as well as from the teaching and education provided all the world's masses by the Soviet Union and other socialist countries.

Therefore, one ought to recognize that the consciousness of those in the vanguard of a given country, based on the general development of the productive forces, can perceive the proper paths by which to lead a socialist revolution to victory in that country, even though, at their level, the contradictions between the development of the productive forces and the relationships of production that would make a revolution imperative or possible (viewing the country as a whole, unique, and isolated) might not exist objectively.

Bettelheim's second serious mistake is his insistence on providing the legal structure with a possibility for independent existence. His analysis stresses the need to take the relationships of production into account in order to establish legal ownership. To think that legal ownership or, more properly, the superstructure of a particular State at a given time has been imposed despite the realities of the relationships of production is to deny precisely the determinism on which he relied in order to assert that consciousness is a social product. Naturally, these are historical rather than physical or chemical processes, and they do not take place in microseconds but rather over the long course of human existence. There are numerous aspects of legal relationships which do not correspond to the relationships of production that characterize the country at the time; which only means that such aspects will be destroyed when the new relationships are imposed over the old ones, but not in the opposite way. Therefore, it might, indeed, be possible to change the superstructure without first changing the relationships of production.

Comrade Bettelheim repeatedly stresses that the nature of the relationships of production is given by the degree of development of the productive forces, and that the ownership of the means of production is the legal and abstract expression of certain relationships of production. He ignores the basic fact that this is perfectly suited to a general situation (whether worldwide or simply within a country). The miscroscopic correlations he attempts to establish between the level of development of the productive forces and legal property relations in every region or situation are impossible.

He attacks those economists who claim to see an expression of socialism in public ownership of the means of production, saying that such legal relationships mean nothing. In a way, he could be right with respect to the word *basis,* but the important thing is that the relationships of production and the development of the productive forces eventually clash. That clash is not mechanically determined by a build-up of economic forces, but rather is a quantitative and qualitative sum, a build-up of forces encountered from the standpoint of economic development, the overthrow of one social class by another, from an historical and political standpoint. In other words, economic analysis can never be separated from the historical fact of the class struggle (until the perfect society is achieved). Therefore, for man, the living expression of the class struggle, the legal basis that represents the superstructure of the society in which he lives has specific characteristics and expresses an obvious truth. The relationships of production and the development of the productive forces are economic and technological phenomena that accumulate during the course of history. Social property is the obvious expression of these relationships just as commodities are the expression of the relationships among men. The commodity exists because there is a mercantile society wherein a division of labor has come about on the basis of private property. Socialism exists because there is a new kind of society in which the expropriators have been expropriated and social property replaces the old, individualized property of the capitalists.

This is the general line that the period of transition should follow. The detailed relationship between this or that stage of society holds interest only for a certain specific analysis. But theoretical analysis should embrace the broad framework delimiting the new relationships among men in a society on the way to socialism.

Starting with these two basic conceptual errors, comrade Bettelheim defends the compulsory identity between the relationships of production and the development of the productive forces at each specific moment and in each specific region, and, at the same time, transplants these same relationships to the level of legal expression.

What is his purpose? Bettelheim says [page 48]:

> Under these conditions, the line of reasoning that bases itself solely on the general notion of "state ownership" in an attempt to embrace the various higher forms of socialist ownership under one designation, reducing the latter to a single reality, encounters insuperable difficulties—above all when it tries to analyze the distribution of commodities within the socialist sector of the State, socialist commerce, the role of money, etc.

And then, analyzing Stalin's two forms of property, he says [page 49]:

> This legal point of departure and the analyses derived from it tend to deny the currently necessary mercantile character of exchange among State socialist enterprises, as well as to obscure, at the theoretical level, the nature of purchases and sales effected among State enterprises, the nature of money, prices, economic accounting, financial autonomy, etc. These categories are thus deprived of all real social content. They appear to be abstract forms or more or less arbitrary technical procedures rather than the expression of objective economic laws, the need for which was brought out by Stalin himself.

For us, comrade Bettelheim's article—despite his apparent opposition to ideas we have expressed on several occasions—is undoubtedly important because it comes from one who is both an economist with profound knowledge and a theorist of Marxism. Starting with an existing situation, in order to build what in our mind is an ill-conceived defense of the use of the categories inherent in capitalism during the period of transition, and of the need for individualized property within the socialist sector, he demonstrates that detailed analysis along the Marxist line (which we would call orthodox) of the relationships of production and social property is incompatible with the maintenance of these categories and points out that there is something of mystery here.

We have exactly the same notion, except that our conclusion is different: We believe that the inconsistency among the defenders of economic calculus stems from their following Marxist analysis to a certain point, then jumping to a new position from which to continue their line of thought (leaving the "missing link" in the middle). In short, the defenders of economic calculus have never correctly explained how the commodity concept is essentially sustained in the State sector, or how the law of value is used "intelligently" in the socialist sector with distorted markets.

Noting the inconsistency, comrade Bettelheim rephrases his terms, beginning the analysis where he should have ended it—

with the legal relationships presently existing in socialist countries and the categories that subsist—verifying the truth that such legal and mercantile categories do exist, and there concluding, pragmatically, that if they exist, it is because they are necessary. Starting from this, he regresses analytically until he reaches the point at which theory and practice collide. At this point, he gives a new interpretation to the theory, submits Marx and Lenin to analysis, and arrives at his own conclusions, erroneously premised as we have noted, which permit him to formulate a process consistent from one extreme to another in the article.

He forgets here, however, that the period of transition is historically young. The moment man arrives at a full understanding of economic reality and masters it by means of planning, he becomes subject to inevitable errors of judgment. Why think that everything that happens in the period of transition is inevitable? Why think that the setbacks dealt by reality to certain bold acts stem exclusively from *boldness* rather than—perhaps entirely—from technical deficiencies in administration?

It seems to us that Bettelheim takes too much importance away from socialist planning, despite whatever technical deficiencies it might have, when he assumes [page 52]:

> This leads to the impossibility of satisfactorily, that is, efficiently, carrying out an integral *a priori* distribution of the means of production and products in general, and to the need for *socialist commerce* and commercial State agencies. Here lies the reason for the role of money within the very heart of the socialist sector. The role of the law of value and a price system must reflect not *only* the social cost of the different products but must *also* express the relationship between supply and demand for these products. It must assure, eventually, a balance between supply and demand when the plan has not been able to do so *a priori* and when the implementation of administrative measures to bring about this balance would compromise the development of the productive forces.

Despite our weaknesses (in Cuba), we nonetheless made an attempt at a basic definition:

> We deny the possibility of consciously using the law of value, basing our argument on the absence of a free market which automatically expresses the contradiction between producers and consumers. We deny the existence of the *commodity* category in relationships among state enterprises. We consider all such establishments to be part of the single large enterprise which is the State (although in practice this is not yet the case in our country). The law of value and planning are two terms linked by a contradiction and its resolution. We can therefore say that centralized planning is characteristic of the socialist society, its definition. It is the point at which man consciously finally succeeds in synthesizing and directing the economy toward his goal, which is the total liberation of the human being within the framework of a Communist society.[2]

To relate the unit of production (Bettelheim's economic entity) with the physical degree of integration is to carry the mechanism to its extreme and to deny us the possibility of doing what, technically, the North American monopolies had already done in many branches of Cuban industry. There is too little confidence in our strengths and abilities [page 43]:

> What may be called a "unit of production" (and what constitutes a true economic entity) obviously varies according to the level of development of the productive forces. In certain branches of production, in which integration of activities is sufficiently advanced, a branch itself can constitute a "unit of production." For example, in the electrical industry, interconnection permits single centralized management of the whole branch.

While engaged in the pragmatic development of our system, we were on the watch for certain of the problems examined above, and attempted to resolve them, following as closely as possible—so far as our preparation would permit—the great ideas of Marx and Lenin. This prompted us to seek the solution to the contradiction existing in the Marxist political economy of the period of transition. In trying to overcome such contradictions—which can stand in the way of socialist development only temporarily as the socialist society does, in fact, exist—we sought the organizational methods most suited to practice and theory that would allow us to propel the new society forward as fast as possible by means of developing consciousness and production. This is the point at which we stand today.

To conclude:

1. We feel that Bettelheim commits two grave errors in analytical method: (a) He mechanically translates the concept of necessary correspondence between relationships of production and development of the productive forces, which is of universal validity, into the "microcosm" of the relationships of production in concrete aspects of a specific country during the period of transition; and thus draws apologetic conclusions, tinged with pragmatism, about so-called economic calculus. (b) He makes the same mechanical analysis of the concept of property.

2. Therefore, we do not agree with his opinion that financial self-management or accounting autonomy "are linked to a given state of the productive forces." Such a conclusion is merely the result of his analytical method.

3. We reject his concept of centralized management based on physical centralization of production (he gives the example of an interconnected electrical network), and instead apply it to centralization of primary economic decisions.

4. We find inaccurate his explanation of the reasons for the necessary unrestricted operation of the law of value and other mercantile categories during the period of transition, although we do not deny the possibility of using elements of this law for comparative purposes (cost, "profit" expressed in monetary terms).

5. For us, "centralized planning is characteristic of the socialist society," etc., and, therefore, we attribute it with much more power of conscious decision than does Bettelheim.

6. We consider the examination of the inconsistencies be-

tween the classical method of Marxist analysis and the survival of the mercantile categories in the socialist sector to be of great theoretical importance and deserving of more thorough research.

7. For the defenders of economic calculus, the following, for the purposes of this article, is appropriate: "God protect me from my friends; I will protect myself from my enemies."

NOTES

1. V. I. Lenin. [Translator's source: *Selected Works* (New York, International Publishers, 1967), Vol. III, pp. 766–767.]

2. "*Sobre el Sistema Presupuestario de Financiamiento*," *Nuestra Industria Económica,* No. 5, 1964, p. 16. [See Chapter 5.]

PART II

Decentralization vs. Centralization: Competing Systems of Economic Organization

4

On Production Costs and the Budgetary System

ERNESTO CHE GUEVARA

AMONG THE MANY PROBLEMS facing a socialist economy in practical planning is how to evaluate enterprise performance in light of new conditions brought about by the progress of the socialist revolution.

The capitalist economy is regulated by the law of value, which is directly expressed in the market. It is, in fact, impossible to consider the law of value outside the context of the market. By the same token, one could say that the expression of the law of value is, in fact, the capitalist market itself. During the process of building the socialist society, many of the relationships of production change as changes in ownership of the means of production take place and as the market sheds the last vestiges of free competition (which before was restricted only by monopolistic actions), acquiring new characteristics under the influence of the socialist sector that consciously regulates the market.*

In the case of Cuba, the shortage of commodities might have

* Guevara uses the term *el fondo mercantil,* which has been loosely translated as the market.

SOURCE: "Consideraciones sobre los costos de producción como base del análises económico de las empresas sujetas a sistema presupuestario," *Nuestra Industria Revista Economica,* Año 1, Junio 1963, pp. 4–12.

produced a rise in market prices until supply and demand again came into equilibrium. But we instituted rigid price-freezes and implemented a rationing system within which the real value of commodities could not be expressed by means of the market mechanism. Although rationing is a transitory measure, as time passes, an economy planned within one country begins to develop its own internal consistencies independent of the realities of the outside world. A price level is determined by the interplay of raw materials and other costs in the intricate process of production and distribution. When all products respond to prices that have an internal relationship among themselves which is distinct from the product relationship in the capitalist market, a new price relationship is brought about which in no way compares with that of the world market. How can prices be made to coincide with value? How can one consciously use the law of value to achieve a balance in the market on one hand, and a faithful reflection of real value on the other? This is one of the most serious problems the socialist economy faces.

The Soviet Union, the first country to build socialism, and those that followed its example determined to develop a planning process that could measure broad economic results by financial means. Relations among enterprises were left in a state of more or less free play. This was the origin of what is now called economic calculus (a poor translation of the Russian term that might better be expressed as auto-financing of enterprises or, more precisely, financial self-management).

Roughly speaking, then, financial self-management is based on establishing broad financial controls over enterprise activities, banks being the principal agencies of control. Suitably designed and regimented material incentives are used to promote independent initiative toward maximum utilization of productive capacity, which translates into greater benefits for the individual worker or the factory collective. Under this system, loans granted to socialist enterprises are repaid with interest in order to accelerate product turnover.

One of our first practical economic steps in Cuba was to centralize the financial activities of all enterprises. This permitted us to resolve major problems as they arose. After a time, we felt that the development of new, more centralized control techniques had become feasible. These would not be unduly bureaucratic and, under certain conditions, would be more efficient for industrial enterprises. Essentially, this system is based on adapting the advanced accounting techniques already being used in capitalist enterprises to our environment. Ours is a small country with a good communications system—not only land or air but also telephone and wireless—which provides a basis for continuous and up-to-date control.

Under our system, the bank supplies enterprises with funds in amounts specified in the national budget. Such funds are interest-free because credit relationships do not exist in these operations. This concept, which has been implemented in only a few branches of the economy, views a product in terms of a long internal flow process through various steps within the socialist sector up to the point of its transformation into a commodity. Such a transformation takes place only when there is a transfer of ownership—i.e., when the product leaves the state sector to become the property of some user.

The transfer of a product from one enterprise to another, whether within one ministry or between ministries, should be construed as merely a part of the production process in which values are added to the product. The bank, in this case, is only a cashier, that carries a record of such movements. The enterprise has no funds of its own and, therefore, all its revenues are reimbursed to the national budget.

Although this system has proved operable, it nevertheless has certain weaknesses that make it subject to serious criticism.

Such criticism is directed primarily at the lack of direct material incentives and at an inherent tendency toward bureaucracy.

At any rate, this is not the time to argue the matter. We would now like to consider the importance of analyzing the economic performance of the budgeted enterprise. How should it be done and under what premises? Here we consider production cost to be the principal factor, or indicator, that will allow the manager of a production unit, an enterprise, or a ministry to observe continuously the overall results of the production operation.

We stress cost analysis because our theory, in part, is based on the fact that the correlation or relationship between production costs and prices in the socialist sector is not necessarily stringent. For a less developed country like Cuba, which conducts a great deal of foregin trade, relations with the rest of the world are of primary importance.

For this reason, we argue that, in general, the domestic price structure must remain tied to the price structure of the foreign market. Clearly, of course, the latter refers only to the socialist trade sphere, in which money is used as a mere arithmetic measuring device.

In this construction, innumerable problems arise from already existing distortions in the world market in respect to foreign prices and technological advances, as well as from distortions of a seasonal nature, or are brought about by monopoly action, which cause prices to fluctuate daily in the international market. Although we have been unable to complete an analysis of this problem, we believe that it could be disposed of by establishing a general system based on a kind of historical average of prices prevailing in the capitalist market, corrected as needed to account for the influence of price movements in the socialist market. (Prices in socialist and capitalist markets are, on the other hand, closely related with respect to the world market.) Prices thus established, including a factor for freight costs, would remain fixed over given periods of time.

If the prices of the most important products in our economy were used as a basis for the estimation of other prices, we would arrive at a weighted historical average of world market prices. This would allow us to weigh the relative efficiency of each and every branch of production in our economy against that of the world market.

On the other hand, it should be seen that such a price structure would yield a distorted picture of the nation's productivity, because prices would merely measure average world efficiency. Such a structure would bring about dangerous propensities to consume temptingly low-priced products on which a much greater amount of labor has been expended than comparison with the world market would suggest.

This is a valid objection. In order to plan correctly, we would have to develop a series of index numbers by which to designate products according to their profitability.* As this system is based on central control of the economy and greater centralization of decision-making, relative profitability would be a mere indicator. What is important is the overall profitability of the production unit. If possible—and it is an enduring hope—this would be measured in terms of world-market value with regard to the level of prices to the consumer. Anything less is really inexcusable.

In no way does this mean that we have already come up with a criterion for evaluating new investments by which, according to current costs in existing industries, planned costs in proposed investment projects, and our potential for capital accumulation, we could decide automatically on the lines to be drawn. This could not happen precisely because the law of value operates in an almost pure form in the world market, while, in our domestic market, its operation will be decidedly influenced by the incidence of the socialist sector and by the amount of labor socially necessary at the local level to produce a given commodity. This is not to mention that it might be in our interest to concentrate much more on producing some kind of product which is not the most profitable, but which, in the long run, has strategic value or is simply of greater benefit to the people. We must again stress that the price to the consumer may bear little relation to the internal accounting price of the enterprises regulated under this system. With this plan, we would immediately have a mirror reflecting the overall progress of the economy at any point in time. By instituting this kind of organization in several industrial branches—not necessarily in the economy as a whole—we could apply an increasingly more accurate system of economic analysis.

Costs would be the real indicator of an enterprise's perform-

* Guevara uses the term *rentabilidad,* which can also be translated as "yield."

ance, whether or not they compared favorably with price levels in the socialist sector or even, in some isolated cases, with that at which the product is sold to the consumer. What matters is the continuous evaluation of the enterprise's performance as measured by its success in lowering costs. In this case, prices reflect the automatic analysis of profits in relation to world prices. A great deal of work must be done on these problems, which until now have received rather sketchy treatment.

We need to develop an entire system of cost accounting that would systematically reward and punish success and failure in efforts to lower costs. We need to develop standards of raw material consumption, indirect costs, goods in process, raw material inventories, and finished goods.

We must continuously upgrade economic performance, systematize inventory controls, and analyze in detail all the above economic indicators.

In our system of accounting, we have divided costs into raw materials, direct materials, indirect materials, cost of labor power, depreciation, and social security. The latter is paid by State enterprises based on the wage fund.

Each and every one of the above components must receive attention. Social security, however, should not be included in this analysis; when in the future all these methods are perfected, the State will simply allocate a portion of its annual budget to social-security payments. Such payments would then be made without regard to the wages received by individual workers.

As to raw-material consumption and other direct costs, we can achieve savings directly by making technological changes and avoiding waste. Indirect cost savings can be achieved by reducing power and fuel consumption, etc., by implementing organizational measures, or by making technological changes. Labor costs can be lowered by raising overall productivity. With regard to depreciation, we have to develop more scientific methods for establishing rates, and must also prolong the useful life of plant and equipment through adequate maintenance, thus allowing depreciation to become a real accumulation fund.

However analyzed, everything is reduced to a common denominator: *increasing labor productivity.* This is essential for building both socialism and communism.

Now then, there are different areas in which cost controls could be established: The first is administration. Controls can be implemented through proper organization and trained administrators that together would accustom all personnel to the job of promptly analyzing costs and would make the handling of cost a routine work habit.

For the time being, of course, we must anticipate numerous difficulties in bringing all this about, because there is little tradition of economic analysis among our administrators; because, in addition, their educational level is low; and because the economy as a whole is not as yet well organized. Still, conscientious efforts along these lines, a task we have already begun, will bear fruit in a very short time.

It should be made clear that cost analysis does not by itself lead to adoption of the measures required to correct observed deficiencies. There are very important objective factors that will stand in the way of this for a while: poor organization of supplies, which so depend on foreign markets; the poor maintenance job we have done until now, which causes unexpected production stoppages; the lack of procedures governing legal relations among enterprises, which causes severe disruptions in plans when, for example, an enterprise fails to retrieve the supplies it has requested and abruptly changes its order. In other words, general defects in planning and problems in foreign supply will for some time make production units and enterprises subject to abrupt changes in cost levels. However, this should not worry us so much as our inability to understand such a phenomenon as soon as it arises.

We can also work on the problem at the level of the individual, who will be able to exercise control over costs as soon as adequate standards have been established to regulate both the quality and the quantity of his labor. Regarding quality, the economization of raw materials can be used as an instrument that will produce substantial results in a short time. This is a task in which we are progressing steadily, though perhaps not as rapidly as need be. We must also stress collective attention to costs. The collective of the production unit will bring this about once cost analysis of its economic performance is accompanied by incentives, primarily of a social nature, that focus the collective's attention on lowering costs in order to obtain benefits. This exacts a deepening of consciousness and a great leap forward in quality of organization. The Party, by taking this task upon itself and thereby bringing it to the people, can in a short time effect a different attitude toward State administration on the part of workers. We cannot, however, even dream that organizational changes can be made with comparable speed; we must, therefore, go through a period during which numerous adjustments will have to be made. We have several pilot factories in operation in which we are studying systems of collective social incentives that would permit the lowering of costs. Clearly, this study *must* be based on a production plan that is to be met without excuses (except where there is extremely unusual justification). The point at which the production plan is met would be the threshold beyond which collective performance could be measured in order to establish whatever incentives might be required.

This broad task is laid out based on the idea that central direction of the economy is possible. But this does not imply that all decisions would stem from the highest level; rather, we must establish various levels of decision-making by which organization itself would secure adherence to principles and would force the independent adoption of whatever measures might be necessary at that particular level. The system's smooth operation depends on the efficacy with which the groundwork is laid in clearly establishing relations among the various levels and in drawing lines of responsibility and authority.

All our efforts must be directed to assuring that the job of administration and control becomes more and more simple so that administrative agencies may concentrate on planning and technological development. Once all the indicators are established and the methods and routines of cost control are brought into effect by improved planning in all sectors of the economy, the administrative task will become mechanical and will present no serious problems. At this point, modern planning methods will take on added importance, and we will approach the ideal of being able to regulate the economy through mathematical analysis, thereby achieving the best allocation of resources between consumption and capital accumulation, as well as among the various branches of production. Clearly, however, we must remember that the human individual, the very reason for being of the Revolution and our hopes, cannot be reduced to a mere formula. His needs will become increasingly complex, going beyond simple material requirements. The various branches of production will become automated, and labor productivity will rise enormously. The worker's free time will be devoted to athletic, cultural, and scientific endeavors of the highest order. Work will become a social need.

The feasibility of bringing this far-distant future nearer to us is conditioned by the technical ability of workers and specialists to maintain the highest standards of service in each industrial sector. It depends on our ability to plan so that the people's material aspirations dovetail with the economy's vital needs, so that we may provide the greatest possible amount of goods while maintaining an adequate rate of economic growth. If economic development is seen in this way, the regulatory function will be simple and can be performed by specialized agencies with the help of machines.

If the numerous technicians in our ministry were relieved from the pedestrian—although necessary—production tasks in which they are engaged and could devote their efforts to research and development, we could immediately perceive great improvements in quality.

We must work to assure that the administrative task is carried out with clocklike precision and to improve production in the greatest possible measure through technological progress.

5

On the Budgetary Finance System

ERNESTO CHE GUEVARA

General Background

THIS SUBJECT has already been discussed to some extent, but not sufficiently, and I consider it imperative to analyze it more thoroughly in order to gain a clear idea of its scope and methodology.

It has its official sanction in the *law regulating the budgetary system of financing state enterprises* and was first used within the Ministry of Industry.

Its history is brief, barely going back to 1960, when it began to be used with some consistency. Our intention, however, is to analyze not its development but rather the system as it is today, with the understanding that its evolution has not by any means come to an end.

We are interested in comparing the budgetary system with so-called economic calculus,* emphasizing financial self-management, which is a fundamental differentiating characteristic of the latter, and attitudes toward material incentives, which are the basis of financial self-management.

* This economic system has also been called auto-finance and self-finance or self-management.

SOURCE: "Sobre el sistema presupuesta de financiamiento," Año 2, Febrero 1964, pp. 3–24.

The explanation of differences is difficult because they are often subtle and obscure; moreover, the budgetary finance system has not been studied thoroughly enough for its description to compete in clarity with that of economic calculus.

We will begin with a few quotations. The first is from Marx's economic manuscripts, which date back to the time when his work was described as that of *the young Marx,* when even his language manifested the influence of the philosophical ideas that contributed to his formation, while his thoughts on economics were less precise. Nevertheless, Marx was in the prime of his life, had already embraced the cause of the meek and explained it philosophically without the scientific rigor of *Capital.* Thinking like a philosopher, he referred to man more specifically as a human individual and stressed the problems of his liberation as a social being. He had not yet begun to study the inevitable break in the period's social structure that would lead to the period of transition under the dictatorship of the proletariat. In *Capital,* Marx emerges as the scientific economist who carefully analyzes the transitory nature of social epochs and their identification with the relationships of production. Here, he does not leave room for philosophical discourse.

The weight of this monument to the human intellect is such that it often makes us forget the humanist nature (in the best sense of the word) of his concerns. The mechanics of the relationships of production and their consequence, the class struggle, obscure to a degree the objective fact that men are the protagonists of history. At the moment, our interest is man. We therefore quote the following, which, while belonging to his youth, is no less representative of the philosopher's thought:

> . . . Communism as the positive transcendence of private property, as human self-estrangement, and therefore, as the real appropriation of the human essence by and for man; communism, therefore, as the complete return of man to himself as a social (i.e., human) being—a return become *conscious,* and accomplished within the entire wealth of previous development. This communism, as fully developed

> naturalism, equals humanism, and as fully developed humanism, equals naturalism; it is the genuine resolution of the conflict between man and nature and between man and man—the true resolution of the strife between existence and essence, between objectification and self-confirmation, between freedom and necessity, between the individual and the species. Communism is the riddle of history solved, and it knows itself to be that solution.[1]

The word *conscious* is emphasized because Marx considered it basic in stating the problem. He thought about man's liberation and saw communism as the solution to the contradictions that brought about his alienation—but as a conscious act. That is to say, communism cannot be seen merely as the result of class contradictions in a highly developed society, contradictions that would be resolved during a transitional stage before reaching the crest. Man is a conscious actor in history. Without this *consciousness,* which embraces his awareness as a social being, there can be no communism. Marx did not abandon his militant attitude while writing *Capital.* When the Gotha congress met in 1875 for the purpose of uniting the existing German labor organizations (the Social Democratic Labor Party and the General Association of German Workers), and the program of the same name was put together, Marx's response was the *Critique of the Gotha Program.*

This paper, prepared during the writing of his principal work, and having a clear bias, is important because in it he touches on the subject of the period of transition. In his analysis of point three of the Gotha Program he deals to some extent with several of the most important issues related to the transitional stage, which he considered to be the result of the breakdown of the advanced capitalist system. He did not anticipate the use of money in this period, but he did foresee individual rewards to labor, because:

> What we have to deal with here is a communist society, not as it has *developed* on its own foundations, but, on the contrary, as it *emerges* from capitalist society; which is thus in

> every respect, economically, morally and intellectually, still stamped with the birthmarks of the old society from whose womb it emerges. Accordingly the individual producer receives back from society—after the deductions have been made—exactly what he gives to it. What he has given to it is his individual amount of labor.[2]

Marx could only intuitively perceive the development of the worldwide imperialist system; Lenin listens to its heartbeat and diagnoses it:

> Uneven economic and political development is an absolute law of capitalism. Hence, the victory of socialism is possible first in several or even in one capitalist country alone. After expropriating the capitalists and organizing their own socialist production, the victorious proletariat of that country will arise *against* the rest of the world—the capitalist world—attracting to its cause the oppressed classes of other countries, stirring uprisings in those countries against the capitalists, and in case of need using even armed force against the exploiting classes and their states. The political form of a society wherein the proletariat is victorious in overthrowing the bourgeoisie will be a democratic republic, which will more and more concentrate the forces of the proletariat of a given nation or nations, to the struggle against states that have not yet gone over to socialism. The abolition of classes is impossible without a dictatorship of the oppressed class, of the proletariat. A free union of nations in socialism is impossible without a more or less prolonged and stubborn struggle of the socialist republics against the backward states.[3]

A few years later Stalin systematized the idea to the point of believing social revolution to be possible in the colonies:

> The third contradiction is the contradiction between the handful of ruling "civilized" nations and the hundreds of millions of the colonial and dependent peoples of the world. Imperialism is the most barefaced exploitation and the most

> inhuman oppression of hundreds of millions of people inhabiting vast colonies and dependent countries. The purpose of this exploitation and of this oppression is to squeeze out super-profits. But in exploiting these countries imperialism is compelled to build railroads, factories and mills there, to create industrial and commercial cities. The appearance of a class of proletarians, the emergence of a native intelligentsia, the awakening of national consciousness, the growth of the movement for emancipation—such are the inevitable results of this "policy." The growth of the revolutionary movement in all colonies and dependent countries without exception clearly testified to this fact. This circumstance is of importance for the proletariat in that it radically undermines the position of capitalism by converting the colonies and dependent countries from reserves of imperialism into reserves of the proletarian revolution.[4]

Lenin's theses are proved in practice by his victory in Russia and the birth of the U.S.S.R.

We confront a new phenomenon: the advent of a socialist revolution in a single, economically backward country covering an area of 22 million square kilometers that is sparsely populated, further impoverished by war, and as if this were not enough, under attack by imperialist powers.

After a period of war communism, Lenin lays the foundations of the NEP [National Economic Plan] and, with it, the basis for Soviet society's development to the present day.

It is important to describe here what the situation in the Soviet Union was, and no one can do this better than Lenin:

> Thus, in 1918, I was of the opinion that with regard to the economic situation then obtaining in the Soviet Republic, state capitalism would be a step forward. This sounds very strange, and perhaps even absurd, for already at that time our Republic was a socialist republic and we were every day hastily—perhaps too hastily—adopting various new economic measures which could not be described as any-

thing but socialist measures. Nevertheless, I then held the view that in relation to the economic situation then obtaining in the Soviet Republic state capitalism would be a step forward, and I explained my idea simply by enumerating the elements of the economic system of Russia. In my opinion these elements were the following: "(1) patriarchal, i.e., the most primitive form of agriculture; (2) small commodity production (this includes the majority of the peasants who trade in grain); (3) private capitalism; (4) state capitalism, and (5) socialism." All these economic elements were present in Russia at that time. I set myself the task of explaining the relationship of these elements to each other, and whether one of the non-socialist elements, namely, state capitalism, should not be rated higher than socialism. I repeat: it seems very strange to everyone that a non-socialist element should be rated higher than, regarded as superior to, socialism in a republic which declares itself a socialist republic. But the fact will become intelligible if you recall that we definitely did not regard the economic system of Russia as something homogenous and highly developed; we were fully aware that in Russia we had patriarchal agriculture, i.e., the most primitive form of agriculture, alongside the socialist form. What role could state capitalism play in these circumstances? . . .

. . . Now that I have emphasized the fact that as early as 1918 we regarded state capitalism as a possible line of retreat, I shall deal with the results of our New Economic Policy. I repeat: at that time it was still a very vague idea, but in 1921, after we had passed through the most important stage of the Civil War—and passed through it victoriously—we felt that the impact of a grave—I think it was the gravest—internal political crisis in Soviet Russia. This internal crisis brought to light discontent not only among a considerable section of the peasantry but also among the workers. This was the first and, I hope, the last time in the history of Soviet Russia that feeling ran against us among large masses of peasants, not consciously but instinctively.

> What gave rise to this peculiar, and for us, of course, very unpleasant, situation? The reason for it was that in our economic offensive we had run too far ahead, that we had not provided ourselves with adequate resources, that the masses sensed what we ourselves were not then able to formulate consciously but what we admitted soon after, a few weeks later, namely, that the direct transition to purely socialist forms, to purely socialist distribution, was beyond our available strength, and that if we were unable to effect a retreat so as to confine ourselves to easier tasks, we would face disaster.[5]

As can be seen, the economic and political situation in the Soviet Union required the cutback of which Lenin spoke. The entire policy, therefore, can be characterized as a tactic closely linked to the country's historical situation. Not everything Lenin says here should be accorded universal validity. It seems to us that two factors are highly applicable with regard to the introduction of socialism in other countries:

1. The characteristics of czarist Russia at the time of the Revolution; levels of technology; the special character of the people; and general conditions in the country—including not only destruction by a world war but also the devastation wrought by the white hordes and the imperialist invaders.
2. The general characteristics of the period with respect to techniques of economic administration and control.

Oskar Lange, in his article, "Current Economic Problems in Poland," says:

> Bourgeois economics performs yet another function. The bourgeoisie and the monopolies do not allocate substantial resources for the creation of schools of higher learning and institutes of scientific study in the field of economics merely to have an aid for the apologetics of the capitalist system. Rather, they expect something more from economists. They expect help in resolving the numerous problems connected with the political economy. During the period of capitalist competition there was little to be done in this area. The

only problems lay in financial administration, monetary and credit policy, customs policy, transportation and so forth. But under the conditions of monopoly capitalism, and especially in light of the increased entry of state capitalism into economic life, problems proliferate. We can list a few: market analysis to facilitate the formulation of monopoly price policy; methods of centralized administration in a complex of industrial enterprises such as reciprocal accounting systems; and planned interlocking of activities, development, location, and amortization or investment policy. All this gives rise to questions concerning the activity of the capitalist State during the present period. These are much the same as those pertaining to criteria for the activity of nationalized industries, particularly investment and location policy (as, for example, in the power field); and to manners of political and economic intervention in the national economy as a whole, etc.

To all these problems has been added a number of technical and economic procedures that we can, in part, use in the process of building socialism. (They will doubtless be used by workers in presently capitalist countries when in the future such countries make the transition to socialism.) Such procedures may be employed, for example, in market analysis; programming the activity of enterprises forming part of a group; internal accounting methods within each factory or group of factories; and amortization or similar policies.[6]

It should be noted that Cuba had not made its transition nor even begun its revolution when this was written. Many of the advanced techniques that Lange describes existed in Cuba; that is, conditions in Cuban society at that time permitted centralized control over some enterprises whose headquarters were in Havana or New York.

The Empresa Consolidada del Petroleo (Consolidated Petroleum Enterprise), formed by the merger of the three existing imperialist refineries (Esso, Texaco, and Shell), maintained and, in some cases, perfected its control systems and is considered a model in this ministry. Where no centralist tradition existed or where practical conditions for centralization were lacking, they were created on the basis of national experience. An example is the Empresa Consolidada de la Harina (Consolidated Flour Enterprise), which took first place among the enterprises under the jurisdiction of the vice-minister of light industry.*

Although the experience of the early days of industrial management fully convinces us of the impossibility of rationally following another course, it would be useless now to ask whether the organizational measures taken then would have yielded similar or better results by introducing self-management at the unit level. The important thing is that it could be done under very difficult conditions and that centralization made possible the liquidation—in the case of the shoe industry, for example—of a great many inefficient shops, and permitted the reallocation of six thousand workers to other branches of production.

Through this series of quotations, we have tried to provide the background needed to understand the budgetary system.

First, communism is a goal consciously pursued by man. Thus, education, which clears the people's consciousness of the old ideas handed down from the capitalist society, is extremely important. It should be kept in mind, however, that without parallel progress in production, communism cannot be achieved.

Second, from a technological standpoint, we should borrow the most advanced forms of economic administration available, from whatever source, so long as they can be adapted for use in the new society. We can use the petrochemical technology of the imperialist camp without fear of being "infected" by bourgeois ideology. The same rule applies with regard to technical standards in production control and administration.

In hope of not seeming too pretentious, we could paraphrase Marx's reference to the use of Hegel's dialectics and say that such techniques can be turned to rights.

* See Chapter 8 for an analysis of the flour industry.

A comparison of the accounting techniques commonly used in socialist countries with those used in Cuba would point up a conceptual difference perhaps comparable to the one between competition and monopoly in the capitalist system. In short, the earlier techniques were the basis for getting both systems "on their feet." After that point, however, their paths separate. Socialism has its own relationships of production and its own requirements.

We might say, then, that as a technique the predecessor of the budgetary finance system was imperialist monopoly as it existed in Cuba after going through changes inherent in the long process of development of administrative and control techniques—a process extending from the dawn of monopoly until today. When the monopolists left, they took their top management—and some middle management—people with them. Meanwhile, our immature idea of the revolution led us to do away with a number of established procedures merely because they were capitalist. Thus, our system has not obtained the degree of efficiency in production control and administration that characterized local monopoly branches. We are on that road, however, and clearing it of whatever dead leaves remain from the past.

General Differences Between Economic Calculus and the Budgetary Finance System

There are differences of varying degrees between economic calculus and the budgetary finance system. We will attempt to divide them into two large groups and explain them briefly. There are methodological differences—practical, we might say —and differences of a more serious nature. The latter, however, because of their nature, can make analysis appear Byzantine if one does not proceed with great caution.

It is important to clarify, at this point, that what we are looking for is a more efficient way of reaching communism. There is no discrepancy in principle. Economic calculus has proved that it yields practical results, and, based on similar principles, both systems seek the same ends. But we believe that our system's plan of action, if properly developed, can increase the effectiveness of economic management by the socialist State and deepen mass consciousness. Moreover, through concerted effort, it can strengthen the bonds of the world socialist system.

The most immediate difference arises with regard to the enterprise. For us, an enterprise is a conglomerate of factories or production units that use similar technology, possess a common market for their output, or are located in some cases, in the same geographical area. The economic calculus system views an enterprise as a production unit with its own legal personality. A sugar mill is an enterprise under the latter system, while under our system all sugar mills as a whole, together with other production connected with the sugar industry, constitute the Empresa Consolidada del Azucar (Consolidated Sugar Enterprise). There have been recent experiments of this type in the U.S.S.R. —conforming, of course, to the specific conditions of that country.[7]

Another difference is the way money is used. Under our system, it functions only as means of measurement, as a price reflection of enterprise performance that is analyzed by central administrative bodies so as to be able to control such performance. Under economic calculus, money serves not only this purpose but also acts as a means of payment, an indirect instrument of control, because without funds the production unit could not operate. Under such circumstances, the production unit's relations with the bank are similar to those of a private producer in the capitalist system who must exhaustively explain plans and prove solvency to his bank. Naturally, in this case, there is no arbitrary decision, rather adherence to a plan, and relations are carried on among state organizations.

Consequently, because of the way in which money is used, our enterprises have no funds of their own. There are separate bank accounts for withdrawals and deposits. The enterprise may withdraw funds in accordance with the plan from the general expense account and the special wages account. But all deposits come automatically under State control.

Enterprises in the majority of our sister countries have their own funds in the banks that they may back up with interest-bearing loans. But the funds that "belong" to the enterprise, as well as the loans, actually belong to the society, and their movement reflects the enterprise's financial state.

As to work standards, enterprises operating under economic calculus use overtime, piecework, and work by the hour. We are trying to institute overtime work in our enterprises as well, with maximum premiums limited to the highest wage scale. We will deal with this subject at greater length below.

Under a fully developed system of economic calculus, there are rigid contractual procedures by which monetary penalties can be invoked for failures to comply. Such procedures are based on a legal scaffolding erected over years of experience. In our country such a structure does not yet exist, even for self-managed entities such as INRA.* It is especially difficult to set up because of the coexistence of two very dissimilar systems. For the time being, we have the Comision de Arbitraje (Arbitration Council), which lacks executive powers but which is gradually growing in importance and may in the future provide a basis for our legal structure. Internally, among entities subject to the budgetary finance system, decision-making is easy, because administrative measures are taken if accounting controls are properly carried and up-to-date (which is already the case in most of this ministry's enterprises). [Industry]

On the basis that under both systems the general State plan is the supreme authority, adherence to which is compulsory, operational analogies and differences can be summed up by saying that self-management is based on overall centralized control and more exaggerated decentralization. The bank exercises indirect control by means of "the rouble," and the monetary results of the enterprise's operation provide a measure for premiums. Material interest is the great lever that moves workers both individually and collectively.

The budgetary finance system is based on centralized control

* The National Institute of Agrarian Reform (INRA) was the fundamental revolutionary institution that transformed Cuban agriculture.

of the enterprise's activity. Its plan and economic activity are directly controlled by central administrative bodies; it has no funds of its own nor does it receive bank credits. And it uses material incentives on an individual basis or, in other words, individual monetary premiums and penalties. At the proper time, it will also institute collective incentives. Direct material incentives, however, are limited by the method of wage payment.

More Subtle Contradictions. Material Incentives Versus Consciousness

Here we come upon more subtle contradictions, which must be better explained. The subject of material versus moral incentives has given rise to many discussions among those interested in such matters. We must make clear that *we do not deny the objective need for material incentives.* But we are unwilling to use them as the primary instrument of motivation. We believe that, in economics, this kind of device quickly becomes a category per se and then imposes its power over man's relationships. It should be recalled that this category is a product of capitalism and is destined to die under socialism.

How do we make it die?

"Little by little, by means of gradually increasing the quantity of consumer goods available to the people, thereby obviating the need for such incentives," we are told. This concept seems too mechanical, too rigid. "Consumer goods"—this is the slogan and great molder of conscience for the proponents of the other system. In our mind, however, direct material incentives and consciousness are contradictory terms.

This is one point at which our differences take on meaningful dimensions. We are no longer dealing with niceties. For advocates of financial self-management, the use of direct material incentives throughout the various stages of building communism does not contradict the "development" of consciousness. But for us it does. It is for this reason that we struggle against the predominance of material incentives—because they would retard the development of socialist morality.

If material incentives are in contradiction to the development of consciousness but, on the other hand, are a great force for obtaining production gains, should it be understood that preferential attention to the development of consciousness retards production? In comparative terms, it is possible within a given period, although no one has made the relevant calculations. We maintain that the development of consciousness does more for development of production in a relatively short time than material incentives do. We take this stance because our society's development is generally projected to lead to communism. This presupposes that work would cease to be a painful necessity and become an agreeable imperative. Such a statement is loaded with subjectivism and requires sanction in the experience we are gaining. If in the course of experience it proves to seriously block the development of the productive forces, then the decision must be made to act quickly in order to get back on familiar paths. This has not happened yet, and the method, which is being improved through practice, is acquiring greater consistency and proving its internal coherence.

How, then, should material interest be handled? We believe that its existence must always be kept in mind whether as a collective expression of the masses' wants, or as an individual presence, a reflection in the worker's conscience of old society's habits. We still do not have a well-defined idea on an approach to collective material interest. There are problems with the planning apparatus that affect its reliability. Moreover, we have been unable until now to devise a scheme that would allow us to steer clear of difficulties. To us, the greatest danger lies in the antagonism between the State administration and the production entities. The Soviet economist Liberman has studied this antagonism and has concluded that methods of applying collective incentive should be changed. He proposes that the old formula of premiums based on plan fulfillment be abandoned in favor of more advanced methods.

Although we do not agree with his stress on material interest (as a motive force), we share his concern about the aberrations that the "plan fulfillment" concept has undergone over the years. Relations between enterprises and central administrative bodies acquire quite contradictory forms, and the methods employed by the former to obtain benefits sometimes acquire characteristics that in fact differ widely with the image of socialist morality.

We believe that, in a way, the possibilities for development offered by the new relationships of production, which could accelerate man's progress toward the "the kingdom of freedom," are being wasted. In fact, in defining the basic arguments for the system, we pointed up the interrelationship between education and the development of production. We can embark on the task of creating the new consciousness because we are confronting new forms of production relationships. And, although in a general historical sense consciousness is a product of the relationships of production, we must still take into account the characteristics of the present era whose principal contradiction is (at the world level) between imperialism and socialism. Socialist ideas act on the consciousness of all the world's peoples; therefore, its development can progress commensurate with the specific state of the productive forces in a given country.

During the early years in the U.S.S.R., the Socialist State characterized the regime despite relationships of a much more backward kind that existed in its midst. Under capitalism there are remnants of the feudal stage, but it is capitalism that characterizes the economy after emerging victorious in its basic sectors. In Cuba, the development of contradictions between the two world systems permitted the establishment of the Revolution's socialist nature. Its nature was determined by a conscious act, thanks to the knowledge acquired by the revolutionary leaders, to the deepening of the mass consciousness, and to the correlation of world forces.

If all this is possible, why not regard education as a persistent aid to the socialist State in eliminating the old aberrations of a society that has died and has taken its old relationships of production to the grave with it? Let us refer to Lenin:

> Infinitely stereotyped, for instance, is the argument they learned by rote during the development of West-European

Social-Democracy, namely, that we are not yet ripe for socialism, that, as certain "learned" gentlemen among them put it, the objective economic premises for socialism do not exist in our country. It does not occur to any of them to ask: but what about a people that found itself in a revolutionary situation such as that created during the first imperialist war? Might it not, influenced by the hopelessness of its situation, fling itself into a struggle that would offer it at least some chance of securing conditions for the further development of civilization that were somewhat unusual?

"The development of the productive forces of Russia has not attained the level that makes socialism possible." All the heroes of the Second International, including, of course, Sukhanov, beat the drums about this proposition. They keep harping on this incontrovertible proposition in a thousand different keys, and think that it is the decisive criterion of our revolution.

But what if the situation, which drew Russia into the imperialist world war that involved every more or less influential West-European country and made her a witness of the eve of the revolutions maturing or partly already begun in the East, gave rise to circumstances that put Russia and her development in a position which enabled us to achieve precisely that combination of a "peasant war" with the working-class movement suggested in 1856 by no less a Marxist than Marx himself as a possible prospect for Prussia?

What if the complete hopelessness of the situation, by stimulating the efforts of the workers and peasants tenfold, offered us the opportunity to create the fundamental requisites of civilization in a different way from that of the West-European countries? Has that altered the general line of development of world history? Has that altered the basic relations between the basic classes of all the countries that are being, or have been, drawn into the general course of world history?

If a definite level of culture is required for the building of

> socialism (although nobody can say just what that definite "level of culture" is, for it differs in every West-European country), why cannot we begin by first achieving the prerequisites for that definite level of culture in a revolutionary way, and *then,* with the aid of the workers' and peasants' government and the Soviet system, proceed to overtake the other nations? [8]

As for the presence of individual material interest, we both recognize (though all the while combating it by means of education) and apply it in designing standards for premiums, overtime, and wage penalties for failures to comply with such standards.

On this subject, one subtle difference with the advocates of self-management resides in the arguments regarding the paying of a wage based on premiums and penalties. The production standard is the average amount of labor that creates a product in a certain time, given average qualifications on the part of the worker, and the specific conditions under which equipment is used. It is the contribution of a work quota to the society by one of its members in fulfillment of his social duty. If quotas are overfulfilled, there is a greater benefit for the society, and it may be assured that the worker who does it fulfills his duties better than the average and deserves, therefore, a material reward. We accept this as a necessary evil during a transitory period, but we do not agree that the maxim *"from each according to his ability, to each according to his labor"* should be literally interpreted as full payment in extra wages for the amount exceeding a given quota. (There are cases in which payment exceeds the percentage of fulfillment as a special incentive to individual productivity.) Marx explains very clearly in the *Critique of the Gotha Program* that a considerable part of the worker's wages goes to purposes far removed from the immediate relationship:

> Let us take first of all the words "proceeds of labor" in the sense of the product of labor, then the cooperative proceeds of labor are the *total social product.*

From this is then to be deducted:

First, cover for replacement of the means of production used up.

Secondly, additional portion for expansion of production.

Thirdly, reserve or insurance fund to provide against mis-adventures, disturbances through natural events, etc.

These deductions from the "undiminished proceeds of labor" are an economic necessity and their magnitude is to be determined by available means and forces, and partly by calculation of probabilities, but they are in no way calculable by equity.

There remains the other part of the total product, destined to serve as means of consumption.

Before this is divided among the individuals, there has to be deducted from it:

First, the general costs of administration not belonging to production.

This part will, from the outset, be very considerably restricted in comparison with present-day society and it diminishes in proportion as the new society develops.

Secondly, that which is destined for the communal satisfaction of needs, such as schools, health services, etc.

From the outset this part is considerably increased in comparison with present-day society and it increases in proportion as the new society develops.

Thirdly, funds for those unable to work, etc., in short, what is included under so-called official poor relief today.

Only now do we come to the "distribution" which the programme, under Lassallean influence, alone has in view in its narrow fashion, namely that part of the means of consumption which is divided among the individual producers of the cooperative society.

The "undiminished proceeds of labor" have already quietly become converted into the "diminished" proceeds, although what the producer is deprived of is his capacity as a member of society.

Just as the phrase "undiminished proceeds of labor" has

> disappeared, so now does the phrase "proceeds of labor" disappear altogether.[9]

All this shows that the size of the reserve funds depends on a series of politico-economic or politico-administrative decisions. As all the goods existing in the reserve always derive from unremunerated labor, we must conclude that decisions regarding the size of the funds that Marx has analyzed imply changes in payments, that is, variations in the amount of labor that is not directly remunerated. One should add to this that no mathematical method is known to exist by which to determine the "fairness" of the premium for overfulfillment (or of even the base wage). It must, therefore, be based primarily on the new social relationships, on the legal structure that sanctions the collective's method of distributing a part of the individual worker's labor.

Our system of standards establishes compulsory professional training for promotion to higher job categories. In time, this requirement will bring about a significant rise in the level of technical skills.

Failure to fulfill a quota means failure to fulfill one's social duty. The society punishes the offender by deducting a part of his wages.* The quota is more than a mere guidepost marking a feasible or conventional measure of labor; it is the expression of the worker's moral obligation, *his social duty*. Here, administrative and ideological control must join forces. The party's role in the production unit is to provide internal motivation and to use the example set by its militant members in order to assure that production, labor, training, and participation in economic matters will become an integral, routine part of the worker's lives.

There is a profound difference (at least in the strict sense of the terms employed) between our position and that of the proponents of economic calculus with regard to the possibility of making conscious use of the law of value.

The *Manual of Political Economy* says:

* This procedure no longer exists in Cuba, where virtually all economic penalties have been eliminated.

> Under capitalism, the law of value operates as a blind, spontaneous force, ruling over men. Under socialism, however, there is an awareness of the law value. The State takes it into account—and *uses* it in the planned administration of the economy.
>
> A knowledge of the operation of the law of value and its *intelligent use* must necessarily help economic leaders to channel production along rational lines, to systematically improve work methods, and to make use of untapped reserves in order to increase and improve production.[10]

The words we have underlined characterize the spirit of the paragraphs.

The law of value would act as a blind force, but because it is known to us, it can be used and controlled by us.

But this law has certain characteristics: First, it is conditioned upon the existence of a mercantile society. Second, its results are not susceptible to measurement *a priori* and must be reflected in the market in which exchange takes place between producers and consumers. Third, it is coherent as a whole, which includes world markets; changes and distortions in certain branches of production are reflected in the total result. Fourth, given its nature as an economic law, it operates basically as a tendency, and, in the period of transition, its tendency must logically be to disappear.

Some paragraphs further on, the *Manual* states:

> The socialist State uses the law of value by exercising—through the financial and credit system—control over production and distribution of the social product.
>
> Domination of the law of value, and its use in conformance with a plan, provide an enormous advantage to socialism over capitalism. Because the law of value is controlled, its operation in the socialist economy does not imply the waste of social labor which accompanies the anarchy of production characteristic of capitalism. This law and its related categories—money, prices, commerce, credit, finance—are used successfully in the U.S.S.R. and other popular democratic countries in the interest of building

> socialism and communism. They are employed in the planned administration of the national economy.[11]

This may be considered accurate only as regards the total amount of the values produced for direct use by the people and the respective funds available for this acquisition—which any capitalist treasury minister could do with relatively balanced finances. Every one of the law's partial distortions fits within that framework.

Further on, the *Manual* states:

> Mercantile production, the law of value, and money will disappear only when the highest stage of communism is achieved. But in order to bring about conditions favorable to disappearance of mercantile production and circulation, it is necessary to *develop* and use the law of value as well as monetary and mercantile relationships while the communist society is being built.[12]

Why *develop?* We understand that the capitalist categories are retained for a time and that the length of this period cannot be predetermined, but the characteristics of the period of transition are those of a society that is throwing off its old bonds in order to move quickly into the new stage.

The *tendency* should be, in our opinion, to eliminate as fast as possible the old categories, including the market, money, and, therefore, material interest—or, better, to eliminate the conditions for their existence. The contrary would be to assume that the task of building socialism in a backward society is in the nature of a historical accident and that its leaders, in order to excuse the *mistake,* should strive to consolidate all the categories inherent in the intermediate society. All that would remain as foundations of the new society would be the distribution of income according to labor and the tendency to eliminate man's exploitation of man. These things alone seem inadequate as the means to bring about the enormous change in conscience needed to face the transition. Such a change must take place through the multiple action of all the new relationships, education, and socialist morality. The individualistic concept instilled in man's consciousness by direct material incentives must be eradicated because it obstructs the development of man as a social being.

To summarize our differences: We consider the law of value to be partially operative because elements of the mercantile society still remain. This is also reflected in the type of exchange that takes place between the State as supplier and the consumer. We believe that, especially in a society with a highly developed foreign trade sector such as ours, the law of value on an international scale must be recognized as a fact governing commercial transactions even within the socialist camp. We recognize the need for this trade to assume a higher form in countries of the new society in order to assume through exchange that the differences between the developed and the more backward countries do not widen. In other words, it is necessary to develop trade formulas that permit the financing of industrial investments in developing countries even though this contravenes the price system prevailing in the capitalist world market. This would allow the entire socialist camp to progress more evenly, which would naturally have the effect of smoothing off the rough edges and of unifying the spirit of proletarian internationalism. (The recent agreement between Cuba and the U.S.S.R. is indicatory of the steps that can be taken in this direction.) We deny the possibility of consciously using the law of value, basing our argument on the absence of a free market that automatically expresses the contradiction between producers and consumers. We deny the existence of the *commodity* category in relationships among State enterprises. We consider all such establishments to be part of the single large enterprise that is the State (although in practice this is not yet the case in our country). The law of value and planning are two terms linked by a contradiction and its resolution. We can therefore state that centralized planning is characteristic of the socialist society, its definition. It is the point at which man consciously finally succeeds in synthesizing and directing the economy toward his goal, which is the total liberation of the human being within the framework of a communist society.

On Price Formation

We also profoundly disagree with some aspects of the theory of price formation. Under self-management, prices are formed "with an eye on the law of value"—but which meaning of the law? The starting point is to calculate the socially required labor needed to produce a given article. Socially necessary labor is an economic and historical concept, however, and is thus changeable not only on the local (or national) level but on the world level as well. Continued technological progress, a result of competition in the capitalist world, reduces necessary labor expenditure and thereby lowers product value. A closed society can ignore such changes for a time, but it must always return to these international relationships in order to compare product values. If a particular society ignores such changes for a long time without developing new and accurate formulas to replace the old ones, it will create internal relationships that shape their own scheme of values. Such a scheme would be consistent in itself but would contradict the tendencies of more highly developed technology (for example, steel and plastics). This could significantly retard progress and, in any case, would produce distortions in the law of value on an international scale, making it impossible to compare economies.

The *"turnover tax"* is an invention of accounting by means of which enterprise can be assured of maintaining given profit levels. Product costs to the consumer are raised in such a way as to equate supply with effective demand. We believe that such a tax is required by the nature of the system but that it is not an absolute necessity, and we are working on other methods that take all such matters into account.

We feel that overall equilibrium between supply and effective demand is essential. The Ministry of Internal Commerce would be in charge of bringing about a balance between public buying power and commodity prices, bearing in mind that many necessities of life must be made available at low prices, while less important goods may be grossly overpriced by openly ignoring the law of value in each specific case.

Here, a serious problem arises. What basis for establishing real prices should the economy use in analyzing the relationships of production? It could be an analysis of necessary labor as regards Cuba. But distortions would immediately occur and world problems obscured because of the automatic interrelationships necessarily brought about. On the other hand, the world-market price could be used. This would obscure domestic problems because in no industrial branch is our productivity up to world standards.

We propose, as an initial approach to the problem, that consideration be given to setting up price indices on the basis of the following principles:

All raw-material imports would have a fixed and stable price based on an average international market price plus a few points to cover the cost of transportation and the facilities of the Foreign Trade Ministry. All Cuban raw materials would be priced on the basis of real production costs in terms of money. To each raw-material classification we would add planned-labor costs plus costs of wear and tear on machinery and equipment. This would be the price of products supplied by one domestic enterprise to another, or to the Ministry of Internal Commerce. Such prices would be constantly adjusted by indices reflecting commodity prices on the world market plus the costs of transportation and the facilities of the Foreign Trade Ministry. Enterprises operating under the budgetary finance system would operate on the basis of planned costs and would make no profits. Instead, all profits would accrue to MINCIN [Ministry of Domestic Trade]. (Naturally, this refers to the commodity portion of the social product, which is essential as stock for consumption.) The indices would tell us (the central administrative body and the enterprise) how effective we are and would prevent our making wrong decisions. The people would not suffer at all as a result of all these changes, since the prices of the commodities they buy are independently established with an eye to demand and need for each product.

For example, in order to calculate the amount of an investment, we would calculate the amount of imported raw materials, machinery, and equipment; expenditure on construction and installation; and planned wage costs. In addition, we would make allowances for contingencies and the cost of construction facilities and equipment. This would yield, at termination of the investment, three figures: one, the real money cost of the project; two, what the project should have cost according to plans; and three, what it should cost in terms of world productivity. The difference between the first and the second would be changed to the inefficiency of construction facilities and equipment. The difference between the second and the third would be the index of our lag in that particular sector.

This would allow us to make basic decisions regarding the alternative use of materials such as cement, iron, or plastics; fiber-cement, aluminum, or zinc roofs; iron, lead, or copper pipes; wood, iron, or aluminum windows, etc.

Decisions could diverge from the mathematical optimum when political or foreign trade factors are to be considered, but we would always have a mirror before us by which to compare our work with what is actually happening in the rest of the world. Prices will always be viewed with an eye toward world-market levels. These will fluctuate in some years in response to technological advances and will change as the socialist market and the international division of labor gain pre-eminence, once a world socialist price system more logical than the one now used is achieved.

We could continue to add to this interesting subject, but it is preferable to outline a few basic ideas here and explain that all this needs further elaboration.

Collective Premiums

With regard to collective premiums to enterprise management, we will first refer to the experiments described by Fikriat Tabeiev, in which he says:

What, then, is the basic, decisive index for evaluating enterprise performance to be? Economic research has yielded several proposals in this regard.

Some economists suggest that the principal index should be average accumulation, while others believe it should be labor costs, and so on. The Soviet press has voiced the extensive discussion caused by an article by Professor Liberman, who proposes that the fundamental indicators of enterprise performance should be the degree of efficiency, average accumulation, and profit. We believe that in judging the operation of an enterprise, the most important thing to consider is the contribution to production made by its personnel. This, which in final analysis does not rule out the struggle for sufficiently high production efficiency, allows the enterprise's personnel to concentrate their efforts on improving the production process. The social organizations of Tartary have proposed an index based on the average value of the manufacture of each product part. In order to verify the feasibility of putting this proposal into practice, they have conducted an economic experiment.

In 1962, average values of manufacture were calculated and approved in Tartary. That year was a transitional period, during which the new index was used in planning alongside the gross production index. The index based on the average value of manufacture embodies technically justified costs, including wages and bonuses paid to workers, plus shop and general plant costs for the production of each article.

It should be noted that the use of this index has nothing to do with the "infernal" labor accounting system employed in capitalist countries. We seek to organize work processes along rational lines, rather than intensify work out of proportion. All the effort devoted to establishing work standards is made with the direct participation of the personnel of enterprises and social organizations, particularly the syndicates.

Unlike the gross production index, the average value of

> manufacture does not include the great majority of material costs—the materialized labor of other enterprises—or profit. In other words, it does not include those components of the value of gross mercantile production which lessen the value of the true volume of the enterprise's production. By more accurately reflecting the labor expended on the manufacture of each article, the index expressing the average value of manufacture allows us to determine on a more realistic basis what measures we should take to raise output, lower costs and increase efficiency of the particular type of production. This index is also better suited from the standpoint of intrafactory planning and organization of economic calculus within the enterprise. Moreover, it admits comparison of labor productivity in related enterprises.[13]

This Soviet research effort deserves study and coincides, in some respects, with our thesis.

Summary of Ideas Regarding the Budgetary Finance System

In order to summarize our idea about the budgetary finance system, we should begin by making clear that it is an overall concept. Its objective operation would begin upon becoming involved in all areas of the economy, in a single whole that, beginning with political decisions and going through JUCEPLAN, would reach the enterprises and production units via ministerial channels. There it would merge with the people to again return to the policy-making body, so forming a giant, well-balanced circle, within which rates of production could be changed more or less automatically because of efficient production controls. The ministries would have the specific responsibility of drawing up and supervising the plans. Enterprises and production units would do this according to levels of decision-making that could be more or less flexible, depending on how thoroughly the enterprise has been organized, the type of production, or the moment at hand. Juceplan [Central Planning

Board] would be in charge of the economy's overall central controls, assisted by the Treasury Ministry in matters of financial control and by the Labor Ministry in matters connected with the planning of labor power.

All this does not really take place so smoothly, so we will describe our present situation—its limitations; its small achievements; its deficiencies and failures, some of them justified or justifiable, some the product of our experience, and others the product of our unembellished faults.

Juceplan furnishes only the broad outlines of the plan, together with target figures for basic products that are fairly rigidly regulated. The central administrative bodies, including the Ministry of Industry, regulate so-called centralized products, while the manufacture of products is regulated by contracts among enterprises. Once the plan is established and made consistent, contracts are signed—sometimes this is done beforehand—and work begins.

The ministry's central office is responsible for assuring the fulfillment of production quotas at the enterprise level. Similarly, the enterprise is responsible for unit production. The important thing is that the accounting system is consolidated at these two points: the enterprise and the ministry. Controls over basic machinery and equipment and inventories must be carried at the central level so that idle resources can be transferred freely among production units. The ministry also has authority to transfer basic machinery and equipment from one enterprise to another. Stocks are not of a mercantile nature. They are debited or credited accordingly. A part of production is passed on directly to the people via MINCIN, while another part is used to supply other production units for which our products are intermediate goods.

Our basic concept is that during this entire process value is successively added to the product by the labor expended on its production but that there is no need for mercantile relations among enterprises.* Supply contracts and the purchase orders corresponding to them—in short, whatever document is required

* Currently, in Cuba, this approach has been generally adopted.

for the transaction—merely confirm that one has fulfilled his obligation to produce and deliver a given product. Acceptance of an article on the part of an enterprise would mean (in somewhat idealistic terms for the moment, it should be noted) acceptance of product quality. The product becomes a commodity once it undergoes a legal change of ownership by passing into the hands of an individual consumer. Means of production used by other enterprises are not commodities, but a value should be placed on them in accordance with the indices proposed above that should then be compared with the necessary labor content of the production quota allocated to consumption in order to arrive at a price for the equipment or raw material under consideration.

Quarterly plans must be met with regard to product quality, quantity, and mix. The production unit, in accordance with labor quotas, would pay wages to its workers directly. One point has not yet been mentioned: the method of rewarding a unit collective for particularly outstanding performance or above average performance with regard to the economy as a whole. Nor have we considered the question of whether to penalize factories that have failed to adequately perform their parts.

Present State of the Budgetary Finance System

What is happening today? One of the most serious things is that the factory can never count on receiving supplies when they are needed. Thus, it fails to fulfill its production plans. But what is worse is that it often receives raw materials for a different production process. This leads to technological changes that increase direct costs, labor requirements, and, sometimes, investment needs. The entire plan is often disrupted and may require frequent adjustments.

Until now, we have had to remain passive at the ministerial level in the face of all these anomalies and simply record them. But we are now entering a phase in which we will be able to act, at least with respect to certain categories of the plan, requiring that such distortions be forecast by methods of accounting or mathematics and thereby be controlled. We do not yet have the automatic devices needed to ensure that controls are put into effect rapidly and that indicators are accurately analyzed and interpreted. We have neither sufficient analytical capacity nor the capacity needed to collect data and develop the indicators for analytical interpretation. The enterprises are in direct contact with their factories, sometimes through telephone or telegraph, or through some provincial delegate. In other cases, they communicate via the controlling ministerial delegations. While in the municipalities, or politico-economic localities of the same type, there are the CILOS, which are nothing but committees of neighboring unit administrators responsible for analyzing the problems of production units. These committees may make decisions regarding small matters of mutual assistance, thus circumventing the red tape of regular bureaucratic channels. In some cases, they may approve loans of machinery and equipment, while always bearing in mind that permanent transfers must meet with the approval of the particular enterprise.

At the beginning of each month, production statistics are sent to the ministry. There they are analyzed even at the highest levels, and basic measures are taken to correct defects. More detailed statistics come in during the days that follow, on the basis of which more specific measures are taken at various levels.

What are the system's principal weaknesses? We believe that its lack of maturity must be placed first. In the second place, there is a scarcity of really qualified cadres at all levels. In the third place, we have failed to publicize the system and clarify its operation so that the people can understand it better. We can also cite the lack of a central planning body that would operate consistently and with an absolute hierarchical order. Such a body would make the job easier. We could list shortcomings in material supply and the transportation system that sometimes force us to accumulate products and at other times hinder production. There are shortcomings in our entire quality-control system. There are problems in relationships (which should be very close, very harmonious, and very well defined) with distribution agencies, particularly MINCIN, and some supply organizations, especially MINCEX [Ministry of Foreign Trade] and INRA [National Institute of Agrarian Reform]. It is still difficult to say exactly which shortcomings have root in the system's inherent weaknesses and which are due largely to our present level of organization.

Neither the factory nor the enterprise employs material incentives of a collective type at the moment. This is not due to any central idea within the scheme. It is, rather, because we are not yet well enough organized to be able to provide this kind of incentive on a basis other than the simple fulfillment or overfulfillment of the enterprise's plans. The reasons for this are given above.

The system is said to have a tendency toward bureaucracy. One point must therefore be constantly stressed: The entire administrative apparatus must be organized on a rational basis. Now, from the standpoint of objective analysis, it is obvious that there will be less bureaucracy the more centralized are enterprises or production units recording and controlling operations. If every enterprise could centralize all its administrative activities, its bureaucracy would be reduced to a small nucleus of unit directors plus someone to collect information for headquarters.

This, for the moment, is impossible. We must, however, proceed with setting up production units of optimum size. Such a move is facilitated by the system through the establishment of labor regulations requiring a single wage level, so as to break through narrow ideas about the enterprise as a center of individual action and stress society as a whole.

General Advantages of the System

To our mind, the budgetary system has the following advantages:

First, by tending toward centralization, it tends toward more rational utilization of national funds.

Second, it tends toward greater rationality in the entire State administrative apparatus.

Third, this same tendency toward centralization compels the creation of larger units—within limits—which economizes on labor power and increases worker productivity.

Fourth, once integrated into a single regulatory system, it converts the entire ministry, on the one hand, and perhaps all ministries together, on the other, into a single, large, State enterprise. Within this complex, a worker could transfer from one part to another, or to different branches or places, with no wage problems. He would simply conform to a national wage scale.

Fifth, with regard to budgeted construction organizations, investment control can be simplified. The contracting investor would look after the physical investment and the Treasury Ministry would supervise the financial end.

It is important to point out that the general idea of mutual cooperation is being instilled in the worker, the idea of belonging to a great whole which is the people. We are developing his social consciousness, the awareness of his duty to society.

The following quotation from Marx is interesting because, absent the phrasing of capitalism, it lays bare the process by which work traditions are formed and might therefore provide us with a background for the building of socialism:

> It is not a case of two independent forces working on one another. *Les des sont pipes.* Capital works on both sides at the same time. If its accumulation, on the one hand, increases the demand for labor, it increases on the other the supply of laborers by the "setting free" of them, whilst at the same time the pressure of the unemployed compels those that are employed to furnish more labor, and therefore makes the supply of labor, to a certain extent, independent of the supply of laborers. The action of the law of supply and demand of labor on this basis completes the despotism of capital. As soon, therefore, as the laborers learn the secret of how it comes to pass that, in the same measure as they work more, as they produce more wealth

> for others, and as the productive power of their labor increases, so in the same measure even their function as a means of the self-expansion of capital becomes more and more precarious for them; as soon as they discover that the degree of intensity of the competition among themselves depends wholly on the pressure of the relative surplus population; as soon as, by Trades' Unions, etc., they try to organize a regular cooperation between employed and unemployed in order to destroy or to weaken the ruinous effects of this natural law of capitalistic production on their class, so soon capital and its sycophant, political economy, cry out at the infringement of the "eternal" and so to say "sacred" law of supply and demand. Every combination of employed and unemployed disturbs the "harmonious" action of this law. But, on the other hand, as soon as (in the colonies, for instance) adverse circumstances prevent the creation of an industrial reserve army and, with it, the absolute dependence of the working class upon the capitalist class, capital, along with its commonplace Sancho Panza, rebels against the "sacred" law of supply and demand, and tries to check its inconvenient action by forcible means and State interference.[14]

The productive forces are developing, the relationships of production change: All awaits the direct action of the worker's State upon the people's consciousness.

With respect to material interest, what we want to achieve with this system is to prevent the lever from becoming something that compels the individual, as an individual, or the collective of individuals, to struggle desperately with others so as to bring about certain conditions of production or distribution that would accord them special privileges. We must make social duty the fulcrum of all the worker's efforts, but keep an eye on his weaknesses, rewarding or penalizing, using material incentives or disincentives, either individual or collective, depending on whether the worker—or unit of production—is able to fulfill his duty to society. Moreover, compulsory training as a requirement for promotion, when it can be implemented on a national scale, stimulates a desire to study on the part of all the country's working masses. Such training is not restricted by local conditions because the framework is the country as a whole. Consequently, it is conducive to substantial improvements in technical skills.

We should also mention that student workers who qualify can, by means of a subsidization policy, easily leave to go on to other jobs. They can go to other parts of the country in order to set up more productive factories, that is, factories more consistent with the central idea of progress toward communism, toward a society of large-scale production and satisfaction of man's basic needs.

It remains for us to emphasize the educational role that the party should play in transforming the work center into the collective expression of the worker's aspirations and concerns and a place where his desire to serve society is fashioned.

Indeed, the work center would be the basis of the future society's political nucleus. Its suggestions, passed on to more complex political organizations, could assist the party and the government in making fundamental decisions about the economy and the cultural life of the individual.

NOTES

1. Karl Marx. [Translator's source: *Economic and Philosophic Manuscripts of 1884* (New York, International Publishers, 1964), p. 135.]
2. Karl Marx, *Critique of the Gotha Program*. [Translator's source: *Critique of the Gotha Program* (New York, International Publishers, c. 1938), p. 8.]
3. V. I. Lenin, "On the Slogan for a United States of Europe." [Translator's source: *Selected Works* (New York, International Publishers, 1967), Vol. I, p. 671.]
4. Joseph Stalin, "Foundations of Leninism." [Translator's source: *The Historical Roots of Leninism* (New York, International Publishers, 1939), p. 14.]
5. V. I. Lenin, "Five Years of the Russian Revolution and the Prospects of the World Revolution." [Translator's source: *Selected Works, op. cit.,* Vol. III, pp. 616, 618.]

6. [No source given.]

7. See "Los combinados de empresas sovieticas: La nueva forma de administración de las industrias," I. Ivonin, *Nuestra Industria: Revista Economica,* No. 4).

8. V. I. Lenin, "Our Revolution." [Translator's source: *Selected Works, op. cit.,* pp. 766–767.]

9. Marx, *Critique of the Gotha Program, op. cit.,* pp. 7–8.

10. [No source given.]

11. *Ibid.*

12. *Ibid.*

13. In "Investigación economica y dirección de la economia," *Revista International,* No. 11, 1963.

14. Karl Marx, *Capital* (Vol. I). [Translator's source: *Great Books of the Western World* (Chicago, Encyclopedia Britannica, c. 1952), Vol. L, p. 317.]

6

On the Operation of the Auto-Financed Enterprise

JOAQUIN INFANTE

AUTO-FINANCE OR ECONOMIC CALCULUS is the method used in the U.S.S.R. and other socialist and popular democratic countries for the economic administration of socialist enterprises. Its main purpose is to incorporate the great working masses into the economic process, to mobilize all the productive forces to the maximum in order to obtain a steady increase in production, a progressive rise in labor productivity, and the lowering of costs, guided always by the socialist principle of reward according to quality and quantity of labor.

This method of administration, by heeding the economic laws in force both during the building of socialism and under socialism itself, helps to assure that countries which were once held in a state of perpetual poverty by international imperialism will grow and develop at a rapid pace so as to quickly attain the material abundance needed for achieving communism.

We should note that the ways and conditions in which such a system is implemented will vary according to specific objective

---

Joaquin Infante was a financial administrator for INRA (National Institute of Agrarian Reform) and is currently Professor of Economics at the University of Havana.

SOURCE: "Características del funcionamiento de la empresa autofinanciada," *Cuba Socialista,* Año IV, Junio 1964, pp. 25–50.

conditions in each country. But the system's basic principles will always hold true.

Socialist enterprises, regardless of the system of economic administration under which they operate, carry out their economic activities within the framework of the National Economic Plan. Accordingly, they draw up financial plans following methods laid down by the Treasury Ministry, abide by Juceplan [Central Planning Board] policies, and are guided by indicators fixed by the central administrative agency governing their activities. Financial plans encompass three basic areas: revenue, costs, and accounts with the budget.

Central administrative bodies are responsible for ensuring that the enterprises under their jurisdiction formulate plans according to the policies emanating from Juceplan. They also assume the burden of presenting such plans on schedule to the Treasury Ministry and the National Bank of Cuba.

The financial plans of both central administrative agencies and enterprises, once approved by the government, form the framework within which they will carry out their economic activities. Such plans cannot be changed with regard to accounts with the budget (in other words, contributions in the form of profits, depreciation, and other revenue may not be reduced, and allocations for investment, losses, or other outlays may not be raised) without prior approval by the Council of Ministers.

One of the basic principles of auto-financing is that the enterprise use available revenue to cover production or operating costs and to meet obligations to the budget. This helps to ensure national financial equilibrium because a balance between costs and revenues in every establishment and enterprise means that aggregate costs incurred in each activity have counterparts in useful material goods.

In order to achieve this, both enterprises and their production units are authorized to hold funds for operating expenses in their own bank accounts. They deposit all revenues received through the sale of articles produced, improved, or handled, as well as services provided, and charge the accounts for all payments made to cover costs related to their activities. Revenue transferred to the national budget derived from profits, depreciation, and reduction of the means of turnover, as well as repayments of loans to the National Bank of Cuba, are also charged against these accounts.

Enterprises and their production units are authorized in addition to hold other bank accounts to be used for specific financial operations such as decentralized investment and the enterprise fund, which we will discuss below.

Payments made to workers and suppliers, as well as to the budget and the National Bank of Cuba, are effected within established terms and procedures so long as the enterprise has sufficient financial resources. When, however, there are insufficient funds to cover all matured obligations, it becomes necessary to establish a schedule of preference for payments.

In determining the order of preference, one must bear in mind the objective conditions in the particular country—the level of organization and the financial situation. Moreover, the order of preference cannot be the same at every stage. In some socialist countries, among them the Soviet Union, obligations to the budget have been given first priority. But this is a mere formality, because there are also certain administrative rules in effect. For example, enterprises are allowed to hold funds in operating accounts during the five days prior to date of wage payment. They are also granted bank credits allocated exclusively to wage payment, which is automatically put in first place.

In Cuba, consistent with our organizational conditions and degree of financial discipline, to remove the wage priority would bring about, among other things, difficulties to some firms which, even when operating with relative economic efficiency, would lack resources as a result of payment default by other enterprises. Besides, bank loans for the payment of wages would have to be made automatically in most cases, without the kind of analysis that should be required.

Even though the order of preference we propose would relieve the pressure of wage payment in enterprises that are managed inefficiently, we believe similar pressure could be applied if enterprises were required to meet the provisions in force regarding collections and payments and if its payments of budget obligations were recorded by date and time.

For all these reasons, we think that at present the schedule of preference that should govern in Cuba is as follows: (a) remuneration of workers; (b) obligations to the national budget; (c) suppliers of commodities and services; (d) amortization of bank credits; (e) other payments.

Socialist enterprises operating under this system must in the first place be cost-accountable, that is, total costs incurred in producing, improving, and handling goods or providing services should be practically equal to revenues perceived by the enterprise for sale or provision of such goods or services. Such a balance cannot be obtained in a mathematical way, because in cost-accountable enterprises revenues may slightly exceed costs or vice versa.

Basically, such accountability of enterprises assures the following:

a. financial equilibrium in each enterprise, as costs incurred have counterparts in useful material goods.

b. Simple reproduction of value, because revenue is used to pay workers' wages and to purchase means of production.

More than cost-accountable, the enterprises should be profitable; in other words, in addition to defraying all costs with revenues, it should obtain a return as a result of its economic operation. Profits are the national budget's prime source of revenue and are used to measure the efficiency of the enterprise's economic operation.

To determine whether an enterprise is operating efficiently and is financially sound, we must observe two indicators: (a) cost plan; (b) production plan.

These two indicators are intimately related, so that enterprise efficiency cannot be gauged by exhaustive analysis of one alone.

We are fully convinced of the importance of production costs as an indicator, because they are an index of the socially necessary labor time expended on production. It is for this reason that the Juceplan, in formulating the control data for the economic plan, establishes cost-reduction goals by sectors and branches. Central administrative agencies set similar goals for the enterprises under their jurisdictions.

The basic factors considered in determining such goals are the following:

a. Savings in past (materialized) labor. To produce more with the same amount of raw materials, fuels, intermediate goods, etc., and, through improved use and maintenance, to prolong the useful life of machinery and equipment.

b. Savings in present labor. Through improved organization and administration of production and labor, incorporation of modern technical advances, and elimination of production halts caused by defective machinery, shortages of raw materials, shortages of other inputs, and absenteeism.

But reducing production costs through savings in past and present labor, while disregarding the quantity and quality of the various outputs, need not imply efficient economic performance, because:

a. While the cost plan for the production unit may be met or surpassed (that is, costs lowered), the production plan may not.

b. While the cost plan may be met or surpassed and while the production plan may also be met with regard to volume, the product may be defective or of such low quality that it cannot be used by consumers.

c. While the cost plan and the production plan may both be met or surpassed in all aspects, the resulting product may not fall within the mix required by other enterprises or the consuming public.

Because profit represents the difference between revenue and total production costs, it is the indicator that controls and measures relationships between the various outputs of an enterprise and its costs. Here, money is used as a measure of value, which is one of its functions during the stage of the building of socialism and during socialism itself.

There are enterprises which for political or economic reasons have to operate temporarily at a loss; but this does not violate the principle, because such enterprises are under obligation to reduce losses to a point at which they become solvent. The measure of their efficiency is controlled by reduction of losses.

The State assigns the socialist enterprise the basic means of production necessary to meet its production plans as established by the respective central administrative body, regardless of the finance system under which the enterprise operates.

These basic means of production may be grouped as follows: (a) machinery, equipment, and installations; (b) basic livestock; (c) transportation equipment; (d) buildings and construction; (e) molds and dies; (f) agricultural plantings; (g) other basic means of production.

The basic means of production used by enterprises cannot be objects of exchange, for which reason their transfer between enterprises—by prior authorization of the corresponding administrative bodies—merely represents the State's distribution of the means of production.

The enterprise may sell to other enterprises surplus basic means of production—that is, machinery and equipment no longer in use because of technological changes or other reasons apart from cyclical activities or temporary supply problems—as well as scrap metal and parts from dismantled machinery and equipment.

This by itself does not represent investment because the mere distribution of such items does not increase the nation's aggregate installed capacity. It does, on the other hand, permit the rational utilization of all the basic means of production belonging to the State.

Moreover, the enterprise may use the proceeds from these sales for investment in plant expansion and modernization. Thus, the enterprise has a material interest in disposing of idle machinery and equipment rather than hold it for a long period of time. In this way, the basic means of production are fully utilized, while at the same time installed capacity is increased.

The enterprise's circulating capital consists of raw materials, direct and indirect materials, fuels, spare parts, goods in process, etc., as well as finished goods in stock, accounts receivable, and cash on hand and in the bank.

In order to rationally utilize such materials and financial resources, the means of turnover must be standardized—that is, unit and cash value quotas or standards must be established for the component items of the means of turnover * according to average annual requirements based on planned output.

Such standards are set primarily for inventories and deferred accounts. In some cases, however, in line with the activities and peculiarities of certain enterprises, it is also necessary to regulate accounts receivable and cash assets.

With regard to inventories, standards or quotas are determined for each component item in accordance with average requirements of production plans, supply plans, and cyclical fluctuations in sales and supply. The other determining factor, of course, is that inventories be sufficient to assure the enterprise's uninterrupted operation. This quota is generally considered as the midpoint between maximum and minimum stocks. For example:

Raw material quota

Average planned daily consumption	104.2	MT
Period for receipt + extra time allowance	3	days
Supply cycle (average period of time between deliveries)	5	days
Average price per ton	$104.50	

Calculus

Minimum stock (daily planned consumption × number of days for receipt + extra time allowance)		
104.2 MT × 3 days	312.6	MT
Maximum stock (number of days for receipt + extra time allowance + the supply cycle × average daily consumption)		
104.2 MT × 8 days	833.6	MT

* The terms "means of turnover" and "circulating capital" have been used interchangeably. [Ed.]

Standard in units

$$(312.6) + (833.6) \text{ divided by } 2 = 573.1$$

Financial standard

$$573.1 \times 104.50 = \$59{,}888.95$$

We should note here that the quarter of least activity is taken as the base in enterprises whose activities are primarily cyclical or seasonal.

It is of vital importance for enterprises as well as for the economy as a whole to assure that circulating capital does not exceed requirements. This represents immobility of both material resources (whether domestically produced or imported) and financial resources. When stocks are below requirements, on the other hand, production may be disrupted or paralyzed.

The aggregate cash value of the various items composing the means of turnover that are standardized according to the above method represents the "standard means of turnover."

The State apportions this amount to the enterprise on a non-reimbursable basis. The circulating capital so assigned is said to "belong" to the enterprise.

Annually, and consistent with the plan, the standard means of turnover are determined and compared with the enterprise's own means of turnover. If the latter are found to be deficient, the State assigns the enterprise the difference. If, on the other hand, they are in surplus, the enterprise transfers the difference to the national budget.

When the enterprise operates efficiently and adequately rotates its inventories and other means of turnover, it can cover the largest part of its own financial requirements without need to resort to bank loans.

In order to achieve the most rational use of resources and to assure that such resources do not become temporarily surplus, the State assigns each enterprise its standard means of turnover. But these do not cover all requirements for the period in question. A socialist enterprise operating under this system may solicit and obtain credits from the National Bank of Cuba as needed to cover financial needs brought about by seasonal fluctuations in production, inventories in surplus of quotas, and accounts-payable documents, as well as other loans properly justified by plan requirements. As soon as the conditions bringing about the additional need for financial resources cease to operate, the enterprise will amortize such credits out of revenues.

The credit plan forms part of the enterprise's financial plan and reflects the requirements of the production, supply, and labor and wage plans.

Bank loans are authorized for use toward specific ends—for example, above-quota inventories, raw-material purchases, warehousing, production expenses—and must be materially guaranteed in full. Such loans are short-term (less than one year) and earn interest.

Bank credits are used to finance the operating costs of socialist enterprises for the following reasons:

a. Rational use of material and financial resources. Without such credits, enterprises would require more loan funds and would therefore pay more interest, thus increasing costs and reducing profits.

b. Financial control over enterprises by the National Bank of Cuba. The bank and its agencies maintain direct daily relations with enterprises because all monetary operations are conducted through the bank. The bank is therefore the best qualified body to exercise such control.

We should clarify that credit between socialist enterprises is totally prohibited. Enterprises must invoice, collect, and pay within established terms and conditions.

The only investments that the enterprise is authorized to make are those included in the plan approved by Juceplan. Such investments are categorized as either centralized or decentralized according to source of financing. The first are financed directly through the national budget, the second by the enterprise itself. The latter are charged to a special investment fund created by the following contributions:

a. A percentage of depreciation.
b. A percentage of the enterprise fund.

c. Revenues derived from sales of surplus means of production.

d. Revenues derived from sales of scrap metal and parts from dismantled machinery and equipment.

e. Contributions by the central administrative body.

The enterprise is authorized to use this fund for the following types of investment:

a. Basic or general repairs regardless of size of expenditure.

b. Expansion and modernization of existing plant and equipment.

c. Construction and repair of homes and sociocultural structures (nonnominal projects).*

In planning investment, we must consider both expansion and replacement. Simple reproduction must be assured before going on to expanded reproduction.

By allowing the enterprise to use that part of depreciation which remains at the enterprise level to make general repairs on basic means of production, and at the same time to expand and modernize plant, simple reproduction is in large part assured. Such expansion and modernization includes innovations made by workers consistent with the slogan "build your machinery."

The remaining investments approved, such as homes and sociocultural structures, are financed through the enterprise and agency funds, and are closely related to the general performance of the enterprise as a whole.

Socialist enterprises exchange goods and services among themselves on the basis of purchase sale. In other words, although these enterprises are owned by the society, in order for the society to exercise economic control over them, they must pay for all commodities and services received.

One enterprise pays another by means of fund transfers between banking agencies. Accounting records are adjusted accordingly as soon as the agency is informed that a collection has been made. As a general rule, the only reason for which a socialist enterprise has to withdraw money from the bank is for payment of wages.

* Projects not exceeding a certain cost ceiling established by Juceplan (presently $100 thousand). (Author's note.)

In order to speak of profitability, we must first explain that the products and services provided by the enterprise must meet quality requirements and specifications. Moreover, product mix must conform to the pattern of consumer demand.

These are economic controls that are exercised automatically among enterprises as follows:

a. by means of paying for all those commodities and services that conform to stipulated quality and specifications at official prices.

b. by not accepting the product or by soliciting and obtaining discounts or price reductions when products do not conform to stipulated quality and specifications.

c. by not accepting or not paying for commodities of the wrong mix, that is, which conforms neither to contractual specifications nor to patterns of consumer demand.

Differences between enterprises sometimes arise through failure to meet obligations under purchasing or sales contracts. The first step toward resolving such differences is to hold a proceeding for conciliation. If this fails to produce agreement, the problem is brought before the Arbitration Council for final resolution. The rulings of this body are compulsory.

As a consequence of independent legal status, an enterprise may:

a. Possess its own patrimony (basic means of production and means of turnover).

b. Sign economic contracts and assume whatever obligations are necessary.

c. Contract bank credits.

d. Be defendant or plaintiff, and pay compensation for damages or injuries caused by failure to comply with its obligations.

e. Open, maintain, liquidate, and close out accounts at any banking agency. Collect and perceive sums of money, withdraw money from its accounts, approve and disapprove statements of account of completed operations and balances resulting from the same.

In order for the enterprise to meet and surpass its economic plan, it must incorporate all its workers into the productive process by making use of individual initiative. Such initiative may be directed and coordinated to permit increasing labor productivity, expansion of output, improved economies, and so forth.

So that this incorporation will lead to the desired goals, the enterprise must employ moral and material incentives in appropriate proportions according to the inherent value of the incentive at each point on the road to communism. As we move toward communism, moral incentives should increase at the expense of material incentives. But the latter do not completely disappear during the building of socialism and communism and, properly used, are an inducement to improve quality, increase productivity, and expand output.

We should note Marx's remark in the *Critique of the Gotha Program:*

> What we have to deal with here is a communist society, not as it has *developed* on its own foundations, but, on the contrary, as it *emerges* from capitalist society; which is thus in every respect, economically, morally and intellectually, still stamped with the birth marks of the old society from whose womb it emerges.[1]

Moral incentives are the society's recognition of the worker's conscientious and revolutionary fulfillment of his duty to society. They may take on various forms. One of them, which workers assign great importance, is to join the prime minister, comrade Fidel Castro, and other leaders of the revolutionary government on the presidential rostrum during parades and mass gatherings.

Not withstanding such incentives, however, one must bear in mind the point that the revolutionary government has made to the working masses regarding the importance of the sugar harvest, where greater production means more foreign exchange for the country and therefore more imported commodities. This point, as the worker reflects on its significance to him personally, leads him to realize that the more he increases production, the more income he will receive and the more consumer goods he will be able to acquire.

Material incentives, both individual and collective, as used in auto-financed enterprises, are based on the socialist principle of reward according to quality and quantity of work performed.

To realize this principle, the enterprise is authorized to set up a fund, with the condition that annual contributions to the fund do not exceed a given percentage of the wage fund (generally 5 per cent) and so long as it conforms to, among other requirements, the following plan: (a) production; (b) delivery; (c) costs; (d) profit or loss.

Contributions to the enterprise fund depend on the enterprise's ability to attain or exceed planned profit levels or to reduce planned losses according to set percentages. Where the enterprise plan is based solely on cost-accounting, contributions are based on a percentage of realized profit.

The resources of the enterprise fund are used primarily to finance the following expenditures:

Collective incentives

a. To build, repair, and maintain homes and sociocultural structures for the use and enjoyment of enterprise workers.

b. To cover costs of child, social, and cultural circles.

c. To cover costs of vacation lodging for enterprise workers.

Individual incentives

d. Individual awards.

e. Cash aid to workers in case of need.

The individual awards to which we have referred several times above are given to workers in the vanguard, winners of the socialist emulation prize, or the most outstanding workers in the various areas of the enterprise.* As to cash aid, we will note in passing that it is granted in order to complement regular wages in case of need due to death or illness in the family.

The agency fund is set up so that awards can be given to workers or brigades of enterprises that have been unable to set

* These material incentives have been virtually eliminated in Cuba (see Introduction).

up funds of their own. The agency fund is also used for special awards and other necessary social expenditures.

It is established through the efforts of the enterprises operating under the agency's jurisdiction. The agency fund's only source of contributions is the enterprise funds themselves. This is handled by the enterprise minister or chief administrator.

The agency fund is generally used for the following purposes: (a) special awards to workers who have attained the goals established by the agency; (b) expenses of the socialist emulation awards in general; (c) special contributions to enterprise funds; (d) other unusual expenses.

As can be gathered from the foregoing, this fund is set up on the basis of the efforts of the workers of the enterprise and is realized through the achievement of goals contained in the economic plan. It therefore fulfills the following main objectives:

a. Application of the socialist principle of reward according to quality and quantity of work performed at the enterprise and agency level.

b. Determination on an economic basis (production of material goods and accumulation) of the amounts and limits of expenditures on individual and collective incentives.

The administrator or director and other members of enterprise management are responsible before the society, as represented by the State administrative agency, for the custody and efficient use of the basic means of production and turnover assigned to the enterprises under their direction as well as for determining how such resources are to be used. They are, moreover, responsible for unjustified failures to meet the approved economic plan, or to comply with the provisions laid down by the administrative agency or established by laws in force.

The enterprise is obliged to use its basic means of production and means of turnover only in those activities in which it specializes. It must never use them for other purposes and must devote maximum attention to the proper use, maintenance, and periodic repair of basic means of production in order to assure maximum-capacity utilization during the estimated operational life of the equipment.

In addition, enterprises are required to use financial resources only for the purpose for which allocated and can in no case whatsoever use them in the following ways:

a. Operating funds for expenditures neither planned nor related to the enterprise's productive activity.

b. Investment funds for unauthorized investments.

c. Investment funds for payment of operating expenses.

d. Funds allocated to specific investments for different investments.

Failure to comply will generally lead to administrative, civil, or criminal action as appropriate. The persons responsible for violations may be required to personally reimburse the enterprise for the losses it incurs.

Socialist enterprises cannot use the economic categories without some perspective on the economy as a whole. Each enterprise is a component of the national socialist economy, and the aggregate of such enterprises together form the principal part of that economy.

In auto-financed enterprises, economic categories are used with a broad economic outlook, which we will analyze shortly.

Production Costs

Production costs are one of the principal categories in a socialist economy because one of the major concerns of such an economy is the lowering of costs, which represents a reduction in the past and present labor time expended on production. The result of such a reduction is increased capital accumulation by enterprises and a larger quantity of consumer goods made available to workers at lower prices—or, in other words, a rise in real wages and accelerated economic development.

The annual lowering of production costs is the basic factor behind economic development under socialism. It is accomplished by totally incorporating workers into the production process. This permits us to root out the irrational use of material and human resources at all levels—enterprise, factory, and shop.

The items that contribute to production costs are grouped under the following headings:

(a) materials consumption; (b) wages; (c) depreciation and amortization; (d) transfers (other expenditures).

WAGES

Wages are the most important item in production costs. A broad economic outlook leads us to understand that the other items are merely accumulated labor. For this reason, increased labor productivity in every enterprise means lower-cost raw materials, intermediate goods, basic means of production, and so on.

In order to bring this about, production standards must be established, work must be organized, and wage scales must be set up in every enterprise. Production standards, which are established according to working conditions and other factors, are based on time or piece rates. If production is highly mechanized and labor is only a marginal factor in increasing production, the first form would be chosen. If, on the other hand, labor, whether manual or technical, is the determinant productive factor, and increased production depends largely on the effort and personal conditions of the worker, then the choice would be the second form.

The wage scale is set up on the basis of job qualification by group or activity, bearing in mind the intricacy of the work performed. In every case, a base rate is established which may include a great number of variables for performance premiums or penalties.

Following the socialist principle of reward according to quantity and quality of work performed—and because the important thing is to increase production and labor productivity—no limit is set on premium payments for surpassing production standards. For example:

Time Standard

Rate: $0.48 per hour
Standard: 96 units per hour
Premiums: $0.0025 units per hour extra
Units produced: 200

Calculus

96 units standard per hour		$0.48
104 units in excess of standard	× .0025	0.26
200		$0.74

Unit of Labor Standard [*piece rates*]

Standard *arrobas* * of sugar cane cut and stacked	Rate
Less than 120 *arrobas*	$1.98
From 120 to 150 *arrobas*	2.20
More than 150 *arrobas*	2.30
Arrobas cut and stacked 300	

Calculus

(300) × (2.30) divided by 100 = 6.90

As can be seen by these examples, there is no limit to the amount the worker can earn through premiums for exceeding quotas.

The ultimate objective is for every worker to devote his maximum effort to increasing production and labor productivity. This method is a means of assuring that workers are not deprived of earnings for reasons of custom, ability, or numerous other limitations deriving from the division of labor; it will not, therefore, cut down on their efforts.

PRICES

Price is the value of commodities expressed in money. Now, because prices have other functions such as stimulating or depressing the production of some commodities and redistributing national income among the various sectors and branches of material production, they may or may not coincide with value. But as those that are above value must be compensated by those that are below, it has been stated that the sum of all prices is equal to the sum of the value of all commodities in circulation. In practice, however, there can be many deviations from this postulate.

* An *arroba* is equal to approximately 25 pounds.

In the U.S.S.R. and the other socialist countries, there are three types of prices: (a) retail, or consumer prices; (b) wholesale prices; (c) warehousing or storage prices.

Retail prices are those set for the sale of commodities or provision of services to the public; wholesale prices are those established in mercantile relations among enterprises; and warehousing or storage prices are those established for purchase of agricultural production.

Retail and wholesale prices are formed as follows:

	Consumer Goods	Producer's Goods
Production cost	65	65
Profit	5	5
Wholesale price enterprise	70	70
Turnover tax	10	—
Wholesale price branch	80	70
Administrative and commercial distribution costs	18	—
Commercial profit	2	—
Retail price	100	—

The above table shows that the enterprise's wholesale price is formed by production costs and a given profit. The latter represents the return to enterprises for producing or importing goods and services. The retail price is formed after the wholesale price and is determined largely on the basis of political and economic factors, such as social need, injuries or benefits to health, available quantities, etc. Once the retail price is established, commercial-enterprise costs and profits are deducted to determine the branch's wholesale price. After these prices have been determined, the turnover tax is calculated by the difference between the two wholesale prices. This tax will be explained below when we deal with the fiscal system.

In the formation of these prices, accumulation takes place

in goods-producing (agricultural and industrial sectors) and importing enterprises.

What we are dealing with here is not cash accumulation as a result of payments and collections among enterprises, but real accumulation of the material goods that are redistributed through the national budget. While money survives, the determination of the value of national income is fundamental, as is its distribution among the workers employed in its creation and its redistribution through the national budget.

In order to determine what part of national income will be redistributed through the national budget, we must take other items into account, such as taxes, the burden of which falls on the public and small private businessmen. But the accumulation that takes place in socialist enterprises has the greatest specific weight and is therefore the most important.

Wages paid to workers (nominal wages) do not themselves determine the quantities of goods and services workers may acquire. Real wages, which are determined by the purchasing power of income, depends primarily on the retail-price level.

Thus, in order to accurately calculate what portion of the material goods or services produced and imported directly corresponds to workers in return for their labor, and what portion is to be redistributed through the national budget, it is essential to measure the accumulation that takes place in those sectors creating such goods or receiving them from other countries.

Moreover, failure to consider accumulation in the productive sectors leads to underestimation of gross social product and national income. Inventory accumulations cannot be gauged during the year.

Fiscal System

Fiscal legislation is also used in socialist enterprises in order to ensure the prompt and proper payment of debts to the national budget. The taxes and contributions gravitating upon the enterprise are as follows: (a) social-security contributions; (b) turnover tax; (c) earnings in the form of profits; (d) earnings from depreciation; (e) other earnings.

The enterprises, either directly or through their production units, are compelled, under established terms, to transfer each of the above items to the national budget.

Social-security contributions take in that portion of production costs represented by expenditures on social benefits to workers that are deferred during the production process and later paid by the State either directly or in the form of services.

The rate of this contribution varies according to branches and sectors because it depends on the number of years actually worked, risks, and other working conditions. In mining enterprises, the percentage of the contribution is much larger than in commercial enterprises in which risks are smaller and the number of years actually worked is usually much greater.

The turnover tax, which has not yet been adopted in Cuba, represents a part of the profit received by the enterprise that is transferred periodically to the budget. The rate or amount of this tax is set after determining prices to the public so that it will not enter into the formation of such prices.

The turnover tax is designed to accomplish the following objectives:

a. To ensure the periodic transfer of a large part of aggregate profit to the budget.

b. To level the profit rate among enterprises within the same branch.

The transfer to the budget of profits and accumulated depreciation may be effected on the basis of planned monthly amounts, adjusted quarterly to take account of how well obligations have actually been met, or according to results reflected in financial statements.

Other transfers encompass reductions in the means of turnover in excess of quotas as well as any other extraordinary revenue that enterprises should transfer to the budget.

Auto-financed enterprises perform their own accounting operations and draw up financial statements and addendums in accordance with the standard accounting system.

In the case of consolidated enterprises, such as we now have in Cuba, each production unit or establishment must comply with this requirement. The national offices of these enterprises have the responsibility of directing, guiding, supervising, and controlling the maintenance of up-to-date statistics and performing regular inspections of the production units or establishments under their jurisdictions. They do not, however, perform paper work and other purely administrative tasks on a centralized basis.

Because each production unit performs its own accounting operations and draws up its own financial statements, the manager and managerial personnel of the production unit can keep abreast of the situation and take prompt action to correct any deficiencies that may be uncovered. This control is achieved by means of periodic checks on the economic and financial status of the unit through income statements, cost statements, balance sheets, and statistical reports.

Financial control (over auto-financed enterprises) is exercised by the central administrative agencies under which they operate, as well as by the National Bank of Cuba and the Treasury Ministry, consistent with the functions and responsibilities assigned to these bodies by the government.

The principal financial controls exercised by these agencies are the following:

Central agencies scrutinize

a. Formulation and fulfillment of economic plans.

b. Reduction of costs.

c. Compliance with contractual obligations to workers, suppliers, clientele, and the National Bank of Cuba.

d. Compliance with obligations to the national budget.

e. Rational use and care of the basic means of production and turnover assigned to the enterprise by the State.

f. Exercise of financial discipline in general.

The National Bank of Cuba

a. Exercises fiscal control over enterprises and production units, assuring that financial resources are used for designated purposes.

b. Controls the use of credits authorized to enterprises.

c. Verifies that the means of turnover do not unjustifiably exceed quotas.

d. Ensures compliance with the regulations in effect regarding collections and payments.

e. Exercises fiscal control over investment expenditures.

f. Controls the use of the planned wage fund and requires that the proper agencies conduct whatever investigations and take whatever measures are necessary with regard to unjustified excesses.

g. Assures compliance with payments preferences when financial resources are scarce.

Treasury Ministry

a. Enforces compliance with all legal and regulatory provisions regarding financial matters by central agencies and enterprises under their jurisdiction.

b. Ensures the fulfillment of reciprocal obligations between enterprises and the national budget and takes whatever measures may be necessary in this respect.

c. Scrutinizes the fulfillment of enterprise financial plans.

d. Maintains surveillance over the exercise of financial discipline.

e. Enforces administrative penalties incurred through failure to comply with legal provisions.

Economic Problems and Harm Caused by Failure to Apply the Principles of Auto-Finance

By analyzing and studying each of the principles of auto-finance, we find that these principles, because they take account of the economic laws in force during the building of socialism and under socialism itself, tend toward increased production and lower costs. Thus, they ensure maximum accumulation and maximum development of the national economy. Likewise, they assure equilibrium between public income and the stock of consumer goods and services. The nation's financial and economic soundness depends on such equilibrium.

In accordance with the above, failure to apply these principles carries implicit, in the national context, a failure to make maximum use of available material resources and labor power and thus to achieve the high rate of growth that we can and must attain. This, combined with inaccurate calculation of national income, and inability to forecast the budgetary distribution and redistribution of that income, implies national disequilibrium.

These problems become manifest at the level of socialist enterprises that do not operate under the auto-finance system—that is, those that operate under the budgetary finance system—in the following ways:

a. Absence of a relationship between the enterprise's production costs and the useful material goods it creates because it does not use its own revenue to cover costs.

b. Spontaneous fluctuations in circulating capital at the enterprise level that cannot be controlled by financial agencies.

c. The National Bank of Cuba cannot control the use of credits to enterprises because such credits are granted indirectly through the Treasury Ministry.

d. Simple reproduction cannot be ensured, and operational efficiency is hindered because enterprises do not properly maintain machinery and equipment, or invest in new equipment as quickly as need be, inasmuch as investment is centralized through the budget.

e. Rational utilization of basic means of production is obstructed because enterprises are prohibited from selling surplus equipment and using the receipts for decentralized investment.

f. Automatic quality control among enterprises is hindered, and product mix is directly affected because exchange relationships, as well as claims and compensations for damages, have been eliminated.

g. Increases in production and labor productivity are limited by restricting the amount a worker can earn through premiums for surpassing production quotas, by placing extremely low limits on material incentives, and by paying such incentives to workers without regard to the enterprise's economic performance.

h. Scheduled transfers to the budget in the amounts due are not assured because the enterprise's revenue comes from the difference between collections and payments, and does not reflect real accumulation.

i. Absence of financial control by the National Bank of Cuba at every level.

In order to try to eliminate or attenuate the deficiencies pointed out above, one must resort to administrative measures that increase paperwork enormously and employ personnel in unproductive activities. Moreover, such measures are not effective in practice.

Auto-Financing in the INRA Enterprises

The INRA [National Institute of Agrarian Reform] enterprises began to operate as such and to have direct relations with the budget as of January 1, 1962, when INRA started being financed through the national budget. Before, there had been such confusion among INRA's enterprises and old departments that it was impossible to tell where one left off and the other began.

The profits earned by enterprises or departments, as well as accumulated depreciation, remained in the central administrative body, INRA, which used them, together with other financing received directly from the government (loans from the Social Insurance Bank, the Postal Savings Fund, and the prime minister), to cover the losses of other enterprises, its own current expenses, and investments in general. The Coffee and Cacao Bureau, however, as well as the Tobacco Bureau and the Commercialization Bureau, received complementary funding in the form of bank credits for use toward storage and warehousing.

During 1962 and 1963, the INRA enterprises have not been operating under the auto-finance system, nor, indeed, could they be presented as examples of such operations. The consolidated enterprises operate under the budgetary finance system. Among these are the people's farms, with more than 250 production units, and the sugar cane farms, with more than 600 production units.

The consolidated enterprises operating under INRA's jurisdiction have been using some of the principles of auto-financing such as covering costs with revenues received from the sale of products and services, the use of bank credit, and direct relations with the budget. But, because at the time the National Bank of Cuba had not come out with the "rules for the concession of credit" and because the government had not yet established payments preferences, such principles have not been strictly followed, even at the enterprise level.

The first step toward progressive development of auto-financing in these enterprises was the establishment of the "quota for the means of turnover belonging to the enterprise," in formulating the 1963 plan. Despite the fact that this quota was fixed very roughly, it served to establish transfers to and assignments by the budget for decreases or increases in the means of turnover; it also provided a basis for the determination of quotas for the 1964 plan, which was drawn up in greater detail. In some enterprises, this determination was made starting with the production units.

In the first six months of 1963, they went over to financial decentralization at the provincial or group level in agricultural enterprises and at the regional level in warehousing enterprises; they also agreed on bank loans to national enterprises at these various levels.

Such measures brought about the more rational use of financial resources, a reduction in needs for bank credit, and scheduled payment of enterprise obligations, especially those of the warehousing enterprises.

The industrial enterprises that operated with bank credit, as well as those that had not made use of such credits, were directed to make use of loans to cover inventories above the established quotas and thus to rationalize resource use and meet their obligations to suppliers and the national budget on schedule.

All these moves were made in conjunction with the National Bank of Cuba and the Treasury Ministry.

The national agricultural enterprises were dissolved on September 30, 1963, and replaced by provincial enterprises as an intermediate step toward this year's creation of the group (regional) enterprises as auto-financed entities. Auto-financing will be implemented this year at the unit level of the national and provincial consolidated enterprises in the industrial, commercial, warehousing, and service sectors.

We are convinced that, generally, the year 1963 will show that the INRA enterprises will not prove to be examples of economic efficiency and financial discipline. Moreover, according to comrade Marcelo Fernández in his article [page 277] appearing in the March issue of this journal, these enterprises rank first in failure to comply with Law 1007. They did not transfer earned profits and accumulated depreciation to the national budget during this period. Neither did they achieve planned reductions in the means of turnover, nor, in the agricultural sector, in production costs. They therefore incurred losses. But these deficiencies are due primarily to two factors. The first is organizational problems that began in 1959, 1960, and 1961, and are now being solved with exceptional speed. The second is that their auto-finance operations are not fully regulated by the corresponding law.

We may point to the Empresa de Acopio y Beneficio de Tabaco as an example of good work. By means of bank credits amortized at the regional level, among other measures, this enterprise managed to incorporate regional administrators and other managerial personnel into the economic activity of the enterprise. Thus, it achieved cost reductions in comparison with 1962 and with those planned for 1963, as well as an increase in labor productivity and planned profits. Moreover, it met all its obligations to the budget, contributing the sum of $22,329.1 million, of which $20,026.0 million are attributed to the planned reduction of means of turnover.

General Considerations

We believe that the auto-finance system is the method of economic administration of enterprises most appropriate to the socialist stage. We do not deny the advantages of certain aspects of the budgetary finance system, but such a system is applicable only in a more advanced stage than the one in which we find ourselves at present.

We should bear in mind that the U.S.S.R. is now in the vanguard of technology and automation, that within this decade its gross and per capita products will surpass those of the United States of North America. Nikita S. Khrushchev recently declared at a meeting of the Central Committee Praesidium of the Communist Party at the Kremlin:

> We must proceed down the path of material incentives with energy and boldness, starting with quality and quantity of production.
>
> Our principal task today is to assure that the people meet their commitments and that the workers are materially interested in raising agricultural production.
>
> Moral incentives are the ideal of the communist society. But to achieve this ideal, we must also employ the great power of material incentives. Lenin said this.

NOTES

1. Karl Marx, *Critique of the Gotha Program.* [Translator's source: *Critique of the Gotha Program* (New York, International Publishers, c. 1938), p. 8.]

7

On the Analysis of the Systems of Finance

LUIS ALVAREZ ROM

ACTUALLY, this article should be about investment financing, but after reading two articles in number 34 of *Cuba Socialista*—one entitled, "The Meaning of Socialist Planning," by comrade Ernesto Che Guevara [page 98], and the other, "On the Operation of the Auto-Financed Enterprise," by comrade Joaquin Infante [page 157]—I have decided to address myself first to the question of the analytical method that I believe should be used to deal with the criteria expressed in these articles. This is important if such criteria are to have any real theoretical value in developing the themes under discussion, themes that are still being treated in socialist countries and that in our own country are peculiarly related to the existence of two systems of finance.

Commander Guevara expressed the same idea in one of his previous articles, saying, in effect, that such discussions are useless unless imbued with a high degree of scientific precision. The thought appears again in "The Meaning of Socialist Planning":

> We consider the examination of the inconsistencies between the classical method of Marxist analysis and the survival of

---

Luis Alvarez Rom was Minister of the Treasury during the period of debate.

SOURCE: "Sobre el método de análisis de las sistemas de financiamiento," *Cuba Socialista,* Año IV, Julio 1964, pp. 64–79.

the mercantile categories in the socialist sector to be of great theoretical importance, and deserving of more thorough research.[1]

Along the same vein, V. I. Lenin said:

Marx did not leave us a Logic (with capital L), but rather the logic of *Capital.* We should make the greatest possible use of this for the problem at hand. In *Capital,* Marx applies logic, dialectic, and the theory of knowledge of materialism to a single science.[2]

Another point intimately related to these statements that should receive special attention is that what we say or write constitutes the use of language as an instrument for communicating our thoughts to others. It is, as Marx said, the immediate reality of consciousness, the raw material of thought.

The reason for which it is erroneously believed that there can be thought without words is based on the fact that Man, by thinking of himself, does not pronounce aloud the words he would have to use if he wanted to communicate a thought to someone else. Sometimes we have great difficulty in even choosing the necessary words and phrases, that is, "we don't find the words" needed to express and make an idea understandable to others which to us is already completely clear. Here, it might seem, they not only fail to express the thought, but even get in the way of its understanding.

Nevertheless, this does not in any way mean that a given thought could exist without an idiomatic wrapping. In thinking to ourselves, we do not always completely dress up our ideas with linguistic clothing. But even if we do not employ *all* the words needed to express our thought fully and in complete detail, still, we always use some words. And in overcoming the difficulties that arise in choosing the appropriate words, we are at the same time developing our own thought.

When the thought receives a definitive verbal expression,

> it acquires clarity, logical consistency and precision. By being dressed in rich idiomatic clothing, the thought acquires greater perfection not only because of its form, but also because of its content.[3]

Comrade Infante's article is divided into four sections. The first deals with purely operational matters, taking as given, with no technical or economic explanation, the existence of mercantile exchange, money as a means of payment, etc., in relations among state enterprises. Infante also believes that the basic means of production are commodities and that material incentives are the principal driving force behind economic development. The second section is entitled, "Economic Problems and Harm Created by Failure to Apply the Principles of Auto-Finance." The third section is called "Auto-Financing in the INRA Enterprises," and the fourth section, "General Considerations."

We will refer here to neither the first nor third sections. As we said, the purely operational nature (and, moreover, subjective, going so far as to assign functions to the National Bank of Cuba and the Ministry of the Treasury) of this section deserves no comment. The author seems to ignore not only what Commander Guevara contributed to the same issue of the journal—which is logical—but even Guevara's previous articles. These articles contained arguments of a technical nature defending ideas contradictory to Infante's, but comrade Infante simply states his concepts formally without bothering to defend them on a similar level. The third section is a brief discussion of INRA's [National Institute of Agrarian Reform] organizational process, which, for obvious reasons, we will not judge.

The very title of the second section, however, is enough to worry anyone: the *economic harm* created by failure to apply the principles of auto-finance—such as our failure to attain the rate of growth that we *can and must* attain, and the fact that socialist enterprises operating under the budgetary finance system *produce disequilibrium in the national economy*. This is all so alarming that it must be examined more closely. Thus, the author describes the ways in which this disaster becomes manifest. They are summarized in nine points, from (a) through (i), which compose the second part of his article, and are expanded under "General Considerations."

We will begin with (a) [page 179]:

> Absence of a relationship between the enterprise's production costs and the useful material goods it creates because it does not use its own revenue to cover costs.

We understand that there is, in the first place, a problem with wording. It should say: "Absence of a relationship between production costs and *the prices* of material goods produced, etc." Unless we make this correction, we will be trying to establish a relationship between production *costs* and *useful* material goods produced. The utility of objects turns them into use-values. As such, they have different qualities, qualitative factors that cannot be compared with costs, factors that in this case are quantitative and whose comparison has nothing to do with what we are trying to relate here, that is, production costs and exchange value. Now that this is clarified, we would point out that in order to establish any value relationship, however "gold-plated" or "silver-plated" such values may be, there is no need to *possess them.*

Marx says:

> The price or money form of commodities is, like their form of value generally, a form quite distinct from their palpable bodily form; it is, therefore, a purely ideal or mental form. Although invisible, the value of iron, linen, and corn has actual existence in these very articles; it is ideally made perceptible by their equality with gold, a relation that, so to say, exists only in their own heads. Their owner must, therefore, lend them his tongue, or hang a ticket on them, before their prices can be communicated to the outside world. Since the expression of the value of commodities in gold is merely an ideal money. Every trader knows that he is far from having turned his goods into money when he has expressed their value in a price or in imaginary money, and

> that it does not require the least bit of real gold to estimate in that metal millions of pounds' worth of goods. When, therefore, money serves as a measure of value, it is employed only as imaginary or ideal money.[4]

In point (b), Infante states [page 179]:

> Spontaneous fluctuations in circulating capital at the enterprise level that cannot be controlled by financial agencies.

Actually, we do not understand what he means by the word spontaneous. But if he is trying to say that inventories of raw materials, goods in process, and finished goods can be varied at will by the manager of the enterprise but cannot be controlled by financial agencies, then his opinion is purely personal. In the budgetary system, inventories must correspond to quotas regulated by a plan and consistent with all categories of that plan. We must confess, however, that on occasion we would have liked freer access to raw materials of which we are sometimes short, in order to avoid production stoppages or improve product quality. At times, the ambition and rigidity of our plan have surpassed its technical and organizational potential. With respect to the above statement, however, we reproduce the following two paragraphs from an article published in the *Economic Gazette,* entitled, "Urgent Tasks of Commerce":

> *I have here the consequences of the lack of attention given the economic aspect of the matter:* At present, inventories exceeding quotas represent hundreds of millions of rubles. The Ministers of Commerce of the Federal Republics must adopt urgent measures in order to get these inventories into circulation.
>
> Commodity inventories which exceed quotas come about where the struggle for high quality has been given up. The planning and accounting systems of factories as well as economic councils often just establish figures rather than bother to thoroughly analyze the causes of deficiencies in the use of production.[5]

This spontaneity is not exactly a trait of the budgetary finance system. Point (c) says [page 179]:

> The National Bank of Cuba cannot control the use of credits to enterprises because such credits are granted indirectly through the Treasury Ministry.

This point is complemented by (i) [page 179]:

> Absence of financial control by the National Bank of Cuba at every level.

These points are consistent with those expressed by comrade Marcelo Fernández, President of the National Bank of Cuba, in an article on the bank's operation appearing in number 30 of *Cuba Socialista* [page 277], which was answered in the following issue by Commander Guevara [page 296].

Commander Guevara responded to Fernández by quoting several paragraphs from Marx regarding the bank credit system. We will transcribe below one of those paragraphs [page 301]:

> On the other hand, the illusions concerning the miraculous power of the credit and banking system, in the socialist sense, arise from a complete lack of familiarity with the capitalist mode of production and the credit system as one of its forms. *As soon as the means of production cease being transformed into capital* (*which also includes the abolition of private property in land*), *credit as such no longer has any meaning*. This, incidentally, was even understood by the followers of Saint-Simon. On the other hand, as long as the capitalist mode of production continues to exist, interest-bearing capital, as one of its forms, also continues to exist and constitutes in fact the basis of its credit system. Only that sensational writer, Proudhon, who wanted to perpetuate commodity-production and abolish money, was capable of dreaming up the monstrous *crédit gratuit,* the ostensible realization of the pious wish of the petty-bourgeois estate.[6]

With respect to financial control by the bank, Che answered as follows [page 299]:

> Lenin, in the article cited by Marcelo Fernández (which was written before the assumption of power), talks of banks as great factors of "accounting and control." He gives the impression that he is seeking the consolidation of the entire financial apparatus so that it might fulfill its primary function, already scored by Marx, of social accounting.
>
> The monopoly bank is, in fact, its own finance ministry in the duality of a State within a State operating at this stage. In periods of building the socialist society, all the concepts that assure the bank's political life change, and another way to use its experience must be found. The centralization that Marcelo seeks can be obtained by making the Ministry of the Treasury the supreme "accounting and control" apparatus of the entire State.[7]

In point (d), the author says [page 179]:

> Simple reproduction cannot be ensured, and operational efficiency is hindered because enterprises do not properly maintain machinery and equipment, or invest in new equipment as quickly as need be, inasmuch as investment is centralized through the budget.

This point merits special attention because economically it represents the greatest "harm." The decision on the degree of investment decentralization is made by the Central Planning Board in accordance with government policy. This decision cannot be based on a formality such as its source of financing, whether that source is the national budget or the total or partial depreciation retained in the enterprise's own fund. But what stands out here is the statement that the budgetary finance system *does not ensure simple reproduction* because it does not allow the enterprise to retain any part of book-value depreciation in its own fund. This is equivalent to saying that simple reproduction in the budgetary system is subject to the whims of fate. To gain some perspective on the magnitude of this accusation and to demonstrate its total lack of technical content, we must go back to the early stages of civilization and briefly review the steps of social evolution.

When man first began to dominate his natural surroundings, and hunting and fishing were the bases of his existence, the regular repetition of the production process was frequently interrupted by periods of widespread hunger. It was only then that the possibility of renewing production depended more or less on the whims of fate. Only then was it necessary to apply tradition, in the form of religious ceremonies, as repeated measures to gain and preserve the means of subsistence. Later, the cultivation of the soil and the use of domestic animals and livestock for food created the regular alternative of production and consumption, which are the characteristics of reproduction. In this sense, reproduction embraces something more than mere repetition: It implies, in economic terms, a certain level of labor productivity.

At every step in social evolution, production as well as reproduction depend on two intimately related factors: technical and social conditions—man's relationship with nature; and his relationships with other men. We are not going to pursue the question of how social forms affect production and, therefore, reproduction, or describe the historically known types of society that preceded capitalism. These matters do not concern us here. Instead, we will move ahead to the capitalist society in which reproduction has a totally unique character. But even here we will have to ignore certain disturbing phenomena such as crises, which, although they may be important in political analysis, represent a purely social condition.

Luckily for humanity, among Marx's lasting services was his presentation of the social-reproduction problem as a whole. Where production is in capitalist form, so, necessarily, is reproduction. And capitalist production is basically composed of countless private producers without any sort of guiding plan. Profit is their ultimate objective, and commodity exchange the only social bond tying them together.

If we regard the formula that expresses total social product, we will see that it is composed of the following elements, which being well-known, we will not define: C plus V plus S equals value of total social product.[8]

This gross product and, therefore, society's total reproduction, is divided into two large sectors:

> a. *Means of Production,* commodities having a form in which they must, or at least may, pass into productive consumption.
> b. *Articles of Consumption,* commodities having a form in which they pass into individual consumption of the capitalist and the working-class.[9]

Even under the capitalist system of production, which is governed by anarchy, this formula has a social application, an objective social existence, and in no way represents a scheme removed from material reality, even though it might appear to be a sum of money. Money is simply the formal expression of value of the means of production and consumption, which must also exist materially. From the standpoint of society as a whole, one may derive from this formulation that the individual, completely autonomous and independent of the existence of capitalist enterprises, is merely the historically conditioned form, while the social connection is the real basis. In this respect, Marx wrote:

> So long as we looked upon the production of value and the value of the product of capital individually, the bodily form of the commodities produced was wholly immaterial for the analysis, whether it was machines, for instance, corn, or looking glasses. It was always but a matter of illustration, and any branch of production could have served that purpose equally well. What we dealt with was the immediate process of production itself, which presents itself at every point as the process of some individual capital. So far as the reproduction of capital was concerned, it was sufficient to assume that the portion of the product in commodities which represents capital-value finds an opportunity in the

sphere of circulation to reconvert itself into its elements of production and thus into its form of productive capital; just as it sufficed to assume that both the labourer and the capitalist find in the market those commodities on which they spend their wages and the surplus-value. This merely formal manner of presentation is no longer adequate in the study of the total social capital and of the value of its products. The reconversion of one portion of the value of the product into capital and the passing of another portion into the individual consumption of the capitalist as well as the working class form a movement within the value of the product itself in which the result of the aggregate capital finds expression; and this movement is not only a replacement of value, but also a replacement in material and is therefore as much bound up with the relative proportions of the value-components of the total social product as with their use-value, their material shape.

Simple reproduction, reproduction on the same scale, appears as an abstraction, inasmuch as on the one hand the absence of all accumulation or reproduction on an extended scale is a strange assumption in capitalist conditions, and on the other hand conditions of production do not remain exactly the same in different years (and this is assumed). The assumption is that a social capital of a given magnitude produces the same quantity of commodity-value this year as last, and supplies the same quantum of wants, although the forms of the commodities may change in the process of reproduction. However, as far as accumulation does take place, simple reproduction is always a part of it, and can therefore be studied by itself, and is an actual factor of accumulation. The value of the annual product may decrease, although the quantity of use-values may remain the same; or the value may remain the same although the quantity of the use-values may decrease; or the quantity of value and of the reproduced use-values may decrease simultaneously. All this amounts to reproduction taking place either under more favourable conditions than before or under

> more difficult ones, which may result in imperfect—defective—reproduction. All this can refer only to the quantitative aspect of the various elements of reproduction, not to the role which they play as reproducing capital or as a reproduced revenue in the entire process.[10]

Following these considerations, can one continue to state that the budgetary system does not ensure simple reproduction? To do so would be to compare it, in effect, to a devastating war or a great epidemic that results in mass annihilation of the working population and the available means of production—or to the despotic will of some personality of the Dark Ages who shifted an enormous number of workers out of the cultivation of huge land tracts into an unproductive project, sometimes permitting almost entire generations to die of starvation.

But let us continue on to point (e) [page 179]:

> Rational utilization of basic means of production is obstructed because enterprises are prohibited from selling surplus equipment and using the receipts for decentralized investment.

The rational distribution of basic means of production among state enterprises through mercantile exchange is a way of using material incentive that, in our judgment, corresponds to neither social nor technical criteria.

Under developed capitalism, when a piece of equipment becomes surplus, its owner tries to get rid of it as fast as possible because otherwise he will have to absorb a depreciation cost that is not transferable, by proper economic technique, to the value of any product. As commodities and mercantile exchange are the only bonds among individual producers in private production, the only method of transfer is through the mechanism that removes the piece of equipment from the sphere of production and returns it to the sphere of circulation. He actually sells it to other representatives of capital, usually less developed, and at a price almost always below its depreciated book value. In economic terms, no new investment is produced by the social order.

Regarding this, Marx writes:

> But the instruments of labour never leave the sphere of production once they have entered it. Their function holds them there. A portion of the advanced capital-value becomes *fixed* in this form determined by the function of the instruments of labour in the process. In the performance of this function, and thus by the wear and tear of the instruments of labour, a part of their value passes on to the product, while the other remains fixed in the instruments of labour and thus in the process of production. The value fixed in this way decreases steadily, until the instrument of labour is worn out, its value having been distributed during a shorter or longer period over a mass of products originating from a series of constantly repeated labour-processes.[11]

In P. Nikitin's *Manual of Economics,* we read the following:

> Labor power is not a commodity; it is neither bought nor sold. The soil and the subsoil cannot be bought or sold, that is, cannot be objects of exchange. Neither are socialist enterprises with their basic resources (machinery, buildings, installations, etc.) bought or sold.[12]

Is it not really contradictory to call means of production commodities merely because they become surplus? In virtue of what economic technique are they given this character if there is no change in State investment? Does this not create an antisocial habit in the enterprise manager who would prefer to charge off the cost of a surplus piece of equipment to depreciation if he could not convert it into money?

The budgetary finance system does not consider the means of production to be commodities in their movement within the State sphere. And we believe that even within the auto-finance system the exchange of basic means of production as a way to their rational distribution is pernicious.

Point (f) says [page 179]:

> Automatic quality control among enterprises is hindered, and product mix is directly affected because exchange re-

lationships, as well as claims and compensations for damages, have been eliminated.

To permit control over the enterprise, over its product quality and mix, to reside automatically in exchange, is to ignore the existence of the supply contract as an instrument of a planned economy and to manifest a certain tendency toward competition. Relative to this and to the subject of compensation for damages, we reproduce below an article from *Pravda,* January 10, 1964:

> HAVE YOU VIOLATED DISCIPLINE? ANSWER. Between us, economic administration and planning are always being improved, excessive losses of goods and material means are being eliminated. Still, losses resulting from low productivity still occur in enterprises in construction, commerce, and transport. The causes of such losses are defective production, failure to meet delivery schedules for equipment, and other violations of state discipline.
>
> In 1962, the *State Arbitration Board,* an adjunct to the Moscow Urban Executive Committee, fined tens of enterprises for a total amount of 2,309,000 rubles. The figure was also considerable last year. It would appear that violators are punished quite severely. Nevertheless, such fines do not always accomplish their objectives. The bad part is that this money comes from the State pocket while the infractors themselves do not usually receive punishment.
>
> The national economy experienced significant losses because of the careless attitude toward the transportation of production. Bad packing, improper loads on railroad cars and trucks, occasional large losses.
>
> Many enterprises and organizations violate the system established for the return of containers. For example: From January to April, 1963, the *State Arbitration Board* fined the Material and Equipment Supply Administration of the Moscow Urban Executive Committee, headed by G. Gorchkov, for the sum of 10,000 rubles for not returning containers to the Iaroslav "Freed Labor" factory.

A great number of fines are imposed on enterprises and organizations for violation of the system for collection and storage of metal scrap. "Moscow Cables," "Kotlotopstroi" and other factories are well-known for this. Example: The construction machine factory was fined three times. And each time the fine was paid with State funds!

It seems to us that this is completely unacceptable. By general rule, those guilty of infractions are: the Manager, the chief Engineer of the enterprise, or their substitutes. What has the State got to do with it then? These punishments contradict the reason for the existence of the system of material sanctions for violation of contractual discipline, which is an important force in the administration of the economy.

It is now necessary to reorganize the agencies of the *State Arbitration Board.* It is necessary to grant them greater freedom and authority in order to eliminate the deficiencies and violations of state discipline.

In order to increase the responsibility of enterprise management, the Presidium of the Supreme Soviet of the U.S.S.R. decreed on June 21, 1961, "Regarding the Demarcation on the Administrative System." *This Decree establishes particularly that fines must be imposed on the responsible parties. It is prohibited to pay such fines with the funds of dependencies, enterprises, and organizations.*

Almost three years have passed since this important decree was issued.

However, the agencies of the *State Arbitration Board* act as they did before the Law came into being. This is motivated by the fact that fines collected on the basis of the Resolutions emanating from the *State Arbitration Board* are not of an administrative nature. Nevertheless, the main idea of the Decree, with respect to the fines' not falling on the enterprise but rather on the persons really responsible, must be reflected in the work of the arbitration board. Not only enterprises, but the persons responsible as well must answer for violation of State discipline. There is need to attract on a broader scale the syndicated organizations and those groups collaborating in Party control in order to determine the persons responsible for violations. There is need to grant the arbitration board the right to deduct given amounts from the salaries of enterprise managers if they have committed serious violations of the law.

The *State Arbitration Board* must be more closely linked to the agencies of Party control and to mass organizations. Then their combined influence will perforce have great educational significance.

The changes proposed in the system for applying patrimonial sanctions for various violations of State discipline would be elevated to the personal responsibility of the Managers of enterprises, dependencies, and organizations.
F. Rabinovich, State Arbiter.
I. Kuzmetzov, honorary Inspector of the Party Control Committee of the District of Leningrad, City of Moscow.

Obviously, administrative sanction is considered an excellent complement to relations among enterprises in the U.S.S.R.

Point (g) goes on [page 179]:

Increases in production and labor productivity are limited by restricting the amount a worker can earn through premiums for surpassing production quotas, by placing extremely low limits on material incentives, and by paying such incentives to workers without regard to the enterprise's economic performance.

Our ideas on production standards and material incentives, with respect to Cuba, conform to those outlined in an article by Commander Guevara, to which we refer the reader [page 296]. The use of material incentives is being contemplated by economists in several socialist countries, and lately literature on the subject has become quite abundant. We believe that this matter cannot be discussed on an abstract, quantitative plane. It requires more thorough analysis. Comrade Infante closes his article with a quotation from a recent speech by Nikita S. Khrushchev, which contains the following points of interest. (We have underlined what we feel is significant.):

1. His remarks are directed to the increase of *agricultural production,* that part of the Soviet economy that has felt little of the impact of technical progress. Lenin makes this point in his early writings on the subject.

2. That "we must proceed down the *path* of material incentives with energy and audacity, starting with *quality and quantity of production.*"

3. That "*moral incentives are the ideal* of the communist society. But to achieve this ideal, we must *also* employ the great power of material incentives."

In point (h) the author states [page 179]:

> Scheduled transfers to the budget in the amounts due are not assured because the enterprise's revenue comes from the difference between collections and payments, and does not reflect real accumulation.

This is stated incorrectly. In order to analyze the point, however, one must have an understanding of the principles behind the budgetary finance system, as well as an ability to distinguish between administrative deficiencies or faults in accounting technique, and what actually has economic relevance for society.

Under the budgetary system, relationships among State enterprises are not relationships between owners of commodities, on the one hand, and owners of money, on the other—and certainly not between debtors and creditors representative of individual patrimonies—but, rather, delivery and receipt of products in accordance with a plan. The enterprise's contribution is calculated in a planned way by the total amount perceived on its operation, plus depreciation. Obviously, this has nothing to do with "collections" and "payments." That part of the contribution which concerns relations among enterprises is nominal, that is to say, merely accountable for the purpose of controlling the enterprise's economic performance. On the other hand, the part connected with the enterprise's relations with non-State sectors or with the people is totally real, or, in other words, has mercantile economic content.

Receipts and payments among State enterprises are, to our way of thinking, no more than compensatory operations in which monetary expression through a bank document, which has a purely arithmetic or accounting content, serves as a means by which the bank, acting as a center of social accounting, records the movements—deliveries and receipts—of products.

The enterprises, having no bank accounts of their own, automatically transfer all their revenues to the national budget. In this way, the State's need to collect its corresponding part of enterprise profit is eliminated. The fiscal nature of such profits in the auto-finance system is a remnant from bourgeois finance and requires that money's function as a means of payment be retained.

The use of money as a means of payment in relations among State enterprises has also been occurring in practice. This applies as much to one system as to the other, because legislation regarding payments is inconsistent with the merely accountable nature of compensatory banking operations in relations among enterprises within the socialist sector.

So long as the idea exists that one commodity owner sells already existing commodities, while the other, acting simply as a representative of money, buys them, the evolution of commodity circulation chronologically separates the act of sale from the act of perceiving the price of the sale. For this reason, the commodity is bought before it is paid for, which makes the seller a creditor and the buyer a debtor. In this process, money unfailingly acquires a function as a means of payment, although theoretically it may be established that such a function does not exist. Indeed, it will exist so long as the debtor's will governs the act of banking compensation.

Socialist banking compensation—because neither anarchy of production nor cooperation exist—should depend on the act of product delivery. Crediting the supplier and debiting the consumer should be simultaneous acts of accounting. This would eliminate the contradiction implied by money as a means of payment in banking compensations, even under premonopoly capitalism. Under monopoly, on the other hand, this contradiction is highly exaggerated, to the point that reciprocal debts among enterprises within the same monopoly are canceled out by consolidating the accounting operation in the "parent company."

Regarding this, Marx wrote:

> The function of money as the means of payment implies a direct contradiction. In so far as the payments balance one another, money functions only ideally as money of account, as a measure of value. In so far as actual payments have to be made, money does not serve as a circulating medium, as a mere transient agent in the interchange of products, but as the individual incarnation of social labour, as the independent form of existence of exchange value, as the universal commodity.[13]

The principles of the budgetary finance system are based on the economic techniques developed in *Capital* and, therefore, are founded on Lenin's scientific abstraction that through the socialization of production the society becomes "a single office and a single factory."

Toward the end of the article under consideration, the author remarks [page 182]:

> We believe that the auto-finance system is the method of economic administration of enterprises most appropriate to the socialist stage. We do not deny the advantages of certain aspects of the budgetary finance system, but such a system is applicable only in a more advanced stage than the one in which we find ourselves at present.

Considering what he believes to be the problems and harm inherent in the budgetary finance system, we will not try to guess what he thinks the system's advantages are. The fundamental thing to note in the above paragraph is the contradiction, or better, confusion, it suggests.

If the author is proposing that the auto-finance system be established today—during the transition from capitalism to socialism—if he is saying that it is the system appropriate to the "socialist stage," and if the next stage is communism, then when should the budgetary finance system be employed?

To conclude, we wish to synthesize the title of our article—"On the Analysis of the Systems of Finance"—with the following paragraphs:

> "For the theory of knowledge," declared the neo-Kantian H. Rickert, "nothing exists but the problem of form. Simple content is held to be completely outside the realm of logic, as it does not yet embrace the problem of truth. And therefore the problems of the theory of knowledge are problems of form . . ."
>
> "To reduce knowledge to a matter of form," says Rosenthal, "separate from its content: I have here the characteristic of the various tendencies of contemporary idealist philosophy, whatever they may be called—'logical positivism,' 'existentialism,' etc." [14]

By failing to look into the content of both systems of finance, by condemning the budgetary system while ignoring its published defense, the author introduces a dialogue for the deaf into the debate and becomes entangled in the web of form.

NOTES

1. *"La Planificación Socialista, su significado," Cuba Socialista,* No. 34, 1964, pp. 23–24.
2. M. Rosenthal, *Los problemas de la Dialectica en* El Capital *de Carlos Marx,* p. 7. *El Alcance Filosófico de* El Capital *de Carlos Marx* (Havana, Editora Politica, 1963).
3. E. V. Konstantinov, *Los fundamentos de la filosofía marxista,* p. 208 (Havana, Editora Politica, 1964).
4. Karl Marx, *Capital* (Vol. I). [Translator's source: *Great Books of the Western World* (Chicago, Encyclopedia Britannica, c. 1952), Vol. L, p. 42.]
5. *Economic Gazette,* May 9, 1964.
6. *"El Banco, el credito y el socialismo," Cuba Socialista,* No. 31, March, 1964, p. 29. Taken from Karl Marx, *Capital.* [Translator's source: *Capital* (New York, International Publishers, 1967), Vol. II, pp. 606–608.]

7. *Ibid.,* p. 27.
8. Where C = constant capital (primarily value of plant and equipment), V = variable capital (primarily wages), S = surplus value (primarily profits). See Karl Marx, *Capital.* [Translator's source: *Capital, op. cit.,* pp. 429–430.]
9. Karl Marx, *Capital, op. cit.,* p. 395.
10. *Ibid.,* pp. 394–395.
11. *Ibid.,* pp. 157–158.
12. P. Nikitin, *Economía Politica,* (Moscow, Ediciónes en Lenguas Extranjeras, 1961), p. 299.
13. Marx, *Capital, op. cit.,* p. 64.
14. M. Rosenthal, *op. cit.,* p. 15.

8

Experiences of Control Under the Budgetary System

ALEXIS CODINA

All of us who are in one way or another involved in "economic administration" have followed the course of the articles that have appeared concerning the finance systems being used in Cuba.

From reading and study, we have noted that most of them are devoted almost exclusively to shedding light on the philosophical aspects, and on the advantages and disadvantages of these systems with regard to achieving a more rapid development of the economy and the revolutionary process in general.

Basically, most of the discussion has focused on the weight that moral and material incentives should have under socialism, on the form assumed by the law of value, and on how this law should be viewed in the context of our economic and social system. In other words, for the most part the discussion has centered on the scientific and political aspects of the system. Except for the articles prepared by the Consolidated Electric Power and Petroleum Enterprises that have appeared in the

---

Alexis Codina was an economic administrator in the consolidated flour enterprise.

Source: "Experiencias sobre el control en el sistema presupuestario," *Nuestra Industria Revista Económica,* Año 2, Diciembre 1964, pp. 52–59.

journal *Nuestra Industria Económica,* we have seen nothing regarding the operational aspects of the new system of economic control that has been introduced in our economy in the last few years.

We do not feel capable of participating in the discussions that have taken place to date because we are unable to treat the issues with the same scientific rigor characterizing the expositions of those comrades who have participated. But we can present our ideas on our working experiences in the operational field and induce our comrades in other enterprises operating under the same system of finance to do the same. Without regard to the philosophical nature of the problem, this system of economic control could become the most apt for a small country like ours in which efficient methods of central administration can be set up with enough flexibility to be made consistent with the special characteristics of the degree of concentration of production in the various enterprises.

Although we do not know whether this system was conceived from the start as a determining factor for the gradual development of the workers' political consciousness, it might be said that it arose from the need "all of a sudden" to control the industries that came under the jurisdiction of INRA's [National Institute of Agrarian Reform] Industrial Administration Bureau during the last half of 1960. We may so conclude by simply reading the following paragraphs taken from an article by comrade Luis Alvarez Rom, treasury minister, entitled "Finance and Political Development" [page 271], which appears in *Nuestra Industria Económica,* number 1:

> Toward the end of 1960, the revolutionary government had to confront its first practical economic and financial problem. The problem had to do with the need to take charge of the administration and control of nationalized enterprises that had been recuperated or intervened.
>
> The usual scarcity of operating funds in small and medium-sized enterprises, together with the nationalization of economically more powerful enterprises, engendered the

first revolutionary decision in matters of finance, which was to centralize the bank accounts of all enterprises, thereby creating a common "central fund." All revenues were deposited in this fund, while financial resources required for evolution of an enterprise's productive activity were made available through specific budget allocations. The fund was administered and controlled by the Department of Industrialization of INRA, and was kept in the Agricultural and Industrial Development Bank, which had already been nationalized.

Later, when the banking system was nationalized and financial bodies were restructured (they were, of course, already serving the nation's needs), the central fund was transferred to the national budget under the jurisdiction of the Treasury Ministry. The new system was administered along the same lines as the central fund, but was modified somewhat by the creation of the consolidated enterprise as a legal entity combining the production and administrative functions of several factories with similar characteristics, as well as by our initial efforts to plan the economy.

The "Year of Organization," the progress achieved in systematizing national economic planning, and the imminent need to strengthen institutional organization, forced us to review our financial organization. The situation in this area was such that the methods in use were evolving by fits and starts. In fact, the most notable characteristic of any advance made in the area was spontaneity.

Both this work by Rom and others by Commander Ernesto Guevara refer to the fact that accounting technique was highly developed in Cuba, especially in the large monopolies such as the Electric Power Company, the Telephone Company, the Petroleum Refinery, and the sugar companies. This development was due to the penetration that North American imperialist capital had achieved in our economy since the end of the last century. In this respect, and in order to demonstrate the degree of development accounting technique had attained in Cuba, we may mention the existence of a great number of public-accounting firms that in many cases were extremely specialized and well-organized enterprises. These enterprises even provided services to the government in matters of systematization and fiscal control of the various state agencies, and obtained juicy profits from such operations. Some of these "firms" had branches in other Latin American countries, and others represented large North American firms, being responsible for checking over the balances being sent to home offices in New York by Cuban monopoly branches.

In some large enterprises, the implementation of the budgetary system was greatly facilitated by this development of accounting technique because the system is oriented toward central administration. Under capitalism, these enterprises had been governed by a budget that projected the output that was to go to the market they controlled, as well as costs of raw-material acquisition, transportation, warehousing, advertising, etc., and the wages they would pay to realize their activities. In other words, they were under the kind of central administration characteristic of monopoly organization.

Our enterprises did not, to our regret, have the above characteristics. A few factories such as the La Estrella, La Ambrosia, and La Pasiega flour mills had more or less efficient accounting and administrative systems. A small number of lesser factories had acceptable systems, but in many cases these were lost because the factories were taken over through interventions due to labor problems, etc., and personnel qualified in administrative and accounting matters left. It was characteristic in such cases that the initial revolutionary administrations threw out these so necessary administrative elements (accounting and economic control) * because at that stage it was more important to avoid a stoppage in a work center than to know whether it was worth the trouble to have it running under current conditions. Except for these factories, however, the rest were workshops with a small number of laborers (*"chinchales"*) which had never even

* These problems are still widespread in Cuba (see Introduction).

kept books. Whey they were visited by some tax inspector, they merely paid him his customary "extra-official" contribution, which was good enough to certify the "fiscal legality of the industrial establishment" in question.

Thus, on the one hand, the distribution and structure of production that characterize this enterprise did not present the favorable conditions existing in others which would permit the immediate implementation of the budgetary system with no major disruptions in organization and production. On the other hand, however, the budgetary system, together with its initial instrument, the "budget program" (established in 1961), helped us to control the economic activity of our factories. The factories were governed by a budget which, though containing defects because of a lack of dependable data, etc., at least served as a framework for the evolution of financial activities. By having a fund availability in the bank limited to within this framework, one could to an extent control the tendency toward waste inherent in the first interventions and nationalizations. Such waste was a product of the overflowing enthusiasm during the early days and of the ignorance of the economic problems faced by the comrades who first had the responsibility of managing production. Clearly, all this had to happen during the embryonic phase of the process in which we were engaged because "between night and morning" we had to place those workers who had the most understanding of the problems of the Revolution in administrative positions. But of course they did not have the knowledge and experience of those who had served the rich and acquired the training needed for enterprise management.

Although the establishment of the budgetary system was a great step forward in the administration and control of economic performance, not everything went as smoothly as it might appear from the above. For one thing, there were inconsistencies in the budget program as well as imperative needs that came up in the production and distribution process. This required frequent revisions in the budget. Moreover, the majority of our factories were well behind in bookkeeping, and the enterprise could not devote its attention to following the budget because of operational matters brought about by the problems referred to above.

To all this we should add that at the time there was no standard accounting system that would enable us to use identical procedures in every factory. On the other hand, we should bear in mind that the principal persons in charge of economic control had abandoned their jobs. Following their masters' lead, they did not intend to serve the working class or be directed by people they had held in disesteem all their lives. Thus, comrades took charge of the accounting operation who, although showing great interest and sacrificial spirit in carrying out their work, even struggling against the failure on the part of many administrators to understand accounting problems, did not have the experience and training needed to perform their tasks well.

At the time (1961), the administrative units had not been formed, and factories operated directly under the enterprise. A number of procedures were adopted in our enterprise as a result of a false and mechanical conception of centralization. In some cases, such procedures contributed to organizational development, but in others they disrupted the elementary control that had already been established. Such was the case, for example, with the centralization of all payments (excluding wages) at the enterprise level. This caused innumerable problems because accounting operations were still decentralized, and the central office had to perform a whole pile of bureaucratic work that improved neither control nor accounting procedures. Instead, it created an anarchy that was only overcome by transferring the activity back to the factories.

In 1961, which may be considered the year of the budgetary system's baptism of fire, the "Regulations of the Standard Accounting System" were established. These regulations marked a new stage in the development of the budgetary system by setting down the standard procedures to be used for recording economic data. Moreover, they provided forms and a timetable for the submission of this data to the upper-level agencies.

The application of these regulations was greatly facilitated by the complementary legislation accompanying Resolution 103. One piece of legislation was Resolution 115, which concerned the cancelation and transfer to the Treasury Ministry of those items that were unnecessary for the performance of the factory's economic activity in the new stage and reflected operations belonging to the decadent capitalist system (securities acquired with surplus funds to speculate in the market, trademarks and patents, concessions, good will,[1] and others). Resolution 110 established that if accounting records were not up to date on July 1 (which was the date on which the system was to be implemented), an inventory of all the means of production and circulation would be taken on that date, and operations would be recorded according to the "regulations" mentioned above. Enterprises were required to bring their records up to date as of June 30 and to make whatever adjustments were necessary before November 30 of the same year. These measures brought about an improvement in enterprise accounting records that allowed them to obtain the best results under the new conditions.

Despite all the facilities provided by law for the implementation of the "regulations," our enterprise could not comply with the conditions of this legislation because of a lack of qualified personnel, in most cases, and because of the anarchic manner, totally lacking in organizational tradition, in which our productive activity was carried out. Thus, in order to be able to begin 1962 with moderately up-to-date accounting records, we had to form a team incorporating the best-trained and most enthusiastic comrades we had available at the time and distribute them over the entire island for the purpose of updating accounting records from July 1 to November 30, and to be able to present our first balance sheets to the Treasury Ministry. This was finally done, but with the deficiencies to be expected in a task of such magnitude carried out in such a short time under adverse conditions. It was accomplished only after several weeks of hard work on the part of these comrades.

In 1962 another step was taken in the development of the budgetary system. A technical-economic plan was formulated which, although containing enormous faults, served to lay out for our inexpert administrators the points to be observed in regulating the productive activity of the factories under their management, and also how to maintain a certain degree of discipline in order to be able to fulfill the role assigned the particular factory in the national economy. Here, we might speculate that the authority of the plan is somewhat weakened at present because of a number of factors. Among these are the degree of subjectivism often inherent in the plan; the want of adequate operational programs to correct the inconsistencies present in drawing up the plan itself; failure to bring all categories of the technical-economic plan down to the factory level; and, as a result of all these things, the constant changes that have to be made in many cases. But apart from the problems we have pointed out, the plan surpassed the budget program as a guide for the factory's economic activity, because now financial availabilities had more real meaning for the factory's economic operation.

In 1961 and 1962 a great many small shops were incorporated into our enterprise. Because it was uneconomical to place someone in each shop for accounting and administrative purposes, and, moreover, because there was a lack of qualified personnel for this kind of work, the enterprise had to come up with a different organizational system—one that would enable it to manage and control the factories vis-à-vis the new situation. The system of administrative units developed out of this need. This system is nothing more than central economic administration and control over the productive operations of the shops located in a production zone (in Havana, by sectors). Thus, we could make better use of the few qualified people available as well as material resources—basic means of production, means of circulation, and others.

The establishment of the administrative units produced a change with respect to financial control, because funds for payment of material purchases and wages were centralized in a single account from which were withdrawn the amounts required to pay daily wages. The amounts of the respective payrolls were transferred to the various shops, where workers were paid directly. This was done so that workers would not have to go elsewhere than their place of work to be paid.

With regard to revenues, two procedures were established based on whether output was transferred to MINCIN [Ministry of Domestic Trade] or distributed directly to the public. In the first case, the funds would be credited directly to the factory-income account for which reason the account number would be entered on all "transfer" forms. In the second case, deposits would be made directly by the comrades of the shop in their nearest banking agency. This procedure has varied of late, adjusting itself to the specific circumstances of each administrative unit (called factories today). In some cases, the daily statements of the shops in a zone are taken to the office of the administrative unit, which then makes the deposit, combining the funds of the shops into a single account. This measure was taken because there are regions with only one banking agency, which was a problem when ten comrades or more from the enterprise made deposits in different accounts at the same time. Although we are still a long way from having the organization and control needed in an enterprise the size of ours, we have been overcoming many of our problems. Today, our statistical records are up to date, and we are working in cooperation with the Methods and Systems Bureau of MININD [Ministry of Industry] in matters such as inventory, payroll, and general and cost-accounting controls that will assure adequate procedures for obtaining such data in the most accurate and convenient way possible. There is, on the other hand, a positive factor present in this entire process: the awareness developed by our administrators with regard to accounting and economic control. It is the experience of this enterprise that our administrators, through interdependent relations with the budgetary system, feel divested of all individualism and are co-participants in the problems concerning the enterprise and the economy in general.

Currently, following an analysis of the size and organizational situation of the enterprise in the last discussion of "Circular 90," we are engaged in a rationalization plan that will assure better use of installed capacity and increased labor productivity by eliminating the workshops. We have divided this job into stages for the purpose of carrying out those acts of integration which require practically no investment funds so that we may go about it by degrees and be consistent with the opportunities that arise. The process should not be forced because of our responsibility to assure that the people are provided with an essential item upon which depends the availability of other consumer food supplies.

Besides the above, vis-à-vis the size and diversity of our output, our agency has proposed the establishment of provincial delegations with enterprise characteristics. The purpose is to avoid excessive centralization, which, far from yielding good results, sometimes hinders solution of some problems and obscures what is happening at lower levels over which the enterprise exercises inadequate control.

Analyzing this question, and the objective fact that the enterprise has to assimilate a great number of private shops, we can see that we are still far from having a firmly established organizational and control system. But we know the road, and we are on our way. We estimate that given the conditions under which we have had to carry out our work, constantly incorporating the private sector without the necessary personnel, the exercise of economic control within the framework of the budgetary system has been of great benefit. Without it, it would have been difficult to attempt to exercise any kind of control over more than one thousand shops producing twenty-two kinds of products of different technological characteristics and distributed throughout the Republic.[2] Aside from all the difficulties, we think that our production has not met with serious disruptions, although we have been compelled to give priority to problems of the moment rather than devote ourselves as needed to the analytical work that should be part of our administrative system. But we are presently directing our efforts to this end.

An important question that should be considered in this article is the point made by detractors of the budgetary system that once administrations are assured of fund availabilities with which to carry out activities, they will neither bother to collect for the commodities they provide nor will they be "interested" in increasing profitability, etc. In our opinion, based on practical experience, this idea is wrong because this attitude is related to the awareness created in this administration of the responsibility in the economic system, backed up by the checks and controls the enterprise exercises over the factory operation. Moreover, the system itself has developed a body of quite practical legislation regulating this aspect of financial discipline. Law 1122, published toward the middle of last year, regulates the application of the budgetary system in State enterprises and finalizes this first stage of instrumentation, so to speak, of the system. We believe that it is the duty of those responsible for the economic administration of enterprises to constantly analyze and review the experiences they undergo in carrying out their work in order to critically enrich the system, which is still young. To close, we wish to state our conclusions on our experiences in this enterprise with regard to the application of the budgetary system:

1. It was an excellent means of controlling the anarchy reigning during the early days of nationalization.

2. The administrative units (today, factories) allowed us to exercise some degree of efficient central control over the large number of diverse shops throughout the Republic.

3. It has permitted us to maintain a degree of discipline that, although broken at times, would hardly have been possible under other conditions.

4. It has allowed the development of a collective awareness in factory administrations concerning the general problems of the enterprise, thus stripping away the individualism characteristic of the capitalist system.

5. We must conduct studies on the practical aspects of the system and use the experiences of the various enterprises operating under it for the purpose of being able to overcome several faults, primarily with regard to the rigidity present in many cases, so that certain situations can be resolved, such as the problem of small investment, the incorporation of shops, matters outside the plan, etc.

NOTES

1. The value of a business that was recognized over and above its active assets, like "prestige," etc.

2. Only through an effort from the small human group that confronted the task was it possible to obtain more or less satisfactory control.

PART III

The Market vs. Planning: The Law of Value During the Period of Transition

9

On the Operation of the Law of Value in the Cuban Economy

ALBERTO MORA

SOME COMRADES HAVE SUGGESTED that the law of value does not presently operate within the State sector of the Cuban economy. These same comrades recognize that the law of value operates in relations between the private and State sectors of the economy but not in relations among State enterprises. For these comrades, the Cuban State or socialized sector as a whole presently constitutes a "single large enterprise."

The purpose of this work is merely to situate a matter that we consider to be of fundamental importance during the present stage of socialist construction in Cuba and to provide some background to the problem by bringing to light several pertinent points of view.

When one says that the law of value operates, he is saying that, as an economic criterion, production is regulated by value, that products are exchanged according to their relative values—in short, that the law of value is a regulator of production.

The question as to whether the law of value operates under socialism is hardly new. It is known that for a time immediately

---

Alberto Mora was Minister of Foreign Trade during period of debate.

SOURCE: "En torno a la cuestión del funcionamiento de la ley del valor en la economía Cubana en los actuales momentós," *Nuestra Industria Revista Económica,* pp. 10–20.

after the triumph of the Soviet Revolution, many authors contended that it does not. Rosa Luxemburg and Nikolai Bukharin, among others, stated that economics as a science would disappear under socialism. In his book, *The Economy of the Period of Transition* (1920), Bukharin said:

> Political economy is a science of the disorganized national economy. Only in a society where production has an anarchical character do the laws of social life appear to be "natural and spontaneous," independent of the will of individuals and groups, acting with the blind compulsion of the law of gravity. In effect, as soon as we begin to deal with an organized national economy, all the basic "problems" of political economy, such as price, value, profit, etc., simply disappear . . . because here the economy is regulated not by the blind forces of the market and competition, but by a consciously prepared plan.[1]

Later, in 1925, Bukharin completely reversed his stance and, during his debate with Evgueni A. Preobrazhenski, called on the peasants to "enrich yourselves."[2] At this point, Bukharin not only recognized that political economy continued to function as a science but even founded his argument against the theory of accelerated industrialization (proposed by Preobrazhenski, V. M. Smirnov, Trotsky, and others) on recognition of the law of value's operation. His attacks on Preobrazhenski's theory of "primitive socialist accumulation"[3]—which lauded the exploitation of agriculture by industry through affixing high prices to industrial products sold to peasants in exchange for low-priced agricultural products—were made on the same basis.

During the stage known as war communism (1918–20), other Soviet authors held that the law of value had ceased to operate in the new Soviet society. There was even an attempt to eliminate money and to put into effect a plan to prepare budgets based on units of labor.[4]

Somewhat later, two Soviet economists, A. Lapidus and K. Osronovitianov, in *An Outline of Political Economy,* stated: "as the principle of planning becomes stronger, the law of value becomes directly transformed into the law of labor expenditure." [5]

Even bourgeois writers were denying that the law of value could operate under socialism. Thus, in the 1920s, Ludwig von Mises proclaimed that socialism could not "operate" because by eliminating the market it eliminated the mechanism determining the "rational" prices needed to organize production. Said Mises in 1920:

> Precisely because no production good will ever be an object of exchange, its monetary value will be impossible to determine. Calculation in monetary terms will be impossible. There will be no means of determining what was rational and, therefore, it is obvious that production will never be governed by economic considerations.[6]

With the NEP (1921), the U.S.S.R. abandoned its attempts to prepare nonmonetary budgets. The NEP [National Economic Plan] recognized the existence of a mixed system. The coexistence of private and socialized economic sectors justified the belief that the law of value continued to operate and that therefore it governed the organization of production. The reestablishment of the market fully restored the monetary economy.

Although the NEP seemed to be a step backward from the standpoint of war communism, it should be pointed out that this was not entirely true with reference to Lenin's ideas right after the Bolsheviks took power. Lenin laid down the basic idea of the NEP in 1918, when he proposed that the Bolsheviks' program should be to secure the economy's "positions of high command." He knew that a period of transition would take place between capitalism and socialism during which elements of both would survive. For this reason, so as to guarantee the worker-peasant alliance, "the Bolsheviks must learn commerce."

Beginning in 1930, for a period lasting until the end of the Second World War, the question of the operation of the law of value was ignored. The dominant criterion at this time was that the problem of value was irrelevant to the building of socialism. This opinion was restricted to theoretical arguments, since in practice everyone, including Gosplan [State Economic Planning Commission], continued to calculate prices and profits.

In 1943, the question arose again. An anonymous article appeared in a Party publication denying that the law of value had been "abolished in the socialist system of the national economy. On the contrary, it operates under socialism, but it operates in a different way." [7]

Later, in 1952, Stalin's final work—*Economic Problems of Socialism in the U.S.S.R.*—appeared, in which he said: "Sometimes it is asked whether the Law of Value exists and operates in our country, in our socialist regime. Yes, it exists and operates." [8] In the course of this anthology, the idea takes form that the law of value operated in the U.S.S.R. because production still had mercantile characteristics and because a private economic sector coexisted with the State sector. But Stalin added:

> . . . does all this mean that the operation of the Law of Value in our country regulates production? No, it does not. In reality, the Law of Value's sphere of operation is rigidly circumstantial and restricted in our economic regime. . . . Clearly, private ownership of the means of production does not exist, and socialization of the means of production, both in the city and in the country, further restricts the law of value's sphere of operation and its influence on production.

In 1956, 1957, and 1958, the subject arose again. During December 1956, May, September, and December 1957, and January 1959, a series of debates developed in Moscow (first in the Economic Institute of the Academy of the U.S.S.R. and afterward in the department of Political Economy of the University of Moscow) which encompassed the views of several Soviet economists (Malyshev, Osronovitianov, Gatovsky Kronrod, Strumlin Leontiev, Nemchinov, Novozhilov, and others) concerning the role of the law of value and the formation of prices under socialism.[9] This debate still goes on. Several points of view have been raised, but the consensus is that the law of value does operate under socialism, at least during the first stage. It should be apparent that the background to this question is quite extensive.

As soon as one begins to analyze the matter, a question arises: "What is value?" Some comrades quickly respond: "Value is the amount of labor socially necessary to produce a given commodity." This definition, they pretend, follows the Marxist line. But they are mistaken. Marx did not say that value was "the amount of labor socially necessary" . . . etc. Marx said that "the magnitude of the value of any article is the amount of labour socially necessary, or the labour time socially necessary, for its production."[10] Marx defined only the "magnitude of value," or the measure of value, in this way. But the measure of something is not the thing itself.

Likewise, Marx in no way identifies value with labor. Rather, he states very clearly that labor is "the creative substance of value."[11] In other words, labor is the creator of value but is not itself value.

In his last economic work, Marx points out:

> He (Rodbertus) focuses on "value" only . . . in (its) manifest form, that is, as exchange value; as this appears only where a part at least of the products of labor, of useful objects, already function as "commodities," and as it does not occur from the start, but rather begins at a certain social phase of development, in other words, upon attaining a certain degree of historical development, we find that exchange value is an historical concept. If Rodbertus had continued to analyze . . . the exchange value of commodities . . . he would have found "value" behind this form of its manifestation.[12]

And in Volume I itself[13]: ". . . exchange value neither is nor can be more than the expression of a content differentiable from it, its form of manifesting itself." This distinction between "value" and "exchange value" (the latter being value's form of manifesting itself in mercantile production) is of major importance, as we will see below.

In short, what is value? In my judgment, if we are going to give some consistent meaning to the category of value, then we must appreciate that it embodies (or better, expresses) a relationship. In the first place, it is a measure, and as such expresses a relationship; in the second place, it is consequently a category created by man under specific circumstances and with a specific purpose, and is therefore bound by man's social relationships.

Here we must emphasize that this concept of value has nothing to do with the subjectivist theories (of Herman Heinrich Gossen, William Stanley Jevons, Karl Menger, Léon Walras, Friedrich von Wieser, Eugen von Böhm-Bawerk, etc.). In effect, the relationship that expresses the category "value" is decidedly objective; it is the relationship between limited available resources and the growing needs of man. . . . The magnitude of value is expressed with respect to this relationship; it is the amount of labor socially necessary to produce some given thing. Remember that only one type of labor creates value: socially necessary labor, that is, the application of limited available resources to the satisfaction of a socially recognized need. It is precisely this relationship, then, that is expressed by the category of value and that is, properly speaking, value.

Accordingly, so long as it is necessary to establish the discrepancy existing in this relationship, the category of value retains meaning. Once (and only once) available resources become fully sufficient, the need to express such a relationship disappears. Once this moment arrives, and only then, could we say that the law of value has ceased to operate. As available resources are then sufficient "to satisfy given socially recognized needs," the need to "exercise caution" in the allocation of such resources will disappear and, it follows, the value relationship will lose its importance, disappearing to all practical effects. We have conscientiously pointed out that the foregoing takes place relative to "given socially recognized needs," because by his very condition man's needs are eternally growing; once some needs are satisfied, new ones arise. For the latter, at least in the beginning, the category of value (as we have defined it above) will retain its meaning; therefore, in such cases, the law of value will operate.

In determining value, this relationship, the discrepancy between available resources and needs, is today recognized in one form or another by several Soviet economists. (Novozhilov, Kantorovich, and Nemchinov are good examples.) [14]

What conclusion can we draw from all the above? Above all, exchange value is value's form (that is to say, the relationship between limited available resources and man's growing social needs) of manifesting itself in the mercantile system of production (that is, production for a market). This relationship (value) manifests itself only in concrete objects. And for the society it takes on its full meaning only in production. In this sense, labor (which creates products) is the "creative substance" of value.

In mercantile production, value manifests itself in the market as exchange value. Products contain (better, express) values, but in the market such values acquire form only as exchange values. And it is through the market that value exercises its role as a regulator of production (law of value).

In a planned economy, value does not disappear. (As we have defined it, the value relationship is something objective that survives so long as the conditions expressed by it exist.) Under socialism, value becomes concrete through planning, or the plan. It is precisely in the conscious decision of the planning authority (Juceplan) where value appears most clearly as an economic criterion, as a regulator of production. That is to say, under socialism, the law of value operates through the plan, or the planning process. In mercantile production, the mechanism is, in a way, automatic—through the market. Thus, under socialism, where the market does not operate (freely, at least), planning methods must be established which take the indicators of the law of value into account. It seems to us that Novozhilov expresses basically the same idea by starting out with the theory that a relative deficiency of productive forces is an economic criterion for investment determination. He points out that this relationship may even survive into communism. For example, new machines, which mean technical progress, will be "deficient" at least at the moment they enter production.

On the other hand, value is not the only valid criterion in

determining investment (and other expenditures) in a planned economy. There are others: political factors, defense needs (conditioned on the existence of imperialism and, thus, the threat of war), etc. But this does not contradict the aforesaid because we have fully clarified that the law of value is an economic criterion for regulating production. Even when noneconomic criteria are given priority, economic realities still limit possibilities, and a "price" must be paid (in the form of limitations in other areas) for applying such criteria. It is a classic adage that one cannot have his cake and eat it too. One cannot provide more resources than he has; therefore, the use of any noneconomic criterion will be cause for certain economic adjustments and limitations. As Stalin says:

> In ancient times the overflow of huge rivers which produced floods and destruction of houses and crops was considered an unavoidable disaster. As time passed, however, man's knowledge increased: he learned to build dams and hydroelectric plants to protect society from such calamities. He learned to dominate natural destructive forces, to make water power serve society by using it to irrigate fields and obtain energy.
>
> Does this mean that man abolished natural and scientific laws, that he created new laws? No, it does not. In reality, everything done to prevent water's destructiveness and to utilize its power in society's interest is done without in any way violating, changing or destroying scientific laws, and without creating new ones. On the contrary, it is done strictly on the basis of natural and scientific laws, because even the smallest infraction of the laws of nature would lead only to frustration and ruin.[15]

How does all this apply to present-day Cuba? Above all, one must keep the characteristics of the Cuban economy in mind. In a country with the size and material wealth of the U.S.S.R., an economic mistake will have much less serious consequences than in Cuba, which is a relatively small country with limited resources. Extraordinary dependence on foreign trade is another differentiating characteristic of the Cuban economy. For all these reasons, it is very important to understand that the law of value continues to operate as an economic criterion and, for the present, retains its full meaning in the Cuban economy. The economic implications of every decision must be analyzed very carefully, as the possible consequences of error are heightened by the limitations characteristic of our economy.

When some comrades deny that the law of value operates in relations among enterprises within the State sector, they argue that the entire State sector is under single ownership, that the enterprises are the property of the society. This, of course, is true. But as an economic criterion it is inaccurate. State property is not yet the fully developed social property that will be achieved only under communism. As Oskar Lange says:

> In a socialist economy the Law of Value continues to operate because production continues to be mercantile production. The reason for which production in a Socialist economy is mercantile production . . . is the existence of numerous product owners. . . . This multiplicity of owners comes about (because). . . . First, the existence of several forms of social ownership of the means of production means that there are many owners of the means of production.[16]

It is enough simply to examine the relations among State enterprises, to note how contradictions arise among them and how some are in opposition to others, in order to realize that in present-day Cuba the state sector as a whole in no way constitutes "a single large enterprise."

Another conclusion is that value as a category will cease to operate (have meaning) only when the development of the productive forces is such that enough resources are produced to satisfy socially recognized needs. That is, value does not disappear simply because labor can be directly measured (in hours)—perhaps the contrary. When resources become fully adequate, the complete mechanization and automation of production will doubtless make direct measurement of labor feasible.

In addition, it should be pointed out that Cuba, despite being a relatively small country, is not really so small (just try to cross Cuba on foot). The Cuban economy presents plenty of complexities.

Another conclusion relates to the stress that some comrades have given the matter of production costs. Their concern has some merit because, as the Cuban economy now stands, any enterprise can be made to appear profitable by merely raising the prices of final products—which have a ready market given the size of demand. Nevertheless, we would warn against an "exclusivist criterion" with respect to costs. One can picture an enterprise with very low (even decreasing) costs that is never profitable because its products are not "socially recognized." It should always be recalled that labor must be socially necessary; therefore, attention must always be given to the production-consumption relationship. It has already been pointed out that the fundamental contradiction in socialism is that which exists between production and consumption.

We may draw the following conclusions:

1. Value is the relationship between limited available resources and the growing needs of man. Its meaning is expressed, then, by a relationship embracing a discrepancy between these factors brought about by inadequate development of the productive forces.

2. The law of value will cease to operate (that is, to be an economic factor regulating production) only when the development of the productive forces creates enough resources to fully satisfy man's fundamental needs (socially recognized needs).

3. Value does not disappear simply because labor can be directly measured. In the end, the quantity of labor is the magnitude of value, but not value itself.

4. Under socialism, the law of value continues to operate, although it is not the only criterion regulating production. Under socialism, the law of value operates through the plan.

5. In present-day Cuba, the law of value maintains its full meaning; it operates as an economic criterion even within the State sector.

6. It is important, then, in Cuba's present situation, to take

the foregoing (Point 5) into account vis-à-vis the possible consequences of a mistake in an economy with Cuba's characteristics.

7. The Cuban State sector does not yet by any means constitute "a single large enterprise."

NOTES

1. Cited by Alex Nove in *The Soviet Economy,* p. 266.

2. "We have to say to all the peasantry, to their entire stratum: enrich yourselves, accumulate, develop your economy." (Cited by Alexander Erlich in *The Soviet Industrialization Debate,* p. 16, from Bukharin's book, *O novoi ekonomicheskoi politike i noshi zadachak,* April 30, 1925.)

3. Preobrazhenski, *Novaya Ekonomica,* Moscow, 1926 (part of the book had been published previously, in 1924).

4. For a description of this period see R. W. Davies, *The Soviet Budgetary System;* Maurice Dobb, *Soviet Economic Development;* and A. Baykov, *El desarrollo del sistema económico soviético.*

5. Cited by M. Dobb, *Soviet Economic Development,* p. 328. (On the same page Dobb says: "During the early days it was commonly denied that the Law of Value operated under socialism: This law was applicable only under conditions of mercantile production and exchange (that is, production for a market) and ceased to be an economic regulator once planning regulated production and product distribution.")

6. Cited by M. Dobb in *On Economic Theory and Socialism,* p. 56.

7. Cited by M. Dobb in *Soviet Economic Development,* p. 328, and Alex Nove in *The Soviet Economy,* p. 268.

8. J. Stalin, "Problemas Económicos del Socialismo, Observaciónes de Economía relacionadas con la Discusión de Noviembre de 1921," No. 3, "La Ley del Valor del Socialismo."

9. Despite its doctrinal leanings, for a statement of the various ideas and theories, see the article by Alfred Zanbermann, "The Soviet Debate on the Law of Value and Price Formation," *Value and Plan,* ed. Gregory Grossman. Also see Alex Nove, *op. cit.,* pp. 271–284. Both authors cite various articles appearing during 1956–58 in the Soviet publications, *Voprosi Economica* and *Pravda.*

10. Karl Marx, *El Capital* (Edición Cartago), p. 36.

11. ". . . How does one measure the magnitude of this value? By the quantity of value creating substance, that is, of labor it contains." *Ibid.,* p. 36. Also, "Human labor power in its fluid state, or, in other words, human labor, creates value, but is not itself value." *Ibid.,* p. 45.

12. Adolph Wagner, "Marginal Notes to the *Treatise on Political Economy.*" *Ibid.,* Vol. I, Appendix III, pp. 695–704.

13. *Ibid.,* p. 34.

14. Others, also Soviet, such as Gatovski, Sakov, Kronrod, etc. have

attacked the earlier economists, accusing them of being too close to the concepts of the Marginalist theories (for example, the attack on Novozhilov made by A. Kats in *Vaprosi Ekonomiki,* No. 11, 1960, and as to Kantorovich, the Gatovski article in *Kommunist,* No. 15, 1960, cited by Alex Nove, p. 278). On this point, we believe that if in developing his theory of value, Marx had no objection to starting with the development attained by Adam Smith and Ricardo, and stripping the analysis of the apologetic nature of nascent mercantile capitalism, he adopted and perfected the labor theory of value, distinguishing between "use-value" and "exchange value" (which stemmed, in turn, from Aristotle), then why completely reject the undeniable development achieved in recent times in the analysis of some bourgeois economists (particularly, microeconomic analysis)? The class character and apologetic nature of capitalism in the bourgeois economists is obvious. They hope (uselessly, we might add) to "justify" and "save" capitalism. But Smith and Ricardo did precisely the same thing. Of course the purity of Marxism must be protected from revisionist tendencies. But clearly the building of socialism presents problems of a kind that cannot be resolved within a framework of rigid, dogmatic academics. Especially when Marx himself says: "according to Mr. Wagner, Marx's theory of Value is the 'cornerstone of the socialist system.' As I have never built a 'socialist system,' this is a fantasy of Messrs. Wagner, Scheffle *e tutti quanti.'* " And, ". . . in order to investigate value I have held specifically to bourgeois conditions, without applying this theory of value to a 'social state' which I have not even bothered to construct. . . ." Marx, "Marginal Notes on the Treatise on Political Economy, Addendum No. 3 to *El Capital, op. cit.,* pp. 695 and 698.

15. J. Stalin, *op. cit.,* Epigraph No. 1, "El caracter de las leyes económicas del Socialismo."

16. Oskar Lange, "Political Economy of Socialism," *Problems of the Political Economy of Socialism,* ed. O. Lange, p. 9.

10

On the Concept of Value

ERNESTO CHE GUEVARA

IN THIS ISSUE of *Nuestra Industria Económica,* we carry an article by Alberto Mora entitled, "On the Operation of the Law of Value in the Cuban Economy [page 219]," which was recently published in the Ministry of Commerce journal *Comercio Exterior.*

The article begins by saying: "Some comrades have suggested that the law of value does not presently operate within the State sector of the Cuban economy." It is important to refute comrade Mora's arguments as well as to identify the persons to whom he refers. "Some comrades" have neither first nor last names, but the subjects toward whom the critique is directed do; they are the Minister of Industry who writes this article, and comrade Luis Alvarez Rom, Minister of the Treasury, not to mention others who can be counted as supporting the budgetary finance system.

We place this at the start because it is important to name not only concepts but also the persons who defend them. We would like to clarify three of Mora's concluding statements. In our opinion, the most important subject discussed in the article is not his disagreement with those who deny the operation of the law of value but his very definition of value, as it does not correspond to the ideas of Marx [page 223].

SOURCE: "Sobre la concepción del valor: contestando algunas afirmaciones sobre el tema," *Nuestra Industria Económica,* Año 1, Octubre 1963, pp. 3–9.

> In short, what is value? In my judgment, if we are going to give some consistent meaning to the category of value, then we must appreciate that it embodies (or better, expresses) a relationship. In the first place, it is a measure, and as such expresses a relationship; in the second place, it is consequently a category created by man under specific circumstances and with a specific purpose, and is therefore bound by man's social relationships.

Let us analyze this paragraph. A few lines before, Mora says: "But the measure of something is not the thing itself," with reference to value. Then, he says, "In the first place, it is a measure and as such expresses a relationship." This seems to be contradictory.

He goes on to say: ". . . and, in the second place, it is, consequently, a category created by man under specific circumstances and with a specific purpose." This clearly contradicts Marx's ideas about the economic laws of society. All his work was dedicated to bringing out the essence of phenomena from beneath their appearance, demonstrating that the various fetishes acquired by humanity serve only to disguise ignorance. We believe that if there is one thing man could not do, it is to create value with a specific purpose. The relationships of production brought about value. Value exists objectively, and whether we know it or not, the reality of its existence does not vary, nor does the spontaneity of expression of the capitalist relationships.

Starting with Marx's analysis, light has been shed on the intricate mechanism of capitalist relationships of production, yet such knowledge hardly changes reality. Man can change society under certain conditions, but he cannot "invent" its laws.

Further on, Mora adds [page 224]:

> Remember that only one type of labor creates value: socially necessary labor, that is, the application of limited available resources to the satisfaction of a socially recognized need. It is precisely this relationship, then, that is expressed by the category of value and that is, properly speaking, value.

We note here that Mora attributes the phrase "socially necessary" with a meaning different from what it has: It really means necessary for society, while here it is taken to mean the measure of labor that society as a whole needs to expend in order to produce a value. Mora finishes by stating that the relationship between needs and resources is value.

Obviously, if the society does not concede utility to a product, the product will have no exchange value (here lies, perhaps, Mora's conceptual error in referring to socially necessary labor), but it is no less obvious that Marx identifies the idea of value with abstract labor. The search for a measure of labor is equated with the search for a measure of value. In *Capital* we find the following: "A use-value, or useful article, therefore, has value only because human labor in the abstract has been embodied or materialized in it. How, then, is the magnitude of this value to be measured? Plainly, by the quantity of the value-creating substance, the labor, contained in the article." [1]

It happens that without use-value there is no value, just as use-value is inconceivable without value (except for some forces of nature) because of the dialectical interrelationship existing between them.

The idea that the need-resource relationship is implicit in the concept of value might come closer to reality. This seems logical because the formula can be substituted by that of supply-demand that exists in the market and that forms one of the links in the operation of the law of value or the value relationship.

This is our first objection so far, which is important because of the risk involved in sketching the problem so roughly as to make it a simple statement of the law of supply and demand.

Going back to the first paragraph of the article, we will say that this is an inaccurate appraisal. We see the problem of value in another way. I will refer to the article published in *Nuestra Industria Económica,* number 1. I said there [page 114]:

> When all products respond to prices that have an internal relationship among themselves which is distinct from the product relationship in the capitalist market, a new price

> relationship is brought about which in no way compares with that of the world market. How can prices be made to coincide with value? How can one consciously use the law of value to achieve a balance in the market on one hand, and a faithful reflection of real value on the other? This is one of the most serious problems the socialist economy faces.[2]

In other words, the fact that the law of value is in force is not being contested; rather, it is felt that the law's most advanced form of operation is through the capitalist market, and that variations introduced into the market by socialization of the means of production and the distribution system bring about changes that obstruct immediate clarification of its operation.

We hold that the law of value is a regulator of mercantile relationships under capitalism; therefore, to the extent that markets are distorted for whatever reason, so will the law of value's action suffer certain distortions.

The manner and degree to which this comes about have not received the same in-depth study that Marx gave capitalism. Marx and Engels did not foresee that economically backward countries might enter the period of transition, and thus failed to study or consider the economic characteristics of such a circumstance.

Lenin, despite his brilliance, had too little time to dedicate his whole life, as did Marx, to long study of the economic problems of that stage of transition in which a society emerging from capitalism before completing that stage (and in which remnants of feudalism still survive) comes together with concentration of ownership of the means of production in the hands of the people.

This is a real event the possibility of which was foreseen by Lenin in his studies regarding the uneven development of capitalism, the birth of imperialism, and the theory of the breaking of the system's weakest links in times of social upheaval such as war. He proved, by the Russian Revolution and the creation of the first socialist State, that such an event was feasible, but had no time to pursue his investigations since he devoted himself fully to consolidating power and to participating in the Revolution, as he stated in the abrupt ending to his book *The State and Revolution.* (The whole of Lenin's works regarding the economy of the period of transition serve as a highly valuable introduction to the matter but lack the development and depth that time and experience would have lent them.)

In his conclusions, comrade Mora states categorically: "Under socialism the law of value continues to operate, although it is not the only criterion regulating production. Under socialism, the law of value operates through the plan."

We are not so sure about this:

Supposing a plan were made that was completely harmonious in all its categories. One would assume there would have to be some means of analysis outside the plan itself that would permit its objective evaluation. It does not occur to me that this could be other than the very results of the plan. But such results are proof *a posteriori* that all goes well or that something is wrong. (With respect to the law of value, it it understood, since there can be defects of other origin.) We would have to begin to study the weak points closely in order to try to take practical measures, again, *a posteriori,* and to remedy the situation through trial and error. In any case, the balance between supply and effective demand would be the control standard; analysis of unsatisfied needs would shed no light on the matter, as, by definition, conditions do not exist for providing man with what he demands during this period.

Supposing something more realistic—that measures must be taken vis-à-vis a given situation: spending on defense, on correction of severe imbalances in domestic production, on investments that absorb part of our capacity to produce for consumption but are necessary because of their strategic importance. (I refer not only to military but also to economic conditions.) Tensions will then be created that will have to be remedied by administrative measures in order to prevent runaway prices, and new relationships will be brought about that will increasingly obscure the operation of the law of value.

Effects can always be calculated; even the capitalists do so in their studies of joint or opportunity costs. But the law of value will be reflected less and less in the plan. That is our opinion on the subject.

We would like to refer to still another part of Mora's article, where he says [page 227]:

> When some comrades deny that the law of value operates in relations among enterprises within the State sector, they argue that the entire State sector is under single ownership, that the enterprises are the property of the society. This, of course, is true. But as an economic criterion it is inaccurate. State property is not yet the fully developed social property that will be achieved only under communism. . . .
>
> It is enough simply to examine the relations among State enterprises, to note how contradictions arise among them and how some are in opposition to others, in order to realize that in present-day Cuba the State sector as a whole in no way constitutes "a single large enterprise."

Alberto Mora is referring either to some conversations we have had, to my address at the close of the term of the School of Administration, or to an unpublished pamphlet by Comrade Alvarez Rom in which the author refers to the subject as one of Lenin's aspirations. In the latter, Rom deals with the treatment of factories as shops of the consolidated enterprise and with the aspiration, consistent with the development of the economy, of raising all relations to the level of those that would prevail in a single large factory.

We would point out here that if it is true that contradictions exist among different enterprises—and we do not refer to enterprises in the economy as a whole but specifically to those under the jurisdiction of the Ministry of Industry—then it is no less true that contradictions exist among the factories of one enterprise or among shops in a factory. Such contradictions may even arise within a workshop's brigade when, for example, it is engaged in work calling for premium pay and refuses to allow one of its workers to take an hour off production to instruct other comrades, on the assumption that by doing so he would lower the group's productivity and thereby its pay. Nevertheless, we are building socialism and doing away with man's exploitation of man.

Do not similar things occur in interdependent factory shops under capitalism? Can it be that the two systems embrace similar contradictions?

Contradictions among men constantly appear in the socialist sector. But when men are not confused by severe misunderstandings or unrevolutionary behavior, such contradictions are not antagonistic and can be resolved within the bounds the society establishes as a framework for its actions. We agree that, as yet, the State sector in no way constitutes a single large enterprise—because of organizational defects, because of our society's lack of development, and because of the existence of two systems of finance. In expressing our concept of a single enterprise, we based ourselves primarily on Marx's definition of commodity: "In order to be a commodity, the product has to pass into the hands of a second party, the one who consumes it, by means of an act of exchange."[2] Added to this is Engels' marginal note explaining that the commodity concept is introduced in order to avoid the error of those who consider a commodity to be any product consumed by a second party other than the producer himself, with the clarification that taxes are not commodities because no exchange takes place.

Engels furnishes an example from feudal society. Might not this concept of commodity with its corresponding examples be valid in the present period, as we build socialism?

We believe that the transfer from one shop or enterprise to another in the budgetary system cannot be construed as an act of exchange: It is merely an act of formation or addition of new values through labor. In other words, if a commodity is that product which changes ownership through an act of exchange, then as soon as all factories become the property of the state under the budgetary system where this phenomenon does not occur, then a product will acquire commodity characteristics only when, reaching the market, it passes into the hands of the consuming public.

Our opinion about costs is reflected in the article already cited which appeared in this magazine under my signature and to which we refer the interested reader [page 113]. As to Cuba's size, by applying Mora's criterion, we could propose that he divide his ministry into nine autonomous parts, one per floor, because of its exaggerated size. If he cannot see this, let him try going up to his office by the stairs. If he uses the telephone, the elevator, and the intercom, it is because they exist for this purpose. Cuba's distances are measured by technical means of modern communication and not by the time it took our ancestors to go from one place to another.

We wish to record that this debate, beginning with our reply, can be of considerable educational value so long as we conduct it with the greatest possible scientific rigor and equanimity. We do not shy from confrontations, but since we are in the middle of a debate that reaches the highest levels of government and party, where two schools of thought reign with regard to the system of finance, we feel it is essential to show concern for the form and method of the debate.

We salute the initiative comrade Mora has shown by entering the public arena with his criticism, although it would be better to name things, and we congratulate him, moreover, on the quality of his ministry's journal, a quality we will try to emulate in our modest publication.

NOTES

1. Karl Marx, *Capital* (Vol. I). [Translator's source: *Great Books of the Western World* (Chicago, Encyclopedia Britannica, c. 1952), Vol. L, p. 15.]

2. "*Consideraciónes sobre los costos de producción como base del analisis económico de las empresas sujetas a sistema presupuestario,*" *Nuestra Industria Económica,* No. 1, 1963, p. 5.

11

Contribution to the Debate on the Law of Value

MIGUEL COSSIO

THE JOURNAL *Comercio Exterior,* number 3, June 1963, contained an article by Commander Alberto Mora [page 219] which concerned the ongoing debate on the operation of the law of value in the Cuban economy.

We consider certain of the ideas set forth in the article to be in error and feel, therefore, that we should express our own thoughts on the subject. It should be borne in mind, however, that the debate is among revolutionary comrades who are all guided by common Marxist-Leninist principles.

In order to develop our exposition in an orderly manner, we will attempt to confine ourselves to Commander Mora's article and comment on some of his statements.

Item I

When one says that the law of value operates, he is saying that, as an economic criterion, production is regulated by value, that products are exchanged according to their rela-

---

SOURCE: "Contribución al debate sobre la ley del valor," *Nuestra Industria Revista Economica,* Año 1, Diciembre 1963, pp. 3–23.

tive values—in short, that the law of value is a regulator of production [page 219].

To our understanding, this explanation of the law of value's operation is actually inconsistent with the concept of the law of value itself. First of all, it would help to clarify a few words.

a. "As an economic criterion." One understands that because the law of value is an objective law that is independent of our will, it also operates independent of our criteria, economic or otherwise. In referring to the law's operation, we speak of an objective fact. The fact can be defined by using any given criterion, but this in no way conditions its operation. "Marxism understands the laws of science—whether one is dealing with Natural Scientific laws or the laws of Political Economy—as reflections of objective processes which operate INDEPENDENT of the will of men." [1]

b. "Exchanged according to their relative values." This phrase does not help us understand what "economic criterion" means, because the word "value" is merely repeated. It is as if we said the law of gravity expresses the fact that bodies fall according to gravity.

However, our principle objections to this definition are as follows:

1. By saying that the law of value is an expression of the fact that ". . . production is regulated by value," one ignores the law's essential meaning, that it implies a necessary and repetitive phenomenon in mercantile societies: exchange among individual, separate producers.

2. By ignoring the definition of the first link conditioning the concept of law, that which "expresses the internal and essential connections of phenomena," [2] the rest of the statement becomes blind approximation.

Our objections regarding repetition (or tautology), which in this case tries to explain the law by its precepts rather than its concepts, have already been expressed. We may therefore close this paragraph by stating our own criterion:

The law of value expresses the existence of mercantile production, which is *exchange among independent producers in accordance with quantities of socially necessary labor.* It is a law because of the constant, necessary, and inevitable nature by which it has ruled for more than five thousand years:

> . . . the Marxian law of value holds generally, as far as economic laws are valid at all, for the whole period of simple commodity-production. . . . Thus the Marxian law of value has general economic validity for a period lasting from the beginning of exchange, which transforms products into commodities, down to the 15th century of the present era . . . thus the law of value has prevailed during a period of from five to seven thousand years.[3]

What are the principal characteristics of the medium within which this law moves and operates?

a. Production for exchange. Use-values have two characteristics for producers: to be useful to buyers and useless to sellers in the change of ownership.

b. Comparison by common denominator of the various commodities to be exchanged. Labor is the only social unit that can be used to measure the multitude of objects produced.

c. Separate, independent production, which, historically, has gone through three stages: (1) production and *exchange* among tribes and communist societies in process of dissolution;[4] (2) simple mercantile production; (3) capitalist production.

In other words, in order for the law of value to operate, the following conditions must prevail:

1. Production of more than the minimum for consumption; thus, the creation of surplus product.

2. Division into tribes or regions (primitive period), or into classes (class society) with various *owners* of the product to be exchanged.

3. That owners exchange their products on the basis of the negative of their ownership (conversion into non-use-values); the *abstraction* of the concrete qualities of their products, and reduction of such qualities to abstract units of "human labor in

general"; and *quantification* of the goods to be exchanged into *socially necessary* proportions.

4. In summary: commodity production.

It is therefore wrong to speak of the operation of the law of value as "production . . . regulated by value." The major stress should be on mercantile production and the exchange of equal quantities of socially necessary labor.

The law of value's operation is not limited to regulating production under capitalism. It has a much more significant meaning.

The law of value is *the form* acquired by the general law of social labor (inherent in the nature of human society) in mercantile societies. It is, thus, an *historical* form in which a law of nature becomes manifest, man being taken as a product of nature, and man's activity or labor as natural because it is human.

Thus, if it is an historical law, then it is a law conditioned on particular social premises. The underlying laws of nature, on the other hand, are not so conditioned, as Marx points out in a letter to Kugelmann:

> That this necessity of distributing social labor in definite proportions cannot be done away with by the PARTICULAR FORM of social production, but can only change the FORM IT ASSUMES, is self-evident. No natural laws can be done away with. What can change, in changing historical circumstances, is the FORM in which these laws operate. And the form in which this proportional division of labor operates, in a state of society where the interconnection of social labor is manifested in the PRIVATE EXCHANGE of the individual products of labor, is precisely the EXCHANGE VALUE of these products.[5]

Referring to this letter, Rosenthal says:

> Thus, the proportional division of labor for production of a corresponding quantity of goods is an objective law of society. . . .

> In a society where private ownership is predominant, the structure of social labor can only come about by means of the exchange of the individual products of labor. Under these conditions, the product becomes a commodity and one commodity can be exchanged for another, both being *bearers of value. In such a society the general law of the proportionate distribution of labor, a law inherent in every social formation,* TAKES ON THE FORM OF THE LAW OF VALUE.[6,7]

In addition to the shortcomings listed above regarding the definition of the law of value, we feel it necessary to press the point that throughout Commander Mora's article he appears to confuse the law of value with a general law of nature. A concrete definition of the law could be stated thus:

The law of value is the historical form acquired by the general law of the distribution of labor in mercantile societies and expresses that commodities must be exchanged according to the quantity of socially necessary labor expended on their production.

Item II

In the midst of a brief account regarding past discussions on this subject, Commander Mora refers on page [207] to Stalin's *Economic Problems of Socialism in the U.S.S.R.* Certainly, this quote was exactly what surprised us most. Stalin completely rejects the comrade's entire argument throughout his exposition, and we could well have limited ourselves to transcribing it intact in order to clarify this debate.

Let us look at the quotation used by comrade Mora [page 208]:

> Sometimes it is asked whether the Law of Value exists and operates in our country, in our socialist regime. Yes, it exists and operates.

Regrettably, the comrade failed to quote what immediately followed in the same paragraph according to the translation by MINCEX [Ministry of Foreign Trade] itself in May of 1963, page 12, a copy of which we have on hand. What followed was this:

> Where there are commodities and mercantile production *the Law of Value cannot but exist.*

Thus, the source itself turns against Mora with respect to his initial definition of the law of value, because he says that "products are exchanged according to their relative values," and then refers to Stalin who says that the law of value exists "where there are commodities and mercantile production."

Moreover, Stalin is quoted again further on, page 14 of the source. (Three lines are now omitted that say: "I have already said that the sphere of operation of mercantile production is *circumscribed and limited* in our regime. The same must be said *of the law of value's* sphere of operation.")

And the paragraphs quoted by Mora contradict his initial thesis by showing that the law of value was not a regulator of production in the U.S.S.R. (with the understanding that the thesis was intended to be sufficiently broad to embrace the U.S.S.R.'s socialist regime)! Without further comment we will proceed to another point.

Comrade Mora concludes his historical account of the ongoing debate on the law of value as follows [page 208]:

> This debate still goes on. Several points of view have been raised, but the consensus is that the law of value does operate under socialism, at least during the first stage.

Regretably, we lack sufficient information about the debate but agree with Marx:

> Within the cooperative society based on common ownership of the means of production, *the producers do not exchange their products;* just as little does the labor employed on the products appear here *as the value* of these products, as a material quality possessed by them, since

> now, in contrast to capitalist society, individual labour no longer exists in an indirect fashion but directly as a component part of the total labour.[8]

On the other hand, the word "operate" does not, in our judgment, indicate clearly just what this law's action is. By "operate," are we to understand, regulates production? Commodity exchange? Or the mere existence of the law within a limited sphere? Social laws do not disappear except when the conditions from which they emanate change. They can therefore exist within a given environment even though they do not "operate" in a general way. Example: During the period of transition, various forms of economy exist—capitalism, small mercantile production, and socialism, schematically—but as the transition is culminated, the capitalist and private forms disappear, as do the special laws that express their presence.

So the debate may go on, but the most concise explanation was made by Marx eighty-eight years ago, and the most superficial analysis tells us that "operate" is not "exist" and that the existence of an historical law is conditioned by that of the given phenomena out of which it emerged and of which men later became aware. "Laws" are human conceptions of dialectical processes of nature and society, and are therefore merely dialectical processes bound and conditioned to each other, and nothing else. What Marxism does is to synthesize the laws of nature, not "build the laws of dialectics into Nature." [9]

Nature is apparent, and its processes are "laws" only in the minds of men. Without men, it exists and operates according to its own internal connections, of which our conceptions are mere images.

Item III

We now come to the question, "What is value?"

In order to counter "some comrades," comrade Mora begins with four theses.

1. The following concept, he says, is mistaken [page 208]:

"Value is the amount of labor socially necessary to produce a given article."

Is this definition true or false? Let us see. Marx says: ". . . A use value, or useful article, therefore, has value only because human labor in the abstract has been *embodied* or *materialized* in it." [10]

Our first concept:

VALUE = MATERIALIZATION OF ABSTRACT LABOR.

Then, we can also say:

VALUE = ABSTRACTION OF CONCRETE LABOR.

Which in proper dialectic means that:

VALUE = MATERIALIZATION AND ABSTRACTION OF HUMAN LABOR.

Where in order for value to exist there must be materialization of human labor THAT MUST BE CONSIDERED IN THE ABSTRACT RATHER THAN IN ITS CONCRETE EMBODIMENT, that is, that a *good* has *value* only if a contradiction is present.

> The reality of the value of commodities thus resembles Dame Quickly, of whom Falstaff said: "A man knows not where to have her." The value of commodities is the very opposite of the coarse materiality of their substance, not an atom of matter enters into its composition. Turn and examine a single commodity, by itself, as we will. Yet in so far as it remains an object of value, it seems impossible to grasp it.[11]

To make it perfectly clear: Value = Expression of a contradiction.

Our second concept:

If we find ourselves facing a contradiction, what is behind it? Let us refer again to *Capital:*

> When I state that coats or boots stand in a relation to linen, because it is true universal incarnation of abstract human labour, the absurdity of the statement is self-evident. Nevertheless, when the producers of coats and boots compare those articles with linen, or, what is the same thing,

> with gold or silver, as the universal equivalent, they express the relation between their own private labour and the collective labour of society in the same absurd form.
>
> The categories of bourgeois economy consist of such like forms. They are forms of thought expressing with social validity the conditions and relations of a definite, historically determined mode of production, viz., the production of commodities. The whole mystery of commodities, all the magic and necromancy that surrounds the products of labour as long as they take the form of commodities, vanishes, therefore, so soon as we come to other forms of production.[12]

Therefore:

What is hidden behind Value, a category of the mercantile society, is PRIVATE EXCHANGE and, it follows, individualized or private property. The axis on which this contradiction turns is PRIVATE LABOR open and in conflict with SOCIAL, COLLECTIVE LABOR. The factor which makes it possible and propagates it is the DIVISION OF LABOR.

"But, while it is true that private exchange implies the division of labor, it does not hold that the division of labor implies private exchange." [13]

Therefore, as already anticipated value is the *historical* expression, based on private exchange and private property, of the social division of labor, which is a natural law.

In short: VALUE = CONTRADICTORY HISTORICAL FORM OF A NATURAL LAW.

Up to this point, we have wanted to establish certain principles before considering comrade Mora's objection to the definition of value in question. It should be noted, too, that this objection is not new: Engels made the same point in 1891 in the introduction to Marx's pamphlet, "Wage Labor and Capital":

> I will remind only, to avoid quibbling, that today this explanation is totally inadequate. . . .

> Therefore, when today we say simply, with economists such as Ricardo, that the value of a commodity is determined by the labour necessary to produce it, *we accept as given the reservations made by Marx.*[14]

Marx himself objected indirectly to this definition in the letter to Kugelman cited above, as well as in other economic works. What is the real limitation of the definition?

When the founders of scientific socialism accepted Ricardo's thesis regarding value, they did so "with Marx's reservations" because Ricardo *did not go into these reservations, into how or why value itself arose.*

> Political economy has indeed analyzed, however incompletely, value and its magnitude, and has discovered what lies beneath these forms. But it has never once asked the question why labour is represented by the value of its product and labour time by the magnitude of that value.[15]

But from here to completely rejecting the definition is a long way. If what one wants is simply to point up the operation and the characteristics of value, it is necessary and proper to explain it precisely as a quantitative relationship, just as Marx and Engels do in the quotations that follow:

a. Criticizing Proudhon and accepting the Ricardian theory of value: "Ricardo shows us the real movement *of bourgeois production* which constitutes value. . . .

Ricardo's theory of value is the scientific interpretation of current economic life. . . ."[16]

b. "We can, then, state the following as a general law: 'The values of commodities are directly proportional to the labour time spent on their production and inversely proportional to the productive forces of the labour employed.'[17]

c. ". . . because value is only a term used to express labour, the term by which our current capitalist society designates the amount of *socially necessary labour embodied in a given commodity.*"[18]

Thus, it would be proper to refer to value in the form that

comrade Mora wishes to disprove so long as the natural reasons and social relationships that bring it about are accepted as parameters. Until now, we have been considering the first thesis.

2. Further on, Commander Mora quotes from *Capital* as follows:

> . . . the magnitude of the value of any article is the amount of labour socially necessary, or the labour time socially necessary for its production.

We believe, however, that in this case the distortion of the quotation may perhaps be due to the different editions we have used. (Mora uses Editorial Cartago, page 36, and ours is Editora Nacional de Cuba, page 7.) But we are doubtless dealing with the same passage.

Comrade Mora OMITTED the following words that go at the BEGINNING of the paragraph.

"In consequence, *that which determines* . . ."

And Marx, after explaining the concept a little more, QUOTES HIMSELF in this way:

"Considered as values, all commodities are no more than given quantities *of crystallized labour time* (emphasis by Marx, quoted from *Contribution to the Critique of Political Economy,* page 6).

In other words, Marx did not say "magnitude," either, but rather "that which determines magnitude." It might seem a little fussy, but it is necessary to clarify that value does not exist if it is not a given magnitude, just as labor is not labor except with a given duration, or the measurement of time is not possible except by a given form of material movement.

The author concludes with a profound thought: "But the measure of something is not the thing itself." This is equivalent to saying: a hectare of land is not land itself, or a meter of cloth is not cloth itself.

The most surprising thing, however, is that we cannot think of land except in terms of hectares, or cloth except in yards.

Here lies, then, the dialectical unit of the concept of magnitudes because, as Engels says:

> We know what an hour or a meter is, but not what time or space is. As if time were something other than a series of hours or space something more than a series of cubic meters! [19]

"The thing itself" that is being sought cannot be found unless it is in a given dimension: and value, very simply, is not value *except in a given amount of socially necessary labor.* To attempt to find "value itself" is much like trying to find the enigmatic "thing itself" of our old friend Immanuel Kant.

Marx substantiates our argument in a phrase:

> The character of having value, when once impressed upon products, obtains fixity only by reason of their acting and reacting upon each other as quantities of value.[20]

Thus, we reject comrade Mora's second thesis.

Commander Mora's last two theses are founded almost exclusively on two quotations from Marx. Regrettably, we were unable to compare the second of these with its original.

3. "Marx clearly says that labor is the 'creative substance of value.' " *Note:* Very frankly, then, why not understand what value is?

4. We would take the quotation on which comrade Mora's fourth thesis is based from the source if we could because it supports our thinking even more:

1. Exchange VALUE = Historical concept.
2. VALUE = Expression of a natural law.

The author reaches the conclusion that Marx differentiates VALUE and EXCHANGE VALUE, but fails to offer a concrete explanation as to what the difference is. The main difference, if one wants to go into it, is that VALUE is the FORM adopted by the product of labor in a mercantile society, while EXCHANGE VALUE is the QUANTITATIVE RELATIONSHIP that mediates two use-values in the process of exchange.

But VALUE and EXCHANGE VALUE are Siamese twins and cannot exist without each other, in the same way that it is impossible to conceive of a commodity without a price. The essence of what differentiates them resides solely in that the former is a MENTAL relationship and the latter a MERCANTILE relationship because BOTH are natural sons of the historical conditions of production under which they operate.

Item IV

On page [223] we come to the theory of value:

> In short, what is value? In my judgment . . . we must appreciate that it embodies (or better, expresses) a relationship. In the first place, it is a measure . . .

We return to magnitude and measure.

> . . . in the second place, it is consequently a category created by man under specific circumstances and with a specific purpose . . .

If we have understood everything up to this point, VALUE is now:

1. A RELATIONSHIP.
2. A MEASURE.
3. A CATEGORY "CREATED BY MAN."

Considering these new concepts more carefully, we would see: (1) that despite comrade Mora's having brought out the difference between value and exchange value, now it turns out that VALUE is also a relationship, though of another "type"; (2) that although it was said that the measure is not the thing itself, now value is a measure that, according to this criterion, would not be "value itself," either; (3) that man created value in the same way that God created man, although in the former case it was "under specific circumstances and with a specific purpose."

So as not to overwork the theme of measure, relationship, and magnitude, we will go on to the "second place":

Comrade Mora says that VALUE is:

1. A CATEGORY CREATED BY MAN.
2. UNDER SPECIFIC CIRCUMSTANCES.
3. WITH A SPECIFIC PURPOSE, ETC.

In other words, now VALUE is no longer a category of an objective law; rather, it is created by man. The will of man can "create" categories and laws. Regrettably, it is just the opposite: value is such a category because it is a mental conception of an objective law that was not "created" by man but arose from the economic milieu within which man performed his NATURAL activity, labor.

Man did not create value "under specific circumstances." Such a statement implies that a man or several men agreed to invent value at a given time. Actually, history proves the contrary. From the earliest times until Ricardo, economic thought could not decipher or explain this category that comrade Mora says men themselves created.

From Aristotle, of whom Marx says:

> . . . an important fact . . . prevented Aristotle from seeing that to attribute value to commodities is merely a mode of expressing all labour as equal human labour, and, consequently, as labour of equal quality, Greek society was founded upon slavery, and had, therefore, for its natural basis, the inequality of men and of their labour powers. The secret of the expression of value (namely, that all kinds of labour are equal and equivalent, because, and so far as, they are human labour in general), cannot be deciphered until the notion of human equality has already acquired the fixity of a popular prejudice.[21]

Until Ricardo, who made the "great and epoch-making" discovery, "The value of a commodity . . . depends on the relative quantity of labour which is necessary for its production,"[22] men were unable to explain value scientifically—

and they had "created" it. In all that time value did not exist. But Engels says that it has existed for "five to seven thousand years!" Clearly, value is not a creation of man, just as labor is not a human creation but a requirement of his nature.

Item V

We will proceed now to the development of his theory [page 224] that ". . . the relationship that expresses the category 'value' is decidedly objective; it is the relationship between limited available resources and the growing needs of man. . . ."

If we accept this new criterion, we are compelled to take one of the following attitudes toward the primitive community, the state of society during which available resources were the most limited in history, the period during which man found himself more unsatisfied than ever before or since:

1. Either we eliminate it from history so as to accommodate value as the "relationship between limited available resources and the growing needs of man . . . ," which is then valid until resources become "unlimited," or until needs are "decreasing";
2. Or we contribute something new to the science and "discover" that inasmuch as the resources of that society were very limited and its needs quite unsatisfied, "value" existed there also, even though naturally in a form unrecognized by men of the time and so obscure that Marx and Engels failed to notice it.

But we are going to leave that detail aside. If value is a relationship ("decidedly objective") between limited available resources and the growing needs of man, when will it disappear as an economic category? For such a thing to occur, there would have to be a point at which resources were greater than or equal to needs. Conversely to what actually takes place in nature and society, the motive force of development would not be needs but resources.

Leaving aside several lines that do nothing but confuse socially necessary labor with "the application of limited available resources to the satisfaction of a socially recognized need"—in the assumption that if resources were unlimited, socially necessary labor would disappear—we come to the following prediction:

> Once (and only once) available resources become fully sufficient, the need to express such a relationship disappears.

But here a question arises: The resources available, for example, to the United States are quite adequate for the time being, at least to satisfy its people's minimum needs, if they were utilized for such a purpose. Could it be that value has disappeared there? Or, on the contrary, is it not an essential condition to the disappearance of value that private exchange and mercantile production disappear?

What follows is truly incomprehensible. First it is said that:

> As available resources are then sufficient "to satisfy given socially recognized needs," . . . the value relationship will lose its importance, disappearing to all practical effects.

And afterward that:

> . . . the foregoing takes place relative to "given socially recognized needs," because by his very condition man's needs are eternally growing; once some needs are satisfied, new ones arise.

Summarizing:

1. It disappears when there are ample resources available.
2. It disappears only in relation to "given socially recognized needs."
3. It does not disappear for those needs that are eternally growing.

How is this explained? Only if the law of value were eternal. In this case, man, besides creating a law, made it eternal. In other words, it is a law that appears and disappears according to the color of the crystal through which it is viewed, as Calderón de la Barca would say.

Permit us now to refer to the marginal note on this matter.

Item VI

On page [225]:

> Under socialism, the law of value operates through the plan, or the planning process.

We have already given Marx's opinion on this but will expand on it further:

> Here obviously *the same principle prevails as that which regulates the exchange of commodities,* as far as this is exchange of equal values. *Content and form are changed,* because under the altered circumstances no one can give anything except his labour, and because, on the other hand, nothing can pass into the ownership of individuals except individual means of consumption. But, as far as the *distribution of the latter* among the individual producers is concerned, the same principle prevails as in the exchange of commodity equivalents, so much labour in one form is exchanged for an equal amount of labour in another form.[23]

Marx clearly established that under socialism the same principle rules as in commodity exchange: AS RESPECTS DISTRIBUTION. He explained, "the distribution of the means of consumption at any time is only a consequence of the distribution of the conditions of production themselves"; and "these defects are as inevitable in the first phase of communist society as it is when it has just emerged after prolonged birth pangs from capitalist society." [24]

But is it possible to speak of value concretized through the plan if this is what regulates the distribution of the conditions of production, of which distribution, as the only area in which the principle of equivalent exchange arises, is a consequence? In what socialist country does the law of value determine the proportions of the plan?

As comrade Mora has quoted Stalin, we feel compelled to use something more of what Stalin said in this respect:

> But does all this mean that the operation of the law of value has free reign in our country, as under capitalism? That the law of value is a regulator of Production in our country? No, it does not mean that. . . .
>
> Clearly, private ownership of the means of production does not exist, and socialization of the means of production, both in the city and in the country, further *restricts* the law of value's sphere of operation and its *influence on production* (page 14).
>
> *Value, the same as the law of value, is an historical category rooted in the economy of mercantile production.* When mercantile production disappears, *so will all the forms of value, and the law of value.*
>
> The statement that the law of value regulates the "proportions" of the distribution of labor among the various branches of production during the initial phase of development of the communist society, in our present economic system, *is also completely wrong.*
>
> If it were so, one could not understand why light industry does not develop at maximum pace in our country. It is the most profitable, which would give it preference over heavy industry, which is often less profitable, sometimes in absolute terms.
>
> *These comrades forget that the law of value can regulate production only under capitalism.* . . . They forget that the sphere of operation of the law of value is *limited* in our country by the existence of social ownership of the means of production, by the operation *of the law of harmonious economic development* and, as a result, by our annual and five-year plans as well, for they are an approximate reflection *of this ultimate law.*[25]

But comrade Mora says [page 225]:

> It is precisely in the conscious decision of the planning authority (Juceplan) where value appears most clearly as an economic criterion, as *a regulator of production.*

The gravity of this error could make one forget that under socialism the law of harmonious development, proportional planning, is what governs the distribution of the means of production and labor—*what regulates production.*

> In this way, the law of proportionally planned development is considered to be a regulatory law of social production.[26]

By suggesting that the plan is the medium through which the law of value operates, one admits that the plan is not such a plan, because the law of value, by presupposing mercantile production and private or individualized property, creates anarchy and competition *on a social scale, where it operates freely.* In other words, a plan that "concretizes value," through which the law of value operates, would necessarily have to be a plan of anarchy and competition rather than one of proportional, harmonious development.

Engels said:

> The seizure of the means of production by society puts an end to commodity production, and therewith to the domination of the product over the producer. Anarchy in social production is replaced by conscious organisation on a planned basis.[27]

Where is the advantage of planning if all it does is to serve as a bridge for the law of value?

The plan obeys the objective need arising under socialism to develop the economy harmoniously in benefit of the people. Because such a plan is created by men, it is a conscious act; because such an objective need is the result of an objective law, it is independent of men.

The law exists and operates with or without a plan, but the scientific accuracy with which it is employed depends on the quality of the plan: if it is good there will be proportionality; if it is not, or if other factors enter, there will be disproportionality. The knowledge of economic laws and their spheres of operation makes it possible for man to conform his actions to the objective needs arising in any social regime, to use them in his own benefit, going "from the kingdom of need to the kingdom of liberty." [28]

How is it possible that a law (that of value) could operate through a plan?

That would be to deny its objective character and to "create it" again, this time "in the planning process."

The author proceeds on the basis that "planning methods must be established which take the indicators of the law of value into account." Certainly, while mercantile production exists, we must know exactly in what area and to what degree this law operates, and use it, as we use others, to obtain better results. But to go from there to turning it into a regulator of production is a long step.

What regulates our production is neither petty interest, nor economic return above all, nor profit, nor capitalization; it is the people's welfare, and this is not satisfied in one year, or two, but during a process of harmonious development over a more or less long period of time.

Finally, it is admitted that "value is not the only valid criterion in determining investment (and other expenditures) in a planned economy. . . . But this does not contradict the aforesaid, because we have fully clarified that the Law of Value is an economic criterion for regulating production."

So far, we have analyzed several explanations of value and its law. Now this one reduces the law of value to "an economic criterion for regulating production."

Is it true that the postulates of the law of value must be taken into account? Certainly. It would be absurd to close one's eyes and march to the tune of one's desires rather than in step with one's possibilities. What happens is that the society, aware for the first time of the phenomena that were imposed upon them before in the midst of chaos, SELECTS its own road, likewise heeding the new laws in its paths.

We again refer the reader to Stalin, who explains this matter in depth.

Item VII

After another quote from Stalin (regrettably none of the passages we have quoted), an explanation is given with which, in general, one can agree. Undoubtedly, there is mercantile production in Cuba, thus value and law of value.

But what we cannot agree with is the following conclusion [page 227]:

> When some comrades deny that the law of value operates in relations among enterprises within the State sector, they argue that the entire State sector is under single ownership, that the enterprises are the property of the society.

To tell the truth, the only argument even *similar* to this is in an article by Commander Guevara appearing in *Nuestra Industria Economica,* number 1. But the thesis he is judging does not appear in this article (if it is to this he refers). Guevara says very clearly:

> This concept, which has been implemented in only a few branches of the economy. . . .[29]

In other words, the thesis must be analyzed within the same framework as it is used. Thus, under circumstances when, "The transfer of a product from one enterprise to another, whether within one ministry or between ministries, is merely a part of the production process in which values are added to the product, while the bank is only a cashier which carries a record of these movements," [30] *we would find ourselves* "Within the co-operative society where . . . producers do not exchange their products," [31] where, simply, "just as little does the labour employed on the products appear . . . *as the value* of these products. . . ." [32]

Comrade Mora errs again when he says that State property "is not yet the fully developed social property which will be achieved only under communism." In the same way, we could say that distribution according to labor is not fully developed distribution, which will be achieved only under communism, etc.

In short, what is State property under socialism? State property is no more than the historical form assumed by social property under the dictatorship of the proletariat.

> Under the dictatorship of the proletariat state property must not be compared to social, socialist property. The first is but an historical form of the second. . . .
>
> Under these conditions no other system is capable of performing the functions of socialist ownership.[33]

To say that "fully developed" social property will be achieved only under communism is to erase with one swipe all Marx's theory regarding the two phases of the communist society, and all Lenin's ideas regarding the dictatorship of the proletariat.

> Accounting and control—that is *mainly* what is needed for the "smooth working," for the proper functioning, of the *first phase* of communist society . . . all citizens become employees and workers of a *single* countrywide state "syndicate." The whole of society will have become a single office and a single factory, with equality of labour and pay.
>
> But this "factory" discipline . . . is by no means our ideal, or our ultimate goal. It is only a necessary STEP . . . for FURTHER progress.[34]

The quote from Oskar Lange with which Mora hopes to corroborate such a statement only supports our view that: (1) the law of value "continues to operate because production continues to be mercantile production . . ."; (2) this is so because there are "numerous product owners" (individual ownership); (3) "there are several forms of social ownership."

What must be determined in Cuba's case is: (1) to what point and in what area is there mercantile production; (2) how many and who are the "numerous owners"; (3) whether there are several forms of social ownership. The answers to these are material for another paper. Here we will restrict ourselves to pointing out that social ownership in Cuba is limited to State ownership—by all the people. Cooperatives in the style of other socialist countries do not exist (although there are cooperative forms in some branches). The steps toward socialization of the entire economy by means of the State are taken at their own accelerated pace within the general laws governing the building of socialism.

Item VIII

Finally, we will consider the problem of costs. Comrade Mora warns ". . . against an 'exclusivist criterion' with respect to costs. One can picture an enterprise with very low (even decreasing) costs which is never profitable because its products are not 'socially recognized.' "

He is right to be concerned about profit, because for the moment it is the only way to assure development. But the problem changes when the phenomenon is closely examined. Profit, savings, or surplus, it is a dialectical function of expanded reproduction, and as such is conditioned simultaneously by the kind of reproduction—capitalist or socialist. In the first case, it will become "production for production's sake,"[35] and in the second, a *means* for satisfying society's growing needs. In the first case, it will be an OBJECTIVE of itself, and the second, an INSTRUMENT subordinated to the collective interest.

Thus an enterprise under socialism *may or may not yield a profit* without serious effect on the society, because the enterprise operates in benefit of the society whether or not it yields a profit.

But what is the only way of ensuring that all enterprises yield profits? "Giving them social recognition?" Reducing costs, production expenses!

For a while, therefore, it is imperative to be concerned with profit, but improvement in this area can be achieved only on a national scale, commensurate with growth in production and decreasing costs.

We should consider the inherent meanings of cost, price, savings, and need at great length, but this would take up a great deal of space.

Permit us to close here. Comrade Mora's seven conclusions are wrong, according to what we have proved or attempted to prove. But we are still willing to fashion our arguments in a different way, and provide them with more substance should this be necessary.

We believe that we will all come out of this debate—which is important in content and open to all studious revolutionaries —more capable men.

NOTES

1. Joseph Stalin, *Economic Problems of Socialism in the U.S.S.R.*
2. M. Rosenthal, "Problems of Dialectic in Marx's *Capital*," p. 33.
3. Friedrich Engels, "Supplement to *Capital*, Volume Three." [Translator's source: Karl Marx, *Capital* (New York, International Publishers, 1967), pp. 899–900.]
4. See, especially, F. Engels, *The Origin of the Family, Private Property and the State.* Also see the Epigraph to the Division of Labor in Volume I of *Capital.*
5. Karl Marx, *Letters to Kugelmann* (New York, International Publishers, 1934), pp. 73–74.
6. Rosenthal, *op. cit.*
7. Also see, *Manual of Economy,* U.S.S.R., p. 73.
8. Karl Marx, *Critique of the Gotha Program.* [Translator's source: *Critique of the Gotha Program* (New York, International Publishers, c. 1938), p. 8.]
9. Friedrich Engels, *Herr Eugen Duhring's Revolution in Science.* [Translator's source: *Anti-Duhring* (New York, International Publishers, 1966), p. 17.]
10. Karl Marx, *Capital,* (Vol. I). [Translator's source: *Great Books of the Western World* (Chicago, Encyclopedia Britannica, c. 1952), Vol. L, p. 15.]
11. *Ibid.,* p. 19.
12. *Ibid.,* p. 33.
13. Karl Marx, *Contribution to the Critique of Political Economy,* p. 39.

14. Karl Marx, *Wage Labor and Capital,* p. 6.
15. Marx, *Capital* (Vol. I), *op. cit.,* p. 35. See especially notes 34 and 35 below, as well as *Contribution to the Critique of Political Economy,* p. 39.
16. Karl Marx, *Misery of Philosophy,* pp. 22–23.
17. Karl Marx, *Salary, Price and Profit* (Editorial Lex), p. 215.
18. Friedrich Engels, "Introduction to *Wage Labor and Capital,*" p. 11.
19. *Natural Dialectic,* p. 201.
20. Marx, *Capital* (Vol. I), *op. cit.,* p. 33.
21. *Ibid.,* p. 25.
22. Engels, *Anti-Duhring, op. cit.,* p. 215.
23. Marx, *Critique of the Gotha Program, op. cit.,* pp. 8–9.
24. *Ibid.,* p. 10.
25. Stalin, *op. cit.,* pp. 15–16.
26. Dr. Iure Jasslo, *National Economic Planning,* Vol. I, p. 73.
27. Engels, *op. cit.,* p. 309.
28. *Ibid.*
29. "Consideraciónes sobre los costos de producción como base del analisis económico de las empresas sujetas a sistema presupuestario," *Nuestra Industria Económica,* No. 1, 1963, p. 6.
30. *Ibid.*
31. Marx, *Critique of the Gotha Program,* p. 8.
32. *Ibid.*
33. Kolesov, "Social Ownership of the Means of Production in the U.S.S.R.," p. 67.
34. V. I. Lenin, "The State and Revolution," *Selected Works* (New York, International Publishers, 1967), Vol. II, pp. 344–345.
35. Marx, *Capital* (Vol. I), *op. cit.*

PART IV

The Function of Finance Under Socialism

12

Finance and Political Development

LUIS ALVAREZ ROM

IT IS A PLEASURE to write about finance because of its important role in achieving the political and economic objectives of every State enmeshed in the process of social transformation.

The word finance derived from the Latin *finatio,* meaning payment. Under capitalism, it is a business term used in connection with monetary matters and might therefore be defined as the use of money for lucrative ends. It has also been employed with reference to the administration of State funds, in which case the word *financier* takes on the meaning of public financier, or an administrator of the public treasury.

In Marxist economics and sociology, finance is defined as "the art of business as related to monetary operations." Thus, although the phrasing is similar, the expression has been given several definitions, all revolving around the operation of procuring, providing, and managing money or other kinds of funds for use in some mercantile activity.

Finance, financier, and similar terms are somehow carried over to the socialist relationships of production. This connotation has nothing to do with the meanings of the words per se; it stems, rather, from the procedures they denote which helped aggravate the exploitation inherent in the capitalist system. For

SOURCE: "Las finanzas como un método de desarrollo político," *Nuestra Industria Revista Económica,* Año 1, Junio 1963, pp. 13–21.

this reason, Marx, in discussing the means of circulation under the credit system, refers to "financiers" as follows:

> They interfere in real production in the most dangerous way, neither understanding nor having anything to do with it.[1]

A socialist revolution, by its very *raison d'être,* must sweep away the mechanisms of the capitalist system. It must abolish the privileges and claims that made the exploitation of labor possible, and place the instruments of finance in the hands of the people. In this way, the most reactionary representatives of capitalism and the most specialized swindlers of the public treasury cease to exist.

Under socialism, the financial system is used by the State to facilitate control and measurement in the formation, distribution, and redistribution of national funds, and thus to define the society's (represented by administrative bodies, enterprises, and the people themselves) monetary relations.

Money, or the expression of value in monetary terms, is employed in the calculation of social labor. In this sense, it is an instrument used in the planning and administration of production and distribution of the social product. Likewise, exchange through the medium of money is circumscribed because the right of ownership is nontransferable within the State sphere.

The concepts of *accounting, finance, and the law of value* are highly interdependent. According to Engels, the law of value became operative some five to seven thousand years ago, long before the birth of capitalism. Although the conditions of its operation are different, and its nature is essentially changed, the law survives even under socialism. Therefore, its conscious use is indispensable in socialist planning.

Accounting is a system for the elaboration, compilation, and recording of economic data. Through its use, one can establish and maintain a precise correlation between labor and material disbursement, on the one hand, and production results on the other.

The system supposedly came about as a result of the merchant's need to keep account of his transactions. There is an article about this which includes photographs of several spinning-mill accounts containing each spinner's name, production quota, wool allotment, and piece output. The article's writer notes that these records date back to 2200 B.C. Accounting technique has developed enormously since then, of course, mainly since the Industrial Revolution. Moreover, the greater the social nature of production becomes, the more important accounting will become as an ideal compendium of economic relations.

Lenin would point out that when the socialist revolution—unlike the bourgeois revolution—comes to power, it finds no readymade relationships. It must organize the accounting system, bring the strongest enterprises under control, and convert the entire State economic system into a single great apparatus so that everyone is governed by a single plan.

Finance and the other concepts explained above are not merely static techniques of economic control and administration. On the contrary, they are essentially dynamic instruments, and play an important role in both political and economic tasks. They can be powerful weapons in the class struggle that takes place during the period of transition; and, during the building of socialism, they are an enormous aid in transforming the national economy. By the time the building of communism has begun, however, such categories—which go through a process of restructuring and change under the impact of dialectical contradictions—reach total atrophy, because monetary relationships of a mercantile nature are inappropriate under communism.

Finance and its related categories form a principle of action based on factors common to all countries where Marxism-Leninism develops. Used intelligently, this principle provides a means for solving the problems of economic reconstruction during the transition from capitalism to socialism in accord with a country's specific national, historical, and cultural circumstances.

Guided by this principle of action, Lenin, in 1921, very effectively stated the problem of the Soviet government's financial policy. The New Economic Plan (NEP) would be the road to socialist transformation. The use of commodity exchange as a means for uniting city and countryside, industry and agriculture, had failed because the peasantry refused to accept any form other than commerce. In response, Lenin declared at the Party's provincial conference in Moscow on October 21, 1921:

> And we have no other choice than to take account of it—unless we want to hide our heads beneath our wings; unless we are too obstinate to recognize our defeat; unless we are afraid to look the dangers in the face. We have to recognize that the retreat has been inadequate, that a new retreat is needed, going back even further, from state capitalism to state regulation of exchange operations and commodity circulation through the medium of money. The exchange of commodities has not yielded results. The private market has shown itself to be stronger than we are, and instead of the exchange of commodities, we find ourselves with the usual purchase-sale, with commerce.

With regard to industry, he also took up the question of reorganizing State enterprises based on the principle of commercial output, which was inevitably linked to the New Economic Policy.

The organization of Soviet State enterprises, abiding by Lenin's principle of commercial output, was originally carried out in the form of "consolidated enterprises," or groups of factories that operated financially independent of the budget under the system initially called "commercial accounting (*kommercheskii rashot*) and later economic accounting (*khozyaistevennyi rashot,* or *Khozraschot*). It is now generally known as "economic calculus." In keeping with its context—that each production unit finance its own costs with its own revenues—however, we prefer to call it auto-financing because no system has exclusive claim to the words "accounting," "calculus," and "economy."

Under this economic policy, finance and similar categories were employed intelligently and with expedience to help restrict and permanently displace capitalist elements as well as to eliminate the *kulaks* as the class on which total collectivization was based.

In Cuba, since the revolutionary victory, finance has followed its own path in response to the rapid development of the political process that began as soon as the Revolution clearly revealed its socialist hue. At no time did a definite financial policy exist, but undoubtedly the high level of accounting technique in our country provided a certain financial framework that helped to contain the disorder naturally brought about by an event with such deep social roots. Financial discipline might have been stronger, or rather, not as weak, had it not been ignored in the beginning that accounting acquires greater importance as production becomes increasingly social in character. On the other hand, this was a natural consequence of the speed with which decisive political and economic measures were taken. This speed was possible because circumstances had created the opportunity and the conditions for putting such measures into practice.

The nature of the financial system employed in the Cuban revolutionary process is most apparent in the nationalized industrial and commercial sector. The origin and development of the system may be synthesized as follows:

Toward the end of 1960, the revolutionary government had to confront its first practical economic and financial problem. The problem had to do with the need to take charge of the administration and control of nationalized enterprises that had been recuperated or intervened.

The usual scarcity of operating funds in small and medium-sized enterprises, together with the nationalization of economically more powerful enterprises, engendered the first revolutionary decision in matters of finance, which was to centralize the bank accounts of all enterprises, thereby creating a common "central fund." All revenues were deposited in this fund, while financial resources required for evolution of an enterprise's productive activity were made available through specific budget allocations. The fund was administered and controlled by the Department of Industrialization of INRA [National Institute of Agrarian Reform], and was kept in the Agricultural and Industrial Development Bank, which had already been nationalized.

Later, when the banking system was nationalized and financial bodies were restructured (they were, of course, already serving the nation's needs), the central fund was transferred to the national budget under the jurisdiction of the Treasury Ministry. The new system was administered along the same lines as the central fund, but was modified somewhat by the creation of the consolidated enterprise as a legal entity combining the production and administrative functions of several factories with similar characteristics, as well as by our initial efforts to plan the economy.

The "year of organization," the progress achieved in systematizing national economic planning, and the imminent need to strengthen institutional organization, forced us to review our financial organization. The situation in this area was such that the methods in use were evolving by fits and starts. In fact, the most notable characteristic of any advance made in the area was spontaneity.

The Central Planning Committee, the Treasury Ministry, and the National Bank of Cuba have been trying to improve this situation for the past two years, but until recently have made little progress toward establishing the organizational principles needed to guide either their actions or those of other State agencies. Thus, the revolutionary government had been unable to formulate policy that would tend to assure the proper exercise of financial discipline.

Of late, however, these agencies have submitted a proposal that, once approved by the National Economic Commission of the ORI,* establishes the organizational principles that in future will regulate the operation of economic and financial bodies.

The budgetary operations law, drawn up by the Treasury Ministry and approved by the Council of Ministers toward the

* Integrated Revolutionary Organizations, which consisted of three parties: the 26th of July Movement, the Directorio Revolucionario, and the Communist Party (the old Party).

end of 1962, represents an improvement in methods of budgetary organization and control. It also combines the various laws still considered useful that were once scattered among several acts of legislation.

Now that the revolutionary government's financial policy has been defined in principle, two additional measures are being taken. Together, these measures encompass the bases and standards that will govern the operation of the existing financial system. The first applies to enterprises operating under the auto-finance system, that is, those which maintain bank accounts with their own funds and replace their means of turnover directly by means of mercantile exchange. The second will regulate the operation of enterprises that rely on the national budget as the sole source of funds allocated in accordance with approved financial plans.

For the moment, however, we must recognize that there are factors that seriously obstruct progress toward the goals pursued by both systems. Some derive from organizational deficiencies stemming from a lack of qualified personnel and others from the need for a further growth of political consciousness. It is for this reason that auto-financing would be impracticable if it were as complex as the sophisticated systems employed in other socialist countries. Moreover, the budgetary system could not yet fulfill its objectives, because it is lacking in organization and political development.

There is little familiarity with the principles of the budgetary finance system. In fact, individual enterprises may mistakenly apply categories that do not conceptually exist in the system. Discussion of the above-mentioned measures should contribute to their understanding and will undoubtedly serve to strengthen financial discipline.

It is important to stress that there are certain inviolable principles common to all socialist countries, no matter what finance system is employed:

1. The law of harmonious and proportional development of the national economy, based on socialist ownership

of the means of production. Through production, which is the basis of this law, the society becomes, to use Lenin's words, "a single office and a single factory," by consciously developing production in order to satisfy the needs of the entire nation.

2. The law of value. This law is described above as is the concept of its operation under socialism. According to this concept, the state consciously employs the law as a means of controlling the amount of the labor contribution and consumption of every member of the society.

3. The principle guiding the distribution of the product of labor, "to each according to his work." This principle also tends to induce a creative attitude toward work.

4. The principle of economic administration based on democratic centralism. This principle is sufficiently flexible to permit the merger of central and local administrations in accordance with technical and administrative qualifications and specializations, thus eliminating unnecessary bureaucracy and paper work, and contributing to the development of the productive forces.

We should add that the essential context of relations among State organizations must in no way diverge from the concepts of social property. The principles guiding such relations are defined by Soviet constitutional law as follows:

> The basic funds of state property may be freely transferred from one state enterprise or institution to another by disposition of authorized state agencies. This transfer does not in any way imply a change of ownership because said agencies and enterprises are of the state itself. The redistribution of means of turnover in accordance with economic calculus implies the transfer of the right to administer and control such funds, but does not suppose a change of ownership. State agencies on an immediately higher level may administer, within the limits defined by law, the goods of subordinate agencies. Property relationships between the latter and higher level agencies are of a

legal and administrative nature.

The state facilitates material and financial resources to given enterprises. The products manufactured by such enterprises are distributed according to procedure established by the state.[2]

As a means of illustration and as a thought that might provide a core for future articles, we reproduce below some of the principles contained in the proposed law regulating budgetary enterprises:

The Revolutionary Government has authorized two systems of control over the exercise of financial discipline in the operations of socialist enterprises. The first is called the budgetary finance system, and the second, the auto-finance system.

The budgetary finance system incorporates all economic activities of the enterprises under its jurisdiction into the national budget. The budget serves as the only source of funds for these enterprises. Such funds are made available through budgeted credit allocations channeled through agencies of the National Bank of Cuba.

Enterprises governed by this procedure may neither hold nor accumulate funds in their own bank accounts. Instead, they must transfer to the budget, whether in real form or as a formality, through pricing, the aggregate of their economic operation expressed in terms of money.

Social ownership of the means of production within the state sphere assures, through the use of this financial system in operations carried out among socialist enterprises, the conversion of mercantile exchange into delivery of products. Thus, by eliminating money as a means of payment, it reduces it to a unit of account. Moreover, it eliminates the credit function of accounts receivable and payable, and turns them conceptually into mere administrative or bookkeeping devices represented physically by orders of compensation which are solely for purposes of bank control.[3]

The financial system is both a means of controlling financial discipline and a political vehicle for the development of creative thought. We feel certain that the above will inspire a number of ideas based on the specific conditions of the country in which a socialist revolution takes shape.

Our final purpose here is to recommend that every financial measure taken attempt to find a balance between necessary financial discipline and unnecessary commercial bureaucracy. In this way, we may discover hidden reserves as well as unfulfilled social obligations at the least possible operating cost.

NOTES

1. [No source given.]
2. [*Ibid.*]
3. [*Ibid.*]

13

Development and Operation of Socialist Banking in Cuba

MARCELO FERNÁNDEZ FONT

Origin and Development of Banks

IN PRIMITIVE TIMES, commodities were exchanged directly in the form of barter; later, money began to be used as the means of payment. Commercial banks, such as exist today, have their origins in medieval Europe. At first, money lenders (the original bankers) considered their principal functions to be money exchange and the holding of temporarily idle money.

Such operations were carried out primarily in public markets, especially during fairs. In fact, the word bank comes from the Italian *banca,* which means seat or bench and refers to public locations in which the bankers of medieval Italy sat to conduct their business.

Banks quickly perfected their work and soon not only performed exchange and deposit operations but also began to use the money entrusted to them for the purpose of making interest-bearing loans to third parties. Although at first this was done

---

Marcelo Fernández Font was President of the National Bank during the period of debate and is currently Minister of Foreign Trade.

SOURCE: "Desarrollo y funciones de la banca socialista en Cuba," *Cuba Socialista,* Año IV, Febrero 1964, pp. 32–50.

without the depositor's knowledge, soon it was done with his consent, and banks that once charged a fee for holding deposits began paying depositors for the right to temporarily administer their money.

The first banks of the modern age were the Bank of Amsterdam (founded in 1609) and the Bank of Hamburg (founded in 1619).

The rapid development of commercial relations and the scarcity of precious metals for coin manufacture led to the appearance of *bank notes.* A bank note is an interest-free security issued by the central bank, expressed in a given amount of money, and made out to the bearer. The first bank note was issued by the Swedish Bank of Issue, created in 1658.

With the development of capitalism and the growth of national and international trade, the active capitalists (landowners, industrialists, merchants) begin to distinguish themselves from the monetary capitalists (bankers). Active capitalists use *commercial credit* among themselves through which goods and services sold are not paid for immediately but over a period of time, generally not exceeding a few months.

The active capitalists' free and idle funds are deposited in banks that serve as intermediaries for placing them at the disposal of other active capitalists in need of funds. This is *bank credit.* Bank credit can be short- or long-term and always earns an interest, which is the bank's principal source of revenue.

During the entire modern era, banks and capitalists in general continued to grow vigorously until the development, beginning in the middle nineteenth century, of monopolistic or imperialistic capitalism. During this period, as Lenin explained in his brilliant work *Imperialism: The Highest Stage of Capitalism,* concentration of production and capital creates monopolies. In addition, bank capital fuses with industrial capital and thus engenders *finance capital* and the financial oligarchy. In Lenin's work, we read:

> Finance capital, concentrated in a few hands and enjoying a virtual monopoly, obtains enormous and ever-growing

> benefits from organizing companies, issuing securities, State loans, etc., consolidating the power of the financial oligarchy and imposing upon society as a whole a tribute in benefit of the monopolists.[1]

Finance capital daily gains greater control over the developed capitalist countries. Banks encourage stock companies and then acquire stock to gain control of them. The large banks absorb the small ones.

The banks of the capitalist powers have established an extensive network of subsidiaries in developing countries. This permits the exportation of investment capital to these countries, which deforms their economies. North American banks have nearly one hundred foreign subsidiaries, French banks approximately two hundred, and English banks more than three thousand.

The Socialist Bank Is Born

Banks exist under certain economic conditions. If a society's means of production are in capitalist hands, its banks will be capitalist. If the class character of the State does not change, the nationalization of banks cannot be of a socialist nature. Such are the cases of bank nationalization in England and France after World War II. Because the class character of these States did not change, their nationalized banks continued to be capitalist banks.

A socialist banking system cannot be built if banks remain in capitalist hands. Marx and Engels were aware of the importance of banks, and in the *Communist Manifesto,* among the ten measures to be adopted by the proletarian Revolution, they foresaw the "centralization of credit in the hands of the state by means of a national bank with state capital and an exclusive monopoly." [2] Marx and Engels also pointed out that the Paris Commune erred by not taking over the Bank of France and using it in benefit of the Revolution.

And Lenin, on the eve of the October Revolution, said the following regarding the decisive role of banks:

> *Without big banks socialism would be impossible . . .* The big banks *are* the "state apparatus" which we *need* to bring about socialism, and which we *take ready-made* from capitalism; our task here is merely to *lop off* what *capitalistically mutilates* this excellent apparatus, to make it *even bigger,* even more democratic, even more comprehensive. Quantity will be transformed into quality. A single State Bank, the biggest of the big, with branches in every rural district, in every factory, will constitute as much as nine-tenths of the *socialist* apparatus. This will be country-wide *book-keeping,* country-wide *accounting* of the production and distribution of goods, this will be, so to speak, something in the nature of the *skeleton* of socialist society.[3]

The Bolsheviks took power, of course, and preceded to nationalize all the banks. The State bank of the U.S.S.R. (Gosbank) was established in 1921 when the NEP [New Economic Policy] was first put into effect following the stage of war communism (1918–20) during which monetary operations had been minimized. For a number of years, several investment banks in the U.S.S.R. specialized according to industrial branches (agriculture, industry, housing construction, local economies). But in 1959 they were consolidated into a single investment bank. In addition, the U.S.S.R. has a foreign trade bank that performs all international operations and a system of savings banks for popular savings.

After the fascist defeat in World War II, the working class triumphed in several European countries. Socialist regimes were established which, among other things, took the measure of nationalizing banks. The structure of banking is now similar in all of them:

a. A central state bank which performs the operations of currency issue, control of monetary circulation, transfer payments, and credits.

b. One or more investment banks in which funds allocated to capital investment in the State budget are deposited and which grant long-term credits for investments.

c. An international operations bank which exercises a monopoly over foreign exchange and performs foreign trade operations.

d. A system of savings banks in which the people's savings are deposited.

It should be noted that although these different banking institutions have been organized in almost all socialist countries, the tendency is toward their concentration in a single bank ("a single State bank, the biggest of the big"). This not only facilitates working with enterprises but also reduces the size of the bureaucracy. The possibility that one enterprise might receive credit for operating expenses at the central bank, investment credit at the investment bank, and at the same time conduct foreign exchange operations through the foreign trade bank, is thus eliminated. In Czechoslovakia, the investment bank merged with the state bank in 1959. In the Soviet Union, the savings banks have just been merged into the Gosbank.

By means of Law 930, the Cuban revolutionary government, on February 23, 1961, created a single state bank embracing the operations of central, investment, international operations, and public savings banks.

The Economic Functions of Socialist Banking

The socialist banking system is not governed by the profit motive, but by the country's economic development. The operations performed by socialist banks, including the National Bank of Cuba, can be summarized as follows:

1. To regulate monetary circulation.
2. To serve as the country's center of settlements and payments.
3. To concede credits.
4. To finance investments.

5. To administer foreign exchange and international operations.
6. To assure the organization of public savings.
7. To perform an economic control function.[4]

Regulating Monetary Circulation

Payments in cash are made primarily for wages, salaries, and social income (scholarships, pensions, retirement benefits). The public spends part of this income on purchases of goods and services (shops, restaurants, transportation, movies, etc.) and on payments of taxes and contributions; it deposits another part in the bank, and the rest remains in circulation. (Individual savings not deposited in the bank are considered to be money in circulation.) Guided by the directives of the economic plan and its own previous experience, the bank prepares an annual *monetary circulation plan* to establish a balance between revenue and expenditure, or, in other words, cash receipts and outlays during the year. The difference between cash receipts and outlays is used as the basis for forecasting fluctuations in the circulating medium during the year. If the public receives much more income than it can reasonably spend on goods and services plus payment of taxes and contributions, even discounting what it saves and deposits in the bank, then the bank's cash outlays (the public's income) will be larger than its receipts (the public's expenditures), and there will be an increase in the quantity of money in circulation. The opposite would occur were there equilibrium between the public's income and the goods and services placed at its disposal. This would bring about a reduction in the circulating medium.

By regulating cash flow and money in circulation, the bank fulfills one of its basic tasks: to assure the steady strengthening of monetary stability and the purchasing power of the monetary unit. To assure monetary stability in a socialist economy implies a systematic increase in production and a steady growth in the quantity of goods placed in circulation.

Changes in the circulating medium are a sensitive indicator of the national economy's development and problems. In order to maintain greater vigilance over such changes, the bank formulates quarterly monetary-circulation plans.

The National Bank of Cuba began to formulate such plans in 1962. The degree of adherence to plans yields important data for the analytical work that the bank has begun to perform.

Serving as the Country's Center of Settlements and Payments

The temporarily free resources of enterprises are deposited in the bank. Enterprises do not effect cash payments among themselves but instead make payments through transfer from one bank account to another.

In Cuba, this system is regulated by Law 1007. The buyer, upon receipt of the invoice and transfer sent to him by the seller, presents a payment order at his banking agency. His account is debited, and a transfer is sent to the seller's banking agency for credit to the seller's account.

Experience has shown that in many cases the buyer has neither initiative nor concern for paying. Consequently, we are looking into an inverse system by which the initiative would reside with the party interested in collecting payment. The seller would present a collection order at his agency which would relay it to the buyer's agency. The buyer's account would be debited and the seller's credited.

This system of payments by adjustment or compensation permits the bank to restrict the volume of money in circulation and to maintain better control over the financial discipline of enterprises.

Credit Concessions

Credit is a typical banking function that does not disappear during the building of socialism. Rather, it serves as a flexible means for helping to assure the proportional and harmonious development of the economy, and the fulfillment of plans.

Just as with the circulation of money, the bank draws up a *credit plan* in the form of a financial balance sheet. The financial resources needed for meeting the plan have several origins: the bank's own resources (capital and reserves); deposits in the accounts of enterprises and agencies; temporarily free popular savings accounts; current resources of the State budget and eventually its accumulated surplus. Such resources are used to provide credits to State enterprises, private contractors, and if need be, the public. Credits may even go to cover State budget deficits. The latter credits have no material backing but are unavoidable until the State budget achieves an operational balance. The financial resources used for this type of credit are usually inordinate issues of money or international credits—which will eventually place a strain on the national economy.

Socialist bank credit must satisfy five conditions: It must be planned (authorized within the plan); direct (the bank authorizes it directly to enterprises because commercial credit among enterprises is prohibited); materially guaranteed (backed by raw materials, goods in process, fuel, growing crops, etc.); reimbursable over a fixed term; and allocated to a specific use.

The objective need for bank credit derives from the irregular evolution of the production and circulation processes in enterprises—seasonal fluctuations, for example. Enterprises must have recourse to funds to cover temporary needs. But fund shortages tend to dovetail with enterprise surpluses—together with private savings—deposited at the bank. The bridge uniting the source of funds with the needs for funds, which brings surplus resources at one point into use at another, is called bank credit.

The credit plan is closely linked to the monetary circulation plan (part of the credits will be taken out in cash), and to the economy's other financial plans, especially the State budget.

Credits granted by the National Bank of Cuba have not always satisfied the principles of socialist credit. They have, however, filled a very important role in national economic development. State agricultural enterprises and private peasants have made considerable use of these credits to improve and develop agricultural and livestock production. The bank authorizes such credits in line with the revolutionary government's economic policy with regard to agricultural development and the worker-peasant alliance. Furthermore, the bank grants credits to enterprises dealing in foreign trade. Certain elements of the system of economic autonomy are employed in the administration of enterprises under the jurisdiction of INRA [National Institute of Agrarian Reform] and MINCEX [Ministry of Foreign Trade]. The system is not used in any other enterprise, however. In the future, the bank will strive to perfect the use of socialist credit principles.

Investment Financing

The financing and control of investment is another of the bank's important functions. Several socialist countries have banks specializing in this function alone.

Investment is a category of the economic plan, and encompasses such areas as construction; acquisition and installation of machinery and equipment; and agricultural investment—pasture improvement, crop development, basic livestock purchases, etc. It accounts for a substantial part of State-budget expenditures. In 1962, state expenditure on investment rose to 500 million pesos, which represents a third of that year's total budgetary expenditures.

We can offer several observations based on the bank's experience in this field. First, it is not infrequent that financial plans calling for more resources than are realistically available for investment are nonetheless approved. Second, investments are sometimes made in projects that have not received prior approval. Third, financial resources are sometimes dispersed among too many projects. Few projects, in this case, possess sufficient funds for start-up.

The National Bank of Cuba has achieved only meager results

in its attempts to solve these problems, because we have limited ourselves to allocating funds among investors and to recording actual expenditures. This year, however, we intend to decentralize investment control by taking it to the agency level. Agency personnel can then work directly with enterprises making investments as well as with those in charge of construction and equipment installation. Thus, in this stage, we will be able to more effectively sway investment toward building the foundations for large-scale agricultural production and socialist industrialization.

Administration of Foreign Exchange and International Transactions

Under socialism, the State has a monopoly on foreign trade excercised through the several enterprises engaged in that activity. The bank also administers the foreign exchange needed for transactions with foreign countries. The Juceplan formulates the General Foreign Exchange Plan, which covers commercial and noncommercial transactions as well as capital transfers. The Bank plays a direct part in this plan by drawing up the projects that have to do with noncommercial transactions and capital transfers.

The bank performs all settlement and payment operations with both socialist and capitalist foreign countries, and maintains relations with a number of banks all over the world.

Moreover, the bank grants credits to enterprises dealing in foreign trade, assuring that they maintain a normal inventory turnover, comply with their payment and collection obligations, repay their loans, and make their regular contributions to the budget.

The bank carries a control of credits with other countries, and makes amortization and interest payments. It also participates in the negotiations of trade agreements and international payments.

There has been some progress toward improving foreign

settlements and payments. On the other hand, a great deal remains to be done with regard to foreign-exchange administration and bank participation in preparing and carrying out the Foreign Exchange Plan.

Organization of Public Savings

Such organization depends on the state of relations between the banking system and the broad masses of the people. Good public relations facilitate the attraction of savings. Money saved leaves circulation, which helps to restore equilibrium between the stock of commodities and the people's buying power. This is particularly important vis-à-vis present conditions in Cuba. In addition, private savings are one of the bank's chief sources of credit funds for the financing of national economic development.

For the last several years, the National Bank of Cuba, in cooperation with the CTC(R) [Confederation of Revolutionary Cuban Workers], the CDR [Committees for the Defense of the Revolution], and other mass organizations, has promoted a fairly successful popular savings campaign. The principal sponsor of this campaign was our departed comrade Raul Cepero Bonilla, ex-president of the bank. By Resolution 933 on December 30, 1961, he created the jobs of "savings manager"—a specialized bank employee at agency level—and a "person responsible for savings"—a worker chosen by his comrades at labor headquarters to collect voluntary deposits from workers so that they do not have to present themselves personally at bank agencies. At present, some ten thousand of the latter collect deposits—without remuneration—in labor headquarters all over the country.

By December 31, 1961, after broadening the popular savings campaign substantially, total private savings had reached $318 million. By December 31, 1962, these savings had risen to $582 million, and by December 31, 1963, to $718 million. Or, in other words, a total increase of 2.26 times in the past two years.

An immediate move to expand and improve service to savings account holders will be to utilize post offices wherever facilities permit.

Economic Control by the Bank

Economic control by the bank is essential to its performance of all the above roles.

The several phases or categories of an enterprise's production process (supplies, production, costs, wages, sales, investments), as well as the results of its economic performance (profit or loss), are commonly expressed in *monetary form.* The use of this common measure or standard allows us to follow the results of an enterprise's economic performance as well as the evolution of its production process. This has come to be known as *control by the monetary unit* (peso, rouble, sloty, crown, etc.). An enterprise may exercise such control over itself or over another enterprise, or the bank may exercise it over an enterprise. The bank's *control by the peso* (applying the expression to Cuba) is known as economic control by the bank.

What does economic control by the bank mean, and how is it performed? In a planned economy, enterprise plans are closely linked. Mistakes or failures to comply in one case will directly reflect in others. It is therefore necessary to maintain rigid control over the production and circulation activities of enterprises.

In order to facilitate the bank's "control by the peso," enterprises are forbidden to conduct credit transactions among themselves. They must resort to bank credit to cover contingency requirements. All payments, except for very small ones, must be made through the system of adjustments or compensations, rather than in cash. Enterprises must deposit daily receipts at the banking agencies in which their accounts are located. Each enterprise must deal at one, and only one, banking agency.

The bank has to exercise a particularly important control over wage funds. An increase in the wage fund is justified only if commensurate with a substantial increase in production.

The bank controls the revenue and expense accounts of enterprises financed through the State budget. No more than the planned amount can be received unless justified by special circumstances. No more than the approved amount can be spent, whether on wages or other operating expenses.

The bank must also control the use of investment funds, assuring that only projected works are started up; that actual investment costs equate with planned costs; and that, if begun, works are completed and do not deteriorate.

The financial activities of an enterprise are the best thermometer by which to appraise its performance; and the banking system that manages the enterprise's funds is the entity best qualified—objective, broadly branched out, and experienced—for appraising such activities.

It should be pointed out that economic control by the bank, "control by the peso," must be strict but not exaggerated. The purpose is not to manage the enterprise but to help it. The purpose is not to create a superstructure of the production unit but to carry a control of the unit's performance as gauged by its financial results. One must be particularly careful about proliferation of controls and creation of parallel apparatus in the planning, production, or finance areas. Imagine a factory with more inspectors inspecting than workers producing.

Economic control by the bank in Cuba should be carried out under specific conditions, because there are, in fact, two systems for financing state enterprises.

Use of the Two Finance Systems in Cuba

The war communism period in the Soviet Union (1918–20) ended in 1921 with the establishment of the NEP. At that time, a type of enterprise management system known as *"khozyaistventnyi raschot"* or in short *"khozraschot"* was instituted—in Cuba, the system known as *economic autonomy*. (In our opinion, "economic autonomy" better suggests the essential meaning of *"khozraschot"* than do "auto-financing," "financial self-management" or "economic calculus," which are other terms used in Cuba.)

The basic principles of this system are still theoretically and practically valid in the U.S.S.R. at present. There is, in fact, a tendency toward broadening and intensifying the system's use. Almost all socialist countries have now accepted these principles. The form and degree in which they are used depends on special conditions in each country and on the amount of effort given to developing their use. In Cuba, several aspects of economic autonomy are being implemented in the INRA [National Institute of Agrarian Reform] and MINCEX [Ministry of Foreign Trade] enterprises.

The principles of economic autonomy as a method for managing socialist enterprises may be outlined as follows:

a. Planned performance, that is, to conform to the broad lines of the State economic plan.

b. Relative economic independence in managing resources and commensurate responsibility for using, conserving, and developing such resources.

c. Direct relations and equal status with other enterprises with regard to product exchange.

d. Profitability: monetary measurement of costs and revenues, covering costs with revenues, and in addition obtaining a profit (through the excess of revenues over costs).

e. Use of bank credit to cover any deficiencies in the enterprise's own (normed) financial resources.

f. Use of material and moral incentives, both individual and collective.

In our country, we have been developing a system of financial management known as the *budgetary finance system.* Its historical origin dates back to the close of 1960 when the then Department of Industrialization of INRA had a number of confiscated or nationalized enterprises under its jurisdiction, many of which lacked operating funds or administrative teams. It was decided to centralize the bank accounts of all these enterprises, thus creating a "centralized fund" to which all revenues would be credited and against which all costs would be charged.

Later, this fund was incorporated into the State budget. Concomitantly, the consolidated enterprises were organized and began to operate in the same fashion as the old enterprises of the Department of Industrialization of INRA: All revenues were credited to the budget and all costs were charged against the budget.

The following are the chief characteristics of the budgetary finance system.

a. Enterprises receive their cost fund allocations for a given period, let us say a quarter, *before* producing revenues and regardless of their origin.

b. Moral incentives, complemented by material incentives, are used to provide the main impetus to production.

c. Cost controls are employed.

d. Because they are tied to the national budget by the sum total of their receipts and outlays, enterprises never use bank credit in a direct way.

In our opinion, the best finance system in Cuba's present stage of development is economic autonomy. We believe that this system provides a better means for achieving two essential goals: financial discipline and economic control.

(We limit ourselves in this article to these two aspects of the problem. The use of economic autonomy to increase profits on production, to improve product mix and quality, to improve relations between buyers and sellers, etc., deserves special study.)

As to *financial discipline,* one should point out the relationship between payments and collections that take place among budgetary enterprises. Apparently, some of these enterprises lack incentive to collect payment for the goods and services they provide. Their costs are already covered, so failure to receive payment only means that they might have to stop contributing to the budget. If they were compelled to collect payment on accounts in order to pay wages, the situation would be different.

This appraisal is based on bank records of payment defaults among enterprises (Law 1007). The budgetary enterprises account for thousands of such violations amounting to millions of pesos weekly (an average of 20 thousand infractions per week for a value of $20 million). One could argue that the economically autonomous enterprises commit violations as well, and we might even point out that since Law 1007 was put into effect, the INRA enterprises have maintained an embarrassing first place as regards number and value of infractions. But the INRA enterprises have, in fact, never really operated as economically autonomous enterprises.

As to *economic control,* it must be said that the system of control over budgetary enterprises—"cost control"—is necessary and useful; but this is an *a posteriori* control requiring a great deal of administrative work in consolidating and studying balances. Such "cost control"—which must be done—cannot, we believe, substitute for general economic control. First, it cannot substitute for the enterprise's self-control "by the peso" in the system of economic autonomy. This form of economic control is premised on the enterprise's obligation to cover costs with receipts and on making use of the material interest of the enterprise's workers as a group. Second, "cost control" cannot substitute for the buyer's "control by the peso" of the supplier's performance. Third, "cost control" cannot substitute for economic control by the bank, a special kind of "control by the peso" that takes account of total financial results rather than costs alone. It also scrutinizes net income, which is a socialist economy's principal source of finance.

The bank is the agency most competent to carry out "control by the peso." The bank is an objective body operating at arm's length from the special interests of enterprises. It has branches throughout the country and is aware of the performance of enterprises that keep accounts in its agencies. The National Bank of Cuba has a number of technicians able to perform this kind of economic control and is preparing to train the economists at its central offices, regional offices, and agencies to assure that the work is done properly. It would be a mistake, in our opinion, to fail to use the "State apparatus that we *need* to bring about socialism and that we *take ready-made* from capitalism."

But is it true that bank credit is not used in the budgetary finance system? Let us see. In 1961, 1962, and 1963, the State budget was in deficit. During the same three years, the budgetary enterprises stopped contributing substantial amounts to the budget or, in other words, failed to achieve planned net income. This was a basic reason for the budget deficits. What really happened was that the bank financed such deficits by automatically granting credits in equal amounts.

But even assuming that all the budgetary enterprises were profitable and that they contributed to the budget according to plan, what happens when the bank makes funds available that have not been received? Well, the bank is simply granting credits indirectly.

In the Cuban economy, monetary resources for this type of credit to the treasury are not yet available. Thus, inflationary pressures are produced and the need for foreign credit increases.

In summary, bank credit, as an economic category within the State sector of the economy, does not disappear. It has only been disguised. But in the process it has lost its relationship to production and circulation, and its possibilities for economic control have diminished in promise.

Now, we wish to stress one point. The system of economic autonomy offers optimal conditions for exercise of economic control by the bank. But such control can also be exercised, though less flexibly, under the budgetary system. Control of collections and payments, use of wage funds, limited fund or petty cash transactions, and physical inspection of factories are important tasks in the budgetary enterprise area that the bank can and must perform.

The revolutionary government has decided, for the moment, to employ both of these financial systems. The bank's obligation, therefore, is to provide the best service and control possible in both systems.

The Bank's Immediate Tasks

Probably no other socialist country has a central bank with a greater number of functions than the National Bank of Cuba. In

Cuba there are no separate banks for investment or foreign trade, nor a system of public savings banks. All banking functions are performed by our 10,000 comrades through the central offices, the 6 regional offices and the 257 agencies of the National Bank of Cuba. We have agencies located throughout the country, from Las Martinas to Baracoa, from Nueva Gerona to Varadero. We conduct foreign-trade exchange operations with both socialist and capitalist countries through our agents in various parts of the world (Moscow, Montevideo, London, Montreal, Paris, Cairo, Mexico, Prague, Zurich, Peking, etc.).

Our Bank is currently completing the job of rationalizing its personnel structure. We have followed the mass line by talking directly with all the workers. Surplus personnel are being located in other agencies and enterprises with no reduction in wages. We have instituted a 40-hour week. With our bureaucratic burden reduced, we can proceed on to greater accomplishments. Our immediate tasks for 1964, the "Year of Economy," might be summarized in the following ten points:

1. To develop economic control over enterprises regulated under both finance systems.

2. To improve the financing and control of investment by delegating the latter function to bank agencies.

3. To improve the planning and supervision of monetary circulation. To scrutinize the evolution of private income, especially wages and salaries, acting to assure equilibrium between consumer buying power and the stock of commodities and services; and to this end, to broaden the popular savings campaign.

4. To improve our work in the field of international operations, making it a more technical job, establishing correspondence with banks in countries with which we have increased our trade.

5. To implement the new system of payment by account adjustment, placing the burden of collection on suppliers. To scrutinize the development of financial discipline.

6. To improve banking services to both enterprises and the public. Open new agencies in regions lacking such services. In-

crease the present service schedule from four to five hours per day.

7. To improve economic and financial analysis in order to define and resolve economic problems at the enterprise, sectoral, and national levels.

8. To bring about the best possible coordination between Juceplan and the treasury in the area of financial planning, with particular reference to the monetary circulation and credit and foreign exchange plans as well as the State budget.

9. To develop the democratic centralist work method by tightening relations among the bank's three levels (central office, regional offices, and agencies).

10. In order to better realize this task, to raise the technical level of bank personnel, and to promote the courses now being developed in the "Raul Cepero Bonilla" School of Banking.

NOTES

1. V. I. Lenin, "Imperialism: The Highest Stage of Capitalism," [Translator's source: *Selected Works* (New York, International Publishers, 1967), Vol.I.]
2. Karl Marx and Friedrich Engels, *Manifesto of the Communist Party*. [Translator's source: *Great Books of the Western World* (Chicago, Encyclopedia Britannica, c. 1952), p. 429.]
3. V. I. Lenin, "Can the Bolsheviks Maintain State Power." [Translator's source: *Selected Works, op. cit.,* Vol. II, p. 398.]
4. K. Podlaha, "El papel del Sistema Bancario para asegurar y controlar el cumplimiento del Plan de Desarrollo de la Economía Nacional," Juceplan publication (Havana, 1961).

14

Banking, Credit, and Socialism

ERNESTO CHE GUEVARA

THE PREVIOUS ISSUE of this magazine [*Cuba Socialista*] carried an article in which comrade Marcelo Fernández, president of the National Bank, analyzes the bank's functions, summarizes historical issues, and passes judgment on the financial systems used in Cuba [page 277]. The article coincides with various public statements by bank administrators as well as other writings that attempt to definitively establish the bank's position. We do not agree with some of the functions they ascribe to the bank during the period of transition, and even less with their opinion regarding the budgetary finance system. We feel that the statements of the bank's president should not go unanswered and wish therefore, to state our own position on the issues.

Regarding the role of banks in the creation of bank notes, Fernández states [page 278]:

> The rapid development of commercial relations and the scarcity of precious metals for coin manufacture led to the appearance of *bank notes*. A bank note is an interest-free security issued by the central bank, expressed in a given amount of money, and made out to the bearer. The first

---

SOURCE: "La banca, el crédito y el socialismo," *Cuba Socialista,* Año IV, Marzo 1964, pp. 23–41.

bank note was issued by the Swedish Bank of Issue, created in 1658.

While recognizing the article's informative nature, we will nonetheless attempt to see why this phenomenon would occur. Marx writes:

> Finally, some one may ask why gold is capable of being replaced by tokens that have no value? But, as we have already seen, it is capable of being so replaced only in so far as it functions exclusively as coin, or as the circulating medium, and as nothing else. Now, money has other functions besides this one, and the isolated function of serving as the mere circulating medium is not necessarily the only one attached to gold coin, although this is the case with those abraded coins that continue to circulate. Each piece of money is a mere coin, or means of circulation, only so long as it actually circulates. But this is just the case with that minimum mass of gold, which is capable of being replaced by paper money. That mass remains constantly within the sphere of circulation, continually functions as a circulating medium, and exists exclusively for that purpose. Its movement, therefore, represents nothing but continued alternation of the inverse phases of the metamorphosis C-M-C, phases in which commodities confront their value-forms, only to disappear again immediately. The independent existence of the exchange value of a commodity is immediately replaced by another commodity. Hence, in this process which continually makes money pass from hand to hand, the mere symbolical existence of money suffices. Its functional existence absorbs, so to say, its material existence. Being a transient and objective reflex of the prices of commodities, it serves only as a symbol of itself, and is therefore capable of being replaced by a token. One thing is, however, requisite: this token must have an objective social validity of its own, and this the paper symbol acquires by its forced currency. This compulsory action of the State can take effect only within that inner

> sphere of circulation which is co-terminous with the territories of the community, but it is also only within that sphere that money completely responds to its function of being the circulating medium, or becomes coin.[1]

It is important to point out, for subsequent purposes, that money reflects the relationships of production: It cannot exist in other than a mercantile society. We may also say that a bank cannot exist without money and, therefore, that bank's existence is contingent upon mercantile relationships of production, whatever high form they may assume.

The article's author continues by quoting several paragraphs from Lenin in order to demonstrate that imperialism is a product of finance capital, that is, the fusion of industrial and banking capital. He again brings up the problem of the chicken or the egg. Does one kind of capital predominate in this relationship? If so, which one? Or are they both of equal power?

Lenin sets forth the following economic conditions for imperialism:

> 1. The concentration of production and capital developed to such a high stage that it created monopolies which played a decisive role in economic life.
> 2. The merging of bank capital with industrial capital, and the creation, on the basis of this "finance capital," of a "financial oligarchy."
> 3. The export of capital, which has become extremely important as distinguished from the export of commodities.
> 4. The formation of international capitalist monopolies which share the world among themselves.
> 5. The territorial division of the whole world among the greatest capitalist powers is completed.
>
> Imperialism is capitalism in that stage of development in which the dominance of monopolies and finance capital has established itself; in which the export of capital has acquired pronounced importance; in which the division of the world among the international trusts has begun; in

> which the division of all territories of the globe among the great capitalist powers has been completed.[2]

Observe that the final stage is considered to be the dividing up of the world and then, as a corollary explained elsewhere, the use of force, or, in other words, war. Why did the monopolies divide up the world? The answer is simple: to obtain sources of raw materials for their industries. That is to say, the objective needs of production bring about, in the developed capitalist system, the functions of capitalists that engender imperialism; or, what is the same thing, industrial capital is the generator of finance capital, and controls it either directly or indirectly. To believe otherwise would be to fall into the fetishism that Marx attacks with respect to bourgeois analysis of the capitalist system. Lenin quotes the following:

> The banking system, Marx wrote half a century ago in *Capital,* "presents indeed the form of common bookkeeping and distribution of means of production on a social scale, but only the form." [3]

The North American economist Victor Perlo has dedicated huge volumes to the analysis of North American monopolies, always finding large branches of production in the midst of these groups. Analysis of their relative development during the last several years demonstrates that the most rapidly growing monopolies are those that bring together the most advanced branches of technology. The DuPont chemical group, the Mellon aluminum group, and the Rockefeller petroleum group, for example, show a relative growth of between 325 and 385 per cent. In contrast, the Kuhn Loeb railroad group shows a slight decline, and the Boston light industry group a growth of only 31 per cent, which clearly reveals an interconnection among production, monopolies, and luck in this competition among wolves.

Lenin, in the article cited by Marcelo Fernández (which was written before the assumption of power) talks of banks as great factors of "accounting and control." He gives the impression that he is seeking the consolidation of the entire financial apparatus so that it might fulfill its primary function, already scored by Marx, of social accounting.

The monopoly bank is, in fact, its own finance ministry in the duality of a State within a State operating at this stage. In periods of building the socialist society, all the concepts that assure the bank's political life change, and another way to use its experience must be found. The centralization that Marcelo seeks can be obtained by making the Ministry of the Treasury the supreme "accounting and control" apparatus of the entire State.

In the following paragraph, Marx stresses the political aspect of capitalist banking:

> At their birth the great banks, decorated with national titles, were only associations of private speculators, who placed themselves by the side of governments, and, thanks to the privileges they received, were in a position to advance money to the state. Hence the accumulation of the national debt has no more infallible measure than the successive rise in the stock of these banks, whose full development dates from the founding of the Bank of England in 1694. The Bank of England began with lending its money to the Government at 8%; at the same time it was empowered by Parliament to coin money out of the same capital, by lending it again to the public in form of banknotes. It was allowed to use these notes for discounting bills, making advances on commodities, and for buying precious metals. It was not long ere this credit-money, made by the bank itself, became the coin in which the Bank of England made its loans to the state, and paid, on account of the state, the interest on the public debt. It was not enough that the bank gave with one hand and took back more with the other; it remained, even while receiving, the eternal creditor of the nation down to the last shilling advanced. Gradually it became inevitably the receptacle of the metallic hoard of the country, and the centre of gravity of all commercial credit. What effect was produced

> on their contemporaries by the sudden uprising of this brood of bankocrats, financiers, bondholders, brokers, stock-jobbers, etc., is proved by the writings of that time, for instance, by Bolingbroke's.[4]

Marcelo Fernández lists seven economic functions of socialist banking. Of these, those that are expressed in point (1), regulation of monetary circulation, and (2), center of the country's settlements and payments, do not basically contradict our way of thinking, except, perhaps, as regards the degree of enterprise autonomy with respect to the maximum financial authority, which is the Treasury Ministry, and to the doubt expressed about the bank's real potential for "regulating" monetary circulation. But this is not the time to argue these points.

As to point (3), credit concession's, the article says [page 283]:

> Credit is a typical banking function that does not disappear during the building of socialism. Rather, it serves as a flexible means for helping to assure the proportional and harmonious development of the economy, and the fulfillment of plans.

Without going into the credit system's origin as a response to usury, we will nevertheless quote a few paragraphs from Marx regarding the issue:

> But it should always be borne in mind that, in the first place, money—in the form of precious metal—remains the foundation from which the credit system, by its very nature, can *never* detach itself. Secondly, that the credit system presupposes the monopoly of social means of production by private persons (in the form of capital and landed property), that it is itself, on the one hand, *an immanent form of the capitalist mode of production,* and on the other, a driving force in its development to its highest and ultimate form.
>
> The banking system, so far as its formal organization and centralization is concerned, is *the most artificial and*

most developed product turned out by the capitalist mode of production, a fact already expressed in 1697 in *Some Thoughts of the Interests of England.* This accounts for the immense power of an institution such as the Bank of England over commerce and industry, although their actual movements remain completely beyond its province and is passive toward them. The banking system possesses indeed the form of universal book-keeping and distribution of means of production on a social scale, but solely the form. We have seen that the average profit of the individual capitalist, or of every individual capital, is determined not by the surplus-labor appropriated at first hand by each capital, but by the quantity of total surplus-labor appropriated by the total capital, from which each individual capital receives its dividend only proportional to its aliquot part of the total capital. This social character of capital is first promoted and wholly realized through the full development of the credit and banking system. On the other hand this goes farther. It places all the available and even potential capital of society that is not already actively employed at the disposal of the industrial and commercial capitalists so that neither the lenders nor users of this capital are its real owners or producers. It thus does way with the private character of capital and thus contains in itself, but only in itself, the abolition of capital itself. By means of the banking system the distribution of capital as a special business, a social function, is taken out of the hands of the private capitalists and usurers. But at the same time, banking and credit thus become the most potent means of driving capitalist production beyond its own limits, and one of the most effective vehicles of crises and swindle.

The banking system shows, furthermore, by substituting various forms of circulating credit in place of money, that money is in reality nothing but a particular expression of the social character of labor and its products, which, however, as antithetical to the basis of private production, must always appear in the last analysis as a thing, a special commodity, alongside other commodities.

Finally, there is no doubt that the credit system will serve as a powerful lever during the transition from the capitalist mode of production to the mode of production of associates labor; but only as one element in connection with other great organic revolutions of the mode of production itself. On the other hand, the illusions concerning the miraculous power of the credit and banking system, in the socialist sense, arise from a complete lack of familiarity with the capitalist mode of production and the credit system as one of its forms. *As soon as the means of production cease being transformed into capital (which also includes the abolition of private property in land), credit as such no longer has any meaning.* This, incidentally, was even understood by the followers of Saint-Simon. On the other hand, as long as the capitalist mode of production continues to exist, interest-bearing capital, as one of its forms, also continues to exist and constitutes in fact the basis of its credit system. Only that sensational writer, Proudhon, who wanted to perpetuate commodity-production and abolish money,* was capable of dreaming up the monstrous *crédit gratuit,* the ostensible realization of the pious wish of the petty-bourgeois estate.[5]

We would note that the article fails to mention here the interest charged state enterprises for money facilitated in the form of bank loans. If Marx proved, as we have seen, that the abolition of private property destroys the meaning of credit as such, what can one say about interest?

Marx says:

The relations of capital assume their most externalized and most fetish-like form in interest-bearing capital. We have here M-M', money creating more money, self-expanding value, without the process that effectuates these two extremes. In merchants' capital, M-C-M', there is at least the

* Karl Marx, *Misere de la Philosophie,* Bruxelles et Paris, 1847.—Karl Marx, *Zur Kritik der* politischen Oeknomie, S. 64. (Marx's note.)

> general form of the capitalistic movement, although it confines itself solely to the sphere of circulation, so that profit appears merely as profit derived from alienation; but it is at least seen to be the product of a social *relation,* not the product of a mere *thing*. The form of merchant's capital at least presents a process, a unity of opposing phases, a movement that breaks up into opposite actions—the purchase and the sale of commodities. This is obliterated in M-M', the form of interest-bearing capital.[6]

At the beginning of the article, still dealing with private banking, interest is mentioned as follows [page 000]:

> This is *bank credit.* Bank credit can be short- or long-term and always earns an interest, which is the bank's principal source of revenue.

If this situation is currently valid—and since interest is not technically an enterprise cost factor but a deduction of the worker's surplus labor for the society that should constitute a national budget receipt—is not interest in fact used to finance the operating expenses of the banking apparatus?

To criticize the budget deficit without analyzing it and to state that the use of "international credits . . . will eventually place a strain on the national economy," is to apply the fetishist concept of classical economics.

As regards (4), investment financing, we feel that Fernández becomes involved in formal and ficticious aspects of the matter, or what is the same thing, in the fetishism that conceals the true relationships of production.

This function would exist only if the bank financed investment using its own resources, which, of course, would be absurd in a socialist economy. What the bank does is to allocate the resources of the national budget in the amounts established by the investment plan.

This aspect of financing and control of investment—particularly with respect to construction—as well as the bank credit system and interest, greatly differentiate the system called economic autonomy in this article from that of budgetary financing. The financing and control of investment will be the subject of an article by comrade Alvarez Rom [page 000] because the theme's importance and comprehensiveness require that it be treated separately. But we will at least discuss the basic principles of the procedure established by the Treasury Ministry.

The Treasury Ministry concludes that all the confusion surrounding investment control owes to a pervading mercantile concept. We still regard the bank as a representative of monopoly—its Cerberus—which scrutinizes every investment it makes.

In a budgetary regime, with properly functioning controls, there is no reason for the bank to be involved in investment decisions. There are political and economic matters (Juceplan). The bank should not concern itself with physical control of investment—this would require the creation of a huge and meaningless apparatus. It is the investment entity directly involved that should be so concerned. Financial control can be exercised by the Treasury Ministry, which is responsible for the State budget. This is the only place to which the surplus product ought to accrue if it is to be effectively employed. The bank should busy itself with scrutinizing fund withdrawals, which is its specific function. There is no need to comment on point (5), administration of foreign exchange and international operations.

In point (6), organization of public savings, the author is carried away by the idea of publicity and propaganda. We do not oppose this and, moreover, defend the use of clear language to explain economic mechanisms. But clarity should not be at odds with the facts. This, however, is exactly what happens [page 000]:

> Such organization depends on the state of relations between the banking system and the broad masses of the people. Good public relations facilitate the attraction of savings. Money saved leaves circulation, which helps to restore equilibrium between the stock of commodities and the people's buying power. This is particularly important vis-à-vis present conditions in Cuba. In addition, private

savings are one of the bank's chief sources of credit funds for the financing of national economic development.

Money saved momentarily leaves circulation. This source of funds can be employed in an economic sense only when used to finance private activity through bank loans. It is absurd to think, in a socialist economy, that interest paid to savers is offset by interest charged to State enterprises.

It would have been much more interesting and useful to discuss the composition and cost of savings, what motivates savings at each income scale, and what economic measures might actually be taken to help "restore equilibrium between the stock of commodities and the people's buying power."

As to the function of providing credit "for the financing of national economic development," we completely disagree.

Finally, point (7), economic control by the bank, falls flat in the controversy raised by Fernández in the section entitled, "Use of the Two Finance Systems in Cuba."

The author again becomes involved with determining the exact meaning of the Russian term that has been the subject of a number of arguments. He manages to come up with a new meaning, which had already appeared in the works of other bank analysts. In our opinion, his new phrase is inappropriate. The statement that "*khozraschot*" is a system of enterprise administration known in Cuba as economic autonomy, and that among the principles of economic autonomy are "relative economic independence" and "planned performance, that is, to conform to the broad lines of the State economic plan," leads us to believe at best that the author has failed to interpret correctly.

In absolute form, the term economic autonomy, together with relative economic independence as one of its principles, is a grammatical construction the content of which we do not begin to comprehend—nor does Fernández furnish any clarification.

Planned performance is not equivalent to conforming to the broad lines of the State economic plan and so merits no consideration.

His method of portraying the two systems of finance does not permit easy comparison. This, however, is understandable, because there is not a great deal of literature on the subject (I refer the reader to number 5 of *Nuestra Industria Economica* where I attempt to systematize the analysis [page 291]). Nonetheless, we believe that he could be more objective in his analysis of the budgetary finance system. This system is sanctioned by the Council of Ministers, and is not, therefore, just someone's idle whim but a recognized fact.

Now for point (a) [page 291]: "Enterprises receive their cost fund allocations for a given period, let us say a quarter, *before* producing revenues and regardless of their origin."

What enterprises receive are not allocations of funds in the bank but fund availabilities equivalent to authorizations for spending in the amounts established by the approved financial plan. These are recorded by the bank on separate accounts for wages and other costs. Such segregation is made to facilitate control of the wage fund. This is not possible under the system of financial self-management presently employed in Cuba. In a recent televised statement, the bank's president proposed a control formula for the wage account that involves discussion of each case at the production-level. This would create serious administrative problems if implemented before its probable consequences were thoroughly analyzed. (It should be recalled that wages are part of the production unit's turnover funds.)

There is an assumption here that direct relations with the bank would assure, first, the analysis of all factors of production, and, second, the impossibility of evading the bank's surveillance. But the bank's relations with self-managing entities are proof positive that this is an illusion under prevailing conditions in Cuba.

In 1931, Stalin made the following observation:

> But this is not all. To this must be added the fact that owing to inefficiency the principles of business accounting are not being applied in a large number of our factories and business organizations. It is a fact that a number of enterprises and business organizations have long ceased to keep proper

> accounts, to calculate, to draw up sound balance sheets of income and expenditure. It is a fact that in a number of enterprises and business organizations such concepts as "regime of economy," "cutting down unproductive expenditures," "rationalization of production" have long gone out of fashion. Evidently they assume that "the State Bank will advance the necessary money anyway." It is a fact that in a number of enterprises, cost of production has begun to increase of late. They were instructed to reduce costs by 10 per cent and more, but instead of that they are increasing costs.[7]

We cite this simply to prove that there is an arduous job of administrative organization to be done before putting any system at all into effect. Our initial thrust must be in this direction.

Points (b) [page 291], "moral incentives, complemented by material incentives, are used to provide the main impetus to production," and (c), "cost controls are employed," are dangerously oversimplified. In my last article, already cited, I mentioned two basic characteristics [page 130]:

> Through this series of quotations, we have tried to provide the background needed to understand the budgetary system.
>
> First, communism is a goal consciously pursued by man. Thus, education which clears the people's consciousness of the old ideas handed down from the capitalist society, is extremely important. It should be kept in mind, however, that without parallel progress in production, communism cannot be achieved.
>
> Second, from a technological standpoint, we should borrow the most advanced forms of economic administration available, from whatever source, so long as they can be adapted for use in the new society. We can use the petrochemical technology of the imperialist camp without fear of being "infected" by bourgeois ideology. The same rule applies with regard to technical standards in produc-

> tion control and administration.
>
> In hope of not seeming too pretentious, we could paraphrase Marx's reference to the use of Hegel's dialectics and say that such techniques can be turned to rights.[8]

We do not see communism as the mechanical addition of consumer goods in a given society, but as the result of a conscious act. Here lies the importance of education. In a society striving to achieve full material abundance, the need to develop individual consciousness is foremost.

The matter of control is discussed in my article, "On Production Costs and the Budgetary System [page 113]."[9] The most important part of the article concerns the possibility of making conscious use of the law of value by setting up an effective broad-based system of control that would convert cost control into a mere mechanical operation [page 120].

> All our efforts must be directed to assuring that the job of administration and control becomes more and more simple so that administrative agencies may concentrate on planning and technological development. Once all the indicators are established and the methods and routines of cost control are brought into effect by improved planning in all sectors of the economy, the administrative task will become mechanical and will present no serious problems. At this point, modern planning methods will take on added importance, and we will approach the ideal of being able to regulate the economy through mathematical analysis, thereby achieving the best allocation of resources between consumption and capital accumulation, as well as among the various branches of production. Clearly, however, we must remember that the human individual, the very reason for being of the Revolution and our hopes, cannot be reduced to a mere formula. His needs will become increasingly complex, going beyond simple material requirements. The various branches of production will become automated, and labor productivity will rise enormously. The worker's free time will be devoted to athletic, cultural,

and scientific endeavors of the highest order. Work will become a social need.

With respect to point (d) [page 291], "because they are tied to the national budget by the sum total of their receipts and outlays, enterprises never use bank credit in a direct way," we believe that the use of bank credit and mercantile exchange in the State sector is unnecessary under the budgetary finance system.

In order to understand the difference between the two systems—as Fernández fails to do—one must keep in mind that such categories come about as a result of individual regard for independent patrimonies. But now that all property is, in fact, in the hands of the masses, they are retained only as a means of economic control. They are fictitious and can be eliminated by use of the budgetary finance system.

Under this system, the principle of commercial yield is strictly formal within the State sphere. It is employed in planning for the purpose of economic calculus, bookkeeping, financial control, etc. But it will never become dominant, a fetish, over the social content of production because the enterprise does not possess its own patrimony as separate from the State. Thus, it neither retains nor accumulates production returns or replacement costs in its own fund. Under the budgetary system, mercantile exchange is appropriate only with regard to State sales to other forms of ownership. The State enterprise that performs this operation collects payment for the commodity and transfers this amount—which is the sum of all internal costs and accumulations perceived in the production and commercialization of the commodity—to the State budget. So long as the final act of exchange is consummated, failure to complete any of the intermediate acts of "payment and collection"—which are mere compensatory, bookkeeping operations devoid of economic significance—would have no serious effect on the national accumulation fund. Such a system weakens the patrimonial concept held by in-

> dividual groups in State factories, and thus encourages the philosophical development of Marxism-Leninism. The need for taxes and interest-bearing loans is obviated because the enterprise neither retains nor accumulates funds. The mercantile categories—and the conflicts they imply—are thereby eliminated in both form and substance. (Unpublished work of Luis Alvarez Rom.)

An enterprise is financed in order, on the one hand, to compensate (for purposes of social accounting and control) another enterprise for the work it performs; and, on the other hand, to remunerate living labor added in each stage of social production. The first is a formality, a compensatory act devoid of economic content. The second is payment of wages, which takes place *after* the worker's labor power has been expended in the production of use-values. In effect, therefore, the worker is the creditor.

Marx explains this as follows:

> The capitalist buys the labor-power before it enters into the process of production, but pays for it only at stipulated times, after it has been expended in the production of use-values. He owns, together with the remainder of the value of the product, also that portion of it which is only an equivalent for the money expanded in the payment of labor-power, that portion of the value of the product which represents variable capital. In this portion of value the laborer has already supplied the capitalist with the equivalent of his wages. But it is the reconversion of commodities into money, their sale, which restores to the capitalist his variable capital in the form of money-capital, which he may advance once more for the purchase of labor-power.[10]

Fernández contends that the bank finances the budget through currency issue and the use of international credit. Moreover, "In the Cuban economy, monetary resources for this kind of credit to the treasury are not yet available. Thus, inflationary pressures are produced, and the need for foreign credit increases." This extends fiction beyond the usual limits. To compare bank credit with the public treasury reveals a mentality that almost confirms Marx's words:

> It was not enough that the bank gave with one hand and took back more with the other; it remained, even while receiving, the eternal creditor of the nation down to the last shilling advanced.[11]

This is not to mention that the bank, as separate from the State, possesses *nothing,* despite the fictitious patrimony granted it by law:

Regarding financial discipline, Fernández says [page 291]:

> As to *financial discipline,* one should point out the relationship between payments and collections that take place among budgetary enterprises. Apparently, some of these enterprises lack incentive to collect payment for the goods and services they provide. Their costs are already covered, so failure to receive payment only means that they might have to stop contributing to the budget.

This is totally unfounded. By the same logic, one could say that an auto-financed enterprise also lacks such incentive because failure to receive payment only means that it might have to default on a bank loan or fail to contribute to the budget or to witholding taxes—which, by the way, has happened.

Following a detailed discussion based on bank records regarding violations of Law 1007 by budgetary enterprises, Fernández says [page 292]:

> One could argue that the economically autonomous enterprises commit violations as well, and we might even point out that since Law 1007 was put into effect, the INRA enterprises have maintained an embarrassing first place as regards number and value of infractions. But the INRA enterprises have, in fact, never really operated as economically autonomous enterprises.

Such statements are inconsistent with the tone and content of the article, and raise several questions:

Why has INRA [National Institute of Agrarian Reform] never really operated under the system of economic autonomy?

Have other agencies attempted to obstruct it?

Have the bank and the treasury failed to cooperate fully?

Has the educational system failed to provide adequate instruction—in any course or at any level?

Can it be that the bank's good intentions, framed by Law 1007, bring about results in name only?

Or can it be that no concrete results should be expected without first organizing the administrative system?

The defenders of self-management have used such arguments for a long while: it is now time that they analyze this system correctly and make it work. Debate on these matters is always useful, but if we continue to bottle ourselves up in it without making any practical progress, we may be too late with the answers.

In summary:

a. The author discusses the genesis of banks in an informative way, but fails to provide the discussion with an adequate theoretical framework. In general, the same failure lies behind the mistaken notions held by bank administrators regarding the bank's role in building the new society.

b. His quotations from Lenin concern only one objective aspect of the problem: the role of banks during the monopoly stage. By no means does Lenin provide any clear insight into their role during the succeeding stage.

c. The author forgets that monopoly banks are the financial arm of the super-States. Hence, he fails to follow through with an analysis of their new role when the State, with its own financial arm, embraces them all. He assumes that the bank continues to maintain its economic hegemony, insulated from socioeconomic changes.

d. He ignores Marx's warning about the nature of the credit system, which leads him to mechanical formulations regarding its function.

e. Marcelo Fernández, in stressing investment control, loses sight of the function fulfilled by the monopoly bank in this respect, ignoring the changes taking place during the period of transition.

f. He has not given enough study to the bases of the budgetary finance system. Thus, his reasoning is too inconsistent in this area of the analysis.

g. So it appears that the bank, possessing its own principal by the work and grace of divine providence, has sound intentions of helping the State resolve its problems by wisely applying a set of financial laws. Regretably, there are a few stubborn people who refuse to recognize this guardianship and who therefore create financial havoc and inflation by not asking the bank for credit "under advantageous conditions."

h. The article as a whole proves that our comrades in the bank employ the economic concepts discussed here in the same fetishist form as in classical and even vulgar economics. With all due respect, therefore, and only because this debate compels us to draw upon the Marxist classics, we offer Marx's words regarding the worshipers of form:

> The capital—profit, or still better capital—interest, land—rent, labor—wages, in this economic trinity represented as the connection between the component parts of value and wealth in general and its sources, we have the complete mystification of the capitalist mode of production, the conversion of social relations into things, the direct coalescence of the material production relations with their historical and social determination. It is an enchanted, perverted, topsy-turvy world, in which Monsieur Le Capital and Madame le Terre do their ghost-walking as social characters and at the same time directly as mere things. It is the great merit of classical economy to have destroyed this false appearance and illusion, this mutual independence and ossification of the various social elements of wealth, this personification of things and conversion of production relations into entities, this religion of everyday life. It did

so by reducing interest to a portion of profit, and rent to the surplus above average profit, so that both of them converge in surplus-value; and by representing the process of circulation as a mere metamorphosis of forms, and finally reducing value and surplus-value of commodities to labor in the direct production process. Nevertheless even the best spokesmen of classical economy remain more or less in the grip of the world of illusion which their criticism had dissolved, as cannot be otherwise from a bourgeois standpoint, and thus they all fall more or less into inconsistencies, half-truths and unsolved contradictions. On the other hand, it is just as natural for the actual agents of production to feel completely at home in these estranged and irrational forms of capital—interest, land—rent, labor—wages, since these are precisely the forms of illusion in which they move about and find their daily occupation. It is therefore just as natural that vulgar economy, which is no more than a didactic, more or less dogmatic, translation of everyday conceptions of the actual agents of production, and which arranges them in a certain rational order, should see precisely in this trinity, which is devoid of all inner connection, the natural and indubitably lofty basis for its shallow pompousness. This formula simultaneously corresponds to the interests of the ruling classes by proclaiming the physical necessity and eternal justification of their sources of revenue and elevating them to a dogma.[12]

NOTES

1. Karl Marx, *Capital* (Vol. I). [Translator's source: *Great Books of the Western World* (Chicago, Encyclopedia Britannica, c. 1952), Vol. L, p. 60.]
2. V. I. Lenin, "Imperialism: The Highest Stage of Capitalism." [Translator's source: *Lenin*, ed. Stefan T. Possony (Chicago, c. 1966), p. 196.]

3. *Ibid.*, p. 276.
4. "If the Tartars overran Europe today, it would be hard indeed to convey to them what a financier is among us."—Montesquieu, *The Spirit of Laws,* Bo. xxx, Chap. 13 (Marx's note.) Marx, *op. cit.,* p. 374.
5. Karl Marx, *Capital.* [Translator's source: *Capital* (New York, International Publishers, 1967), Vol. III, pp. 606–608.]
6. *Ibid.,* p. 391.
7. J. Stalin. [Translator's source: *Leninism* (New York, International Publishers, c. 1942), pp. 217–218.]
8. "Sobre el sistema presupuestario de financiamiento," *Nuestra Industria Económica,* No. 5, 1964, pp. 7–8.
9. "Consideraciónes sobre los costos de producción como base del analisis económico de las empresas sujetas a sistema presupuestario," *Nuestra Industria Económica,* No. 1, 1963, p. 11.
10. Karl Marx, *Capital, op. cit.,* Vol. II, p. 399.
11. [Source not given.]
12. Marx, *Capital, op. cit.,* Vol. III, *Editorial Nacional de Cuba,* 1966, pp. 836–837.

PART V

Socialism: Theory and Practice

15

On Certain Problems of Building Socialism

ALBERTO MORA

SEVERAL OF THE PROBLEMS that come about during the process of building the new socialist society have lately required a certain immediacy and have begun to draw a great deal of much needed attention. There have been a number of suggestions for their solution, some of which are based on more thorough analysis than others, and not all of which show the same degree of ideological commitment. But the most important thing is that the analysis is improving. Analysts are getting away from simple schematic approaches and are no longer postponing consideration of these problems, which have become vital to man's continued historical development.

Our interest here centers on two such problems. The first is practical economic administration under socialism; and the second is the basic question of man in the new society. Nothing, of course, is farther from our mind than trying to exhaust—or even consider—all the implications of such complex problems. But we deem it opportune vis-à-vis the present Cuban reality to at least open the door to their study, which, in our opinion,

---

SOURCE: "Sobre algunos problemas actuales de la construcción del socialismo," *Nuestra Industria Revista Económica,* Año 3, Agosto 1965, pp. 15–27.

is essential if we are to accomplish the tasks demanded of us by our Revolution's role in history.

Economic Administration under Socialism

Clearly, the methodology of economic administration under socialism has received scant attention in the development of Marxist economic theory. Even Marx, consistent with the tasks history called upon him to perform, focused his efforts on analyzing the capitalist economy and made only a few relatively shallow observations on the problems of socialism. This is understandable because at the time it was believed that socialism would logically and inevitably succeed capitalism. Historically, it was to be the stage during which the contradictions of capitalism would be resolved. One could not, then, without risk of generalization, predetermine the problems of the socialist society. Marx did foresee, however, that the revolutionary proletariat had no hope of automatically establishing a communist society immediately after taking power. He also knew that there would be a fairly long transitional period during which the survival of capitalist categories (in a somewhat different form than before) would give rise to a number of problems.

Thus, in his *Critique of the Gotha Program,* he says:

> What we have to deal with here is a communist society, not as it has *developed* on its own foundations, but, on the contrary, as it *emerges* from capitalist society; which is thus in every respect, economically, morally and intellectually, still stamped with the birthmarks of the old society from whose womb it emerges. Accordingly the individual producer receives back from society—after the deductions have been made—exactly what he gives to it. . . . Here obviously the same principle prevails as that which regulates the exchange of commodities, as far as this is exchange of equal values. Content and form are changed. . . . But, as far as the distribution of the latter

> among the individual producers is concerned, the same principle prevails as in the exchange of commodity equivalents.[1]

Although Engels, too, failed to consider these problems at any length, he did make a few general observations:

> The seizure of the means of production by society puts an end to commodity production, and therewith to the domination of the product over the producer.[2]

And:

> From the moment when society enters into possession of the means of production and uses them in direct association for production, the labor of each individual . . . is immediately and directly social labor. The quantity of social labor contained in a product has then no need to be established in a roundabout way; daily experience shows in a direct way how much of it is required on the average. Society can calculate simply how many hours of labor are contained in a steam-engine, a bushel of wheat of the last harvest, or a hundred square yards of cloth of a certain quality. It could therefore never occur to it still to express the quantity of labor put into the products, which it will then know directly and in its absolute amount in a third product, and moreover in a measure which is only relative, fluctuating, inadequate, though formerly unavoidable for lack of a better, and not in its natural, adequate and absolute measure, *time*. . . . On the assumptions we made above, therefore, society will also not assign values to products. . . . It is true that even then it will still be necessary for society to know how much labor each article of consumption requires for its production. It will have to arrange its plan of production in accordance with its means of production, which include, in particular, its labor forces. The useful effects of the various articles of consumption, compared with each other and with the quantity of labor required for their production, will in the last analysis determine the plan. People will be able to manage every-

thing very simply, without the intervention of the famous "value." [3]

Engels oversimplifies and makes no reference at all to the problems of a transitional period. Following the October Revolution, however, Rosa Luxemburg and Nikolai Bukharin concluded by these statements that there was no place in socialism for economics as a science.[4] The same kind of analysis lay behind the Soviet Union's attempts to eliminate money during the latter part of the war communism period.[5]

Marxism is the only theory that can provide a thorough interpretation of reality, but the founders neglected to analyze fully the economic problems of socialism. This is perfectly understandable. Knowledge comes from experience, so it was impossible for Marx and Engels to be fully aware of all the complex problems of a society that, although clearly foreseen, had not yet been born and thus had not given rise to such problems.

Only when "praxis" creates a need does thought become possible: one thinks only what he feels ("lives") necessary. Marx and Engels could in no way "live" the problems of a nonexistent society. Still, they left us basic scientific premises that can be developed to coincide with the requirements of a reality that is forever changing. There is nothing farther from Marxism than statics. Its basic premises, which have been substantiated time and again, are precisely what enable the theory to develop in step with reality. It is here, however, that the theory's deficiency, which must be resolved without delay, becomes apparent.

Nothing could be expected from the Second International. Not only had there been no experience with a socialist society but also the "praxis" of socialism had been negative because of the opportunistic, revisionist character of the principal representatives of German social democracy, who were considered for some time to be the chief continuers of the founders of Marxism. Thus, Kautsky referred only casually to the fact that money and prices would surely survive in the socialist society. In a talk given in 1902 entitled "The Day After the Revolution," Kautsky declared:

> Money is the simplest means known up to the present time which makes it possible in as complicated a mechanism as that of the modern productive process, . . . to secure the circulation of products and their distribution to the individual members of society. . . . since the laborers cannot be assigned by military discipline and against their wishes to the various branches of industry, so it may happen that too many laborers rush into certain branches of industry while a lack of laborers is the rule in the others. The necessary balance can then only be brought about by the reduction of wages where there are too many laborers and the raising of them in those branches of industry where there is a lack of laborers until the point is reached where every branch has as many laborers as it can use.[6]

And, later, in his book *The Labor Revolution,* written in 1922, he states:

> The valuation of commodities according to the labor contained in them, which could not be achieved by the most complicated State machinery imaginable, we find to be an accomplished fact in the shape of the transmitted prices, as the result of a long historical process, imperfect and inexact, but nevertheless the only practical foundation for the smooth functioning of the economic process of circulation.

Further on in the same book, he concludes a sentence as follows, revealing his accursed "praxis," already so far afield from Marxism:

> As the measure of value and means of circulation of products money will continue to exist in a socialist society until the dawn *of that blessed second phase of communism which we do not yet know whether will ever be more than a pious wish, similar to the Millennial Kingdom.*[7]

Lenin embodies all the essential characteristics of a Marxist theoretician: a brilliant intellect, total commitment to principle, and revolutionary "praxis." But the "praxis" in which Lenin evolves is conditioned by the history of the time and the enormous job to be done: basically, it becomes political "praxis." In this case, while it promotes the rapid advance of Theory, it also restricts the development of Theory. For this reason, Lenin, before as well as after he takes power and begins to live the "praxis" of the new socialist society, comes out essentially as a politician. The political "praxis" conditions even the theoretical development of his thought. And the concrete conditions of the historical moment intensify the process after the taking of power. As he begins to live with the problems of the new society in all their complexity, therefore, problems that come about (that is, exist) for the first time in the history of mankind, his thinking becomes more specifically conditioned by political "praxis." Understand well. By no means do we imply that Lenin's contribution to the development of Marxist Theory (in its broadest context) has been at all limited to the political environment. What we are saying is that his contributions in the various aspects of the theory—philosophy, economy, etc.—were always primarily conditioned by political "praxis," especially after the taking of power. This, in fact, is what enables him to perform his enormous role as the motive force behind the most far-reaching event in the history of man: the birth of the socialist society.

As to the economic problems of the new society, Lenin is fully aware before taking power that a transitional period will necessarily intervene between capitalism and the fully communist society. This awareness is clearly revealed in *The State and Revolution*. But as to the complexity of these problems, he himself says after reaching power:

> Very often . . . the proverb "measure thrice and cut once" has not been applied. Unfortunately, things are not so simple in regard to the organization of the economy on socialist lines as they are expressed in that proverb. . . . it will become immediately understandable that . . . in such a gigantic task, we could never claim, and no sensible socialist who has ever written on the prospects of the future ever even thought, that we could immediately establish and

compose the forms of organization of the new society according to some predetermined instruction and at one stroke.[8]

The concrete conditions of the time in history and the magnitude of the task during the final stage of the revolutionary victory shape Lenin's economic thought. In *The State and Revolution,* he had already said: "Accounting and control—that is *mainly* what is needed for the 'smooth working,' for the proper functioning of the *first phase* of communist society."[9] At the beginning, then: "It was essential to organize the exchange of products and introduce regular accounting and control. . . ."[10]

In the sphere of the economic building of socialism, the essence of the present situation is that our work of organizing the country-wide and all-embracing accounting and control of production and distribution, and of introducing proletarian control of production, lags far behind the direct expropriation of the expropriator. . . . This is the fundamental fact determining our tasks.[11]

After completely diagnosing the concrete conditions under which the Russian Revolution took place, Lenin says in 1918:

Yesterday, the main task of the moment was, as determinedly as possible, to nationalize, confiscate. . . . Today, only a blind man could fail to see that we have nationalized, confiscated, beaten down and put down more *than we have had time to count.* The difference between socialization and simple confiscation is that confiscation can be carried out by "determination" alone, without the ability to calculate and distribute properly, *whereas socialization cannot be brought about without this ability.* . . . state capitalism would be a *step forward* as compared with the present state of affairs in our Soviet Republic. If in approximately six months' time state capitalism became established in our Republic, this would be a

> great success and a sure guarantee that within a year socialism will have gained a permanently firm hold and will have become invincible. . . . No one, I think, in studying the question of the economic system of Russia, has denied its transitional character. Nor, I think, has any Communist denied that the term Socialist Soviet Republic implies the determination of Soviet power to achieve the transition to socialism, and not that the new economic system is recognized as a socialist order.[12]

In 1921, arguing in favor of the NEP [National Economic Plan], Lenin used an excerpt from this article to begin his pamphlet "The Tax in Kind": "It was the war and the ruin that forced us into War Communism. It was not, and could not be, a policy that corresponded to the economic tasks of the proletariat. It was a makeshift."[13]

Again, in 1921, he writes:

> Borne along on the crest of the wave of enthusiasm, rousing first the political enthusiasm and then the military enthusiasm of the people, we expected to accomplish economic tasks just as great as the political and military tasks we had accomplished by relying directly on this enthusiasm. We expected . . . to be able to organize the state production and the state distribution of products on communist lines in a small-peasant country directly as ordered by the proletarian state. Experience has proved that we were wrong. It appears that a number of transitional stages were necessary—state capitalism and socialism—in order to *prepare* —to prepare by many years of effort—for the transition to communism. Not directly relying on enthusiasm, but aided by the enthusiasm engendered by the great revolution, and on the basis of personal interest, personal incentive and business principles, we must first set to work on this small-peasant country to build solid gangways to socialism by way of state capitalism. Otherwise we shall never get to communism. . . . That is what experience, the objective course of the development of the revolution, has taught us.[14]

To summarize: Only when "praxis" brings about a "need" does thought and, consequently, theoretical solution of problems become possible. (It would be redundant to discuss the fact that the use of Theory is essential in order to fully comprehend reality and to arrive at accurate solutions for the problems it poses.) Thus, it was impossible for the founders of Marxism, or even Lenin, to "think out" the many complexities involved in the general (and, therefore, economic) problems of the socialist society. (Just as neither Marx nor Engels could "think out" the problems that would arise during the highest stage of capitalism-imperialism, while, on the other hand, Lenin could.) Nor could they have handled them theoretically. It would be absurd to think otherwise; one cannot analyze something that does not exist (that is, the problems of the new society could only come about with the advent of the society itself).[15] Only after the taking of power do the problems of the new society—their complexity exposed—turn up in Lenin's "praxis," because then, and only then, do they come into existence. But this means that specific concrete conditions determine his theoretical approach to such problems. In other words, if political "praxis" always conditions Lenin's thought, and hence his contribution to the development of Theory (including its economic aspects) after taking power, then the specifics of Russia's 1917 socialist revolutionary victory determine his theoretical approach to problems and the development of Theory itself. In other words, Lenin's "praxis" is individualized by the concrete conditions surrounding the birth of the Russian socialist society in 1917. And the abstract character of the socialist society is concretized, comes into existence, in such individuality. The general, basic precepts of the Theory (which is considered to be the structural whole of knowledge) are present, of course, because it is a Marxist, Lenin, and a Marxist movement—the Bolshevik Party—that bring about the victory and progress of the Revolution. But this "general" part of the Theory is concretized in the specific nature of the conditions that determine the way in which the new society comes about. For this reason, the development of the Theory of the "praxis" of that new society is limited to the immediate: It even materially reduces the time for theorizing. But there is another consequence. The "concrete conditions" encompass and, at the same time, are synthesized in a given historical moment. And this determines in addition the need to defend the new society at all cost, just as it was born—in one country. Which is to say that the "concrete conditions" also determine the characteristics of the "need" that will demand and polarize the attention of thought. It is precisely this that later brings about the concept of socialism in one country. Moreover, it explains, in our opinion, the whole outlook of Soviet policy in the international Marxist movement during the stage commonly referred to as that of "the personality cult."

Russia's concrete conditions in 1917, together with those of the historic moment of the socialist Revolution's victory in one country, determined the extent to which the Theory of the "praxis" of the new society would develop. In this way, theory (in lower case, in order to differentiate it from the aggregate of the basic principles that serve as the exact interpretation of reality as a whole) has root in the immediate, in the "praxis" of the "current moment." It does not respond to a subjective desire. The early attempts by Bukharin, Prebrazhenski, Larin, and others to carry it further are the proof. Because their theories did not correspond to "concrete conditions," they lose all perspective and nearly always come to lamentable conclusions.

The new Russian society born in 1917 develops into the U.S.S.R. The specific concrete conditions under which it develops continue for a long while (long if attention is focused on the length of its existence, but short relative to the course of human history) to determine practical theory in the new society. The basic precepts of Marxist Theory are still present, of course, but its nature as a pragmatic theory is accentuated. As Louis A. Althuser says in his article (responding to criticism on one of his previous articles) appearing in the magazine *La Pensée:*

> Regarding Dialectical Materialism . . . that practice can exist and develop very well . . . without experiencing, at

> least for a while, the need to form a theory of practice, a Theory of its "method." It can exist, survive, and even progress without it . . . until its object (the actual world of the society that the practice transforms) offers enough resistance to force it to fill the vacuum, to question and consider its very method so as to come up with appropriate solutions and the means for carrying them out, and particularly to infuse "the theory" serving as its base (the theory of the existing social structure with the new facts which correspond to the context of the new "stage" of its development).[16]

What Althuser says about political practice is generally applicable, we believe, to "praxis" in all areas of the new society. In our judgment, it is also what has happened to the theory of economic practice. And, in fact, it shapes the current situation in those socialist countries in which problems concerning how the economy should be regulated under socialism (in general, the economic problems of the "period of transition" to communism) stubbornly resist solution. This urgently demands the development of Theory in such areas.

In effect, the absence of an economic Theory of socialism (the "period of transition" and its characteristics as accurately defined by theoretical analysis deriving from fifty years of economic practice in the new society) lends an air of "crisis" to the present situation in socialist countries. The apologetic nature of the pragmatic theory of economic practice obscured many fundamental problems that today have become paramount. Indeed, it is in response to this situation that various European socialist countries are experimenting with new methods of economic administration. The situation corresponds to the change in "concrete conditions" and to the historic moment of the new socialist society. While the new society existed in only one country, it was characterized by apologetics and the pragmatism of economic theory, which focused on solving the problems associated with concrete conditions in the Soviet Union. But the change in these "concrete conditions" (not only those of the U.S.S.R.,* development of the productive forces, but mainly, and more decisively, those of socialism as a new historical stage in the development of man, that is, the beginning of the building of the new society in a growing number of countries) revitalizes theoretical thought. In the area of economics, the publication of Stalin's *Economic Problems of Socialism in the U.S.S.R.* had a corresponding impact. Pragmatism in theorization still survives here, as suggested by the title's specific reference to the U.S.S.R., but the need for economic Theory in the new society is restated through the formulation of several problems arising in practice during the "period of transition."

The change that comes about in "concrete conditions" continues to expose the problems arising from the "praxis" of socialism. This happens on all planes: political, economic, and ideological. On the economic plane, recognition is given for the first time to problems such as economic relations among countries undergoing the building of the new society. These changes caused such a turnabout in the situation that the rudimentary methods that had governed economic practice before became inoperative. Thus, problems arose relative to the administration of economic practice—for example, planning techniques—that had to be confronted.

In search of objective bases permitting rational decision-making in economic matters, some European socialist countries have recently begun to experiment with new methods of economic administration which, though having different roots in the various countries, share in common the use of indirect means (such as prices; the market mechanism to prove the "efficiency" of enterprise decisions and performance; material incentives; extension of the organizational principle of auto-financing of enterprises; greater enterprise autonomy, etc.). The development of the productive forces has complicated the economies of these countries, exaggerating the need for improved methods of administration. These problems, in their majority, are not

* At this point a number of words were omitted in the transcript.

new, and neither are the "solutions" now being tried out. The only new problems are those that have arisen from new conditions—for example, trade among socialist countries or, in part, the greater significance of the foreign trade sector in the economies of some countries now building the new society. By 1920, a bourgeois economist, Ludwig von Mises, attempted (consistent with his class interest) to prove that socialism was impossible, and in doing so raised the question of objective bases for economic calculation that would assure rational capital-investment decisions in the absence of a capital market.[17] And Oskar Lange, completely rejecting Mises' conclusions in a work published in 1938,[18] developed the idea of using prices as a tool of economic administration under socialism, despite the absence of a market for means of production.

There are serious doubts as to whether the "new" methods of economic administration mentioned above might, in fact, compromise the realization of socialism in light of their implications regarding the use of mercantile categories. There are special reservations concerning the use of "material incentives" and the "profit" motive as standards for the measurement of enterprise efficiency. Such devices could become basic economic motivations, thus inhibiting the development of socialist consciousness. Some have even mentioned the danger of an eventual return to capitalism.

Though undoubtedly much of this criticism is accurate, we believe that it fails to correctly evaluate the magnitude of the economic problems involved. Because of the development of the productive forces, the economy has become very complex. Hence, it has become apparent that yesterday's methods of economic administration are no longer adequate to today's needs. It is also apparent that a most difficult problem lies in determining objective bases under socialism for rational economic decision-making.

The heart of the matter resides, in our judgment, in a failure to properly analyze current economic practice in countries building socialism, and thereby to develop the Theory in accord with current reality. "Solutions" are tested by theorizing on the expediency of the economic practice. Solutions are sought by focusing exclusively on economic factors. Clearly, economic practice in the new society has proved that serious problems exist with regard to economic administration under socialism and, moreover, that there is need for a system assuring the rationality of economic decisions. But the deficiency, in our estimation, lies in the fact that the Theory of the "praxis" of socialism has not been adequately developed. And this is a problem that requires the thorough treatment of all categories of problems. The new society must be built as a whole rather than as the simple aggregate of various practices. An infinity of questions exist which have received not the slightest consideration. For example, analysis of problems associated with the superstructure and its influence on the base might yield some knowledge with regard to the new society's sociological aspects. An understanding and firm grasp of such matters is, to our mind, the only possible way to resolve the problems of the new man's socialist consciousness. Within this frame of reference, indirect methods of economic control will doubtless be adopted in order to bring about a degree of automation in economic relations, while at the same time assuring that decisions are made rationally.

To summarize: In our judgment, the problems currently facing countries now building the new society stem from the inadequate development of the Theory of "praxis" in the socialist society. In economic practice this translates into the absence of an economic Theory of socialism. In the *Pravda* article cited above,[19] Lenin said: "Experience has proved . . . that a number of transitional stages were necessary—State capitalism and socialism—in order to prepare—by many years of effort—for the transition to Communism." Do the experiments with new methods of economic administration mentioned above still correspond to the stage of State capitalism? Can it not be that the stage of State capitalism is actually much longer than was thought (as Lenin foresaw in Russia) and that its end will become feasible only when "national economies" are overcome? Consider the influence—with regard to survival of the mercantile categories—of the commercial nature of present trade relations among socialist countries.

These problems are pressing and impossible to postpone further. The type of economic administration to be used in the new society must be chosen. Objective bases for rational decision-making (through accurate economic calculus) must be established.

But these matters cannot be resolved except by accurately diagnosing reality or, in other words, by bringing Marxist Theory up to date with changes in reality brought about by the "praxis" of the socialist society. This demands broad and thorough treatment of the problems of that society as a whole, which would in turn allow one to draw accurate conclusions at the various levels: economic, political, ideological, and the interrelationship among these.

Socialist Consciousness and the Future

The second category of problems we wish to mention, if only briefly, have to do with the future man and the present state of socialist consciousness.

The communist society is the culmination of human development. In it man fully becomes Man. This implies a concomitant development of consciousness. But consciousness is a result of "praxis," that is, man's acting upon reality and changing it. Consciousness is conditioned by the way in which the realization of "praxis" is organized. For this reason, so as to assure the transformation of consciousness, it is necessary to change the form in which, in the society, man's "praxis" comes about. To pretend that mere "political work"—consisting, really, of the repetition of code words—can bring about such a transformation of consciousness is, to our mind, pure idealism, and has nothing to do with Marxism. If code words and appeals to conscience are not enough for man to organize his economic, political, and ideological relations, then we see no way to assure the real, effective transformation and development of socialist consciousness that the coming of communist man would suggest. Here, in our opinion, lie the greatest dangers of obstructing the development of the socialist consciousness that leads in turn to frustrations created by lack of communication and alienation among men, by problems belonging to the capitalist society. If the relationships of production and their determination in the superstructure were not objectively organized so as to assure that work would eventually lose its quality of alienation, then we fail to see how we could develop a consciousness of nonalienated—that is, voluntarily contributed—work in men as a whole. In any case, such a course leads to opportunism, which has nothing to do with socialist consciousness. The enthusiasm and fervor awakened during the first years of the Revolution must not be damaged. The history of the new society proves that frustrations arise when such feelings are not translated into the way that "praxis" is organized.

Here, more than in any other area concerning the evolution of the new man, which implies the growth of social consciousness in present generations, we need to achieve a "total" focus encompassing the many factors that condition his evolution. It must embrace not only the relationships of production but also the political and ideological superstructure. The only real way to assure the evolution of man's socialist—and progressively communist—consciousness is to establish relationships of production within the framework of the new society's political organization (relationship of the individual to the State, the role of the Party, etc.) and ideological perception (of art, etc.). These are factors that objectively influence the shape of the new man. Since the interrelationships in these areas are so strict, we are probably unable to assure the evolution of consciousness—and therefore the new man—by simply eliminating the desire for personal gain as a motive for social behavior (which is risked by using material incentives as a motivation in the relationships of production). Rather, we must at the same time assure that the superstructure is so organized as to prevent the substitution of the money motive by the power motive.

In summary, we feel that the relationships of the superstructure must coincide with the socialist relationships of production in order to assure the objective development of man's socialist consciousness. Otherwise, contradictions will arise to inhibit such development.

In our opinion, this matter is vitally important. The very purpose of the revolutionary struggle is to develop man's socialist consciousness. In other words, we must realize Engels' proposition (stated in *Anti-Duhring*):

> Men, finally in possession of their own social existence, become owners of nature, of themselves—they become free men.

NOTES

1. Karl Marx, *Critique of the Gotha Program.* [Translator's source: *Critique of the Gotha Program* (New York, International Publishers, c. 1938), pp. 8–9.]
2. Friedrich Engels, *Herr Eugen Duhrings Revolution in Science.* [Translator's source: *Anti-Duhring* (New York, International Publishers, 1966), p. 309.]
3. *Ibid.,* pp.337–338.
4. "The end of capitalism and the mercantile society means the end of political economy." Bukharin, *The Economy of the Period of Transition* (1920).
5. See R. W. Davies, *The Soviet Budgetary System;* A. Baykov, *El Desarrollo del Sistema Económico Sovietico;* Maurice Dobb, *Soviet Economic Development;* and E. H. Carr, *The Bolshevik Revolution.*
6. Cited by Oskar Lange, *On the Economic Theory of Socialism* (New York, McGraw Hill, 1964), pp. 134–135.
7. *Ibid.,* pp. 136–137. Emphasis is Mora's.
8. V. I. Lenin, "Speech at the First Congress of Economic Councils," (May 26, 1918). [Translator's source: *Selected Works* (New York, International Publishers, 1967), Vol. II, pp. 727–728.]
9. V. I. Lenin, "The State and Revolution." [Translator's source: *Selected Works, op. cit.,* Vol. II, p. 344.]
10. V. I. Lenin, "Report on the Economic Condition of Petrograd Workers and the Tasks of the Working Class—Delivered at a Meeting of the Worker's Section of the Petrograd Soviet of Workers' and Soldiers' Deputies" (December 1917). [Translator's source: *Selected Works, op. cit.,* Vol. II, p. 682.]
11. V. I. Lenin, "Six Theses on the Immediate Tasks of the Soviet Government." [Translator's source: *Selected Works, op. cit.,* Vol. II, p. 682.]

12. V. I. Lenin, " 'Left-wing Childishness' and the Petty-Bourgeois Mentality." [Translator's source: *Selected Works, op. cit.,* Vol. II, pp. 692–694.]

13. V. I. Lenin, "The Tax is Kind." [Translator's source: *Selected Works, op. cit.,* Vol. III, p. 595.]

14. V. I. Lenin, "Fourth Anniversary of the October Revolution." [Translator's source: *Selected Works, op. cit.,* Vol. III, p. 642.]

15. Understand well. By no means are we denying that it might be possible to forecast a future event or anything else within the realm of knowledge, including its most important general aspects. The quotation from Marx regarding his foresight of the "period of transition" should be proof enough. But full, detailed knowledge of something that has never before existed is impossible (Mora).

16. It is from this work by Althuser that we have derived the aforesaid regarding the conditioning of Lenin's thought by political "praxis," and later, its determination by Russia's concrete conditions. Incidentally, we believe that these works by Althuser about the fundamental characteristics that differentiate and individualize the Marxist dialectic constitute one of the most important contributions to the development of Marxist Theory in recent times (Mora).

17. L. von Mises, "Economic Calculation in the Socialist Commonwealth," 1920. Later, this article was translated into English and included in a book by F. A. Hayek published in London, in 1935.

18. Lange, *op. cit.*

19. Lenin, "Fourth Anniversary of the October Revolution," *op. cit.,* p. 642.

20. [No source given.]

16

Man and Socialism in Cuba

ERNESTO CHE GUEVARA

Dear Comrade:

I am finishing these notes while traveling through Africa, moved by the desire to keep my promise, although after some delay. I should like to do so by dealing with the topic that appears in the title. I believe it might be of interest to Uruguayan readers.

It is common to hear how capitalist spokesmen use as an argument in the ideological struggle against socialism the assertion that such a social system, or the period of building socialism on which we have embarked, is characterized by the extinction of the individual for the sake of the State. I will make no attempt to refute this assertion on a merely theoretical basis, but will instead establish the facts of the Cuban experience and add our commentaries of a general nature. I shall first broadly sketch the history of our revolutionary struggle both before and after taking of power.

As we know, the exact date of the beginning of the revolutionary actions that were to culminate on January 1, 1959, was July 26, 1953. A group of men led by Fidel Castro attacked the

---

Letter to Carlos Quijano, editor-publisher of the Uruguayan weekly *Marcha,* written early in 1965, then published in Cuba as "El Socialismo y el Hombre en Cuba" (Havana, Ediciones R.). Official government translation by Margarita Zimmermann.

Moncada military garrison in the province of Oriente in the early hours of the morning of that day. The attack was a failure. The failure became a disaster, and the survivors were imprisoned, only to begin the revolutionary struggle all over again, once they were amnestied.

During this process, which contained only the first seeds of socialism, man was a basic factor. Man—individualized, specific, named—was trusted, and the triumph or failure of the task entrusted to him depended on his capacity for action.

Then came the stage of guerrilla warfare. It was carried out in two different environments: the people, an as yet unawakened mass that had to be mobilized, and its vanguard, the guerrilla, the thrusting engine of mobilization, the generator of revolutionary awareness and militant enthusiasm. This vanguard was the catalyst that created the subjective condition necessary for victory. The individual was also the basic factor in the guerrilla, in the framework of the gradual proletarianization of our thinking, in the revolution taking place in our habits and in our minds. Each and every one of the Sierra Maestra fighters who achieved a high rank in the revolutionary forces has to his credit a list of noteworthy deeds. It was on the basis of such deeds that they earned their rank.

It was the first heroic period in which men strove to earn posts of greater responsibility, of greater danger, with the fulfillment of their duty as the only satisfaction. In our revolutionary educational work, we often return to this instructive topic. The man of the future could be glimpsed in the attitude of our fighters.

At other times of our history, there have been repetitions of this utter devotion to the revolutionary cause. During the October crisis and at the time of Hurricane Flora, we witnessed deeds of exceptional valor and self-sacrifice carried out by an entire people. One of our fundamental tasks from the ideological standpoint is to find the way to perpetuate such heroic attitudes in everyday life.

The revolutionary government was established in 1959 with the participation of several members of the "sell-out" bourgeoisie. The presence of the rebel army constituted the guarantee of power as the fundamental factor of strength.

Serious contradictions arose that were solved in the first instance in February 1959, when Fidel Castro assumed the leadership of the government in the post of prime minister. This process culminated in July of the same year with the resignation of President Urrutia in the face of mass pressure.

With clearly defined features, there now appeared in the history of the Cuban Revolution a personage that will systematically repeat itself: the masses.

This multifaceted being is not, as it is claimed, the sum total of elements of the same category (and moreover, reduced to the same category by the system imposed on them), and which acts as a tame herd. It is true that the mass follows its leaders, especially Fidel Castro, without hesitation, but the degree to which he has earned such confidence is due precisely to the consummate interpretation of the people's desires and aspirations, and to the sincere struggle to keep the promises made.

The mass participated in the agrarian reform and in the difficult undertaking of the management of the state enterprises; it underwent the heroic experience of Playa Giron; it was tempered in the struggle against the groups of bandits armed by the CIA; during the October crisis, it lived one of the most important definitions of modern times, and today it continues the work to build socialism.

Looking at things from a superficial standpoint, it might seem that those who speak of the submission of the individual to the State are right; with incomparable enthusiasm and discipline, the mass carries out the tasks set by the government whatever their nature: economic, cultural, defense, sports, etc. The initiative generally comes from Fidel or the high command of the Revolution: It is explained to the people, who make it their own. At times, local experiences are taken up by the Party and the government and are thereby generalized, following the same procedure.

However, the State at times makes mistakes. When this occurs, the collective enthusiasm diminishes palpably as a result of a quantitative diminishing that takes place in each of the elements that make up the collective, and work becomes paralyzed until it finally shrinks to insignificant proportions; this is the time to rectify.

This was what happened in March 1962 in the presence of the sectarian policy imposed on the party by Anibal Escalante.

This mechanism is obviously not sufficient to ensure a sequence of sensible measures; what is missing is a more structured relationship with the mass. We must improve this connection in the years to come, but for now, in the case of the initiative arising on the top levels of government, we are using the almost intuitive method of keeping our ears open to the general reactions in the face of the problems that are posed.

Fidel is a past master at this; his particular mode of integration with the people can only be appreciated by seeing him in action. In the big public meetings, one can observe something like the dialogue of two tuning forks whose vibrations summon forth new vibrations each in the other. Fidel and the mass begin to vibrate in a dialogue of growing intensity that reaches its culminating point in an abrupt ending crowned by our victorious battle cry.

What is hard to understand for anyone who has not lived the revolutionary experience is that close dialectical unity which exists between the individual and the mass, in which both are interrelated, and the mass, as a whole composed of individuals, is in turn interrelated with the leader.

Under capitalism, certain phenomena of this nature can be observed with the appearance on the scene of politicians capable of mobilizing the public, but if it is not an authentic social movement, in which case it is not completely accurate to speak of capitalism, the movement will have the same life span as its promoter or until the rigors of capitalist society put an end to popular illusions. Under capitalism, man is guided by a cold ordinance that is usually beyond his comprehension. The alienated human individual is bound to society as a whole by an invisible umbilical cord: the law of value. It acts upon all facets of his life, shaping his road and his destiny.

The laws of capitalism, invisible and blind for most people, act upon the individual without his awareness. He sees only the broadness of horizon that appears infinite. Capitalist propaganda presents it in just this way, and attempts to use the Rockefeller case (true or not) as a lesson in the prospects for success. The misery that must be accumulated for such an example to arise and the sum total of baseness contributing to the formation of a fortune of such magnitude do not appear in the picture, and the popular forces are not always able to make these concepts clear. (It would be fitting at this point to study how the workers of the imperialist countries gradually lose their international class spirit under the influence of a certain complicity in the exploitation of the dependent countries and how this fact at the same time wears away the militant spirit of the masses within their own national context, but this topic is outside the framework of the present note.)

In any case, we can see the obstacle course that may apparently be overcome by an individual with the necessary qualities to arrive at the finish line. The reward is glimpsed in the distance, and the road is solitary. Furthermore, it is a race of wolves: He who arrives does so only at the expense of the failure of others.

I shall now attempt to define the individual, the actor in this strange and moving drama that is the building of socialism, in his twofold existence as a unique being and a member of the community.

I believe that the simplest approach is to recognize his unmade quality. He is an unfinished product. The flaws of the past are translated into the present in the individual consciousness, and constant efforts must be made to eradicate them. The process is twofold: On the one hand, society acts on the individual by means of direct and indirect education, while on the other hand, the individual undergoes a conscious phase of self-education.

The new society in process of formation has to compete very hard with the past. This makes itself not only in the individual consciousness, weighed down by the residues of an education and an upbringing systematically oriented toward the isolation of the individual, but also by the very nature of this transition period, with the persistence of commodity relations. The commodity is the economic cell of capitalist society: As long as it exists, its effects will make themselves felt in the organization of production and therefore in man's consciousness.

Marx's scheme conceived of the transition period as the result of the explosive transformation of the capitalist system torn apart by its inner contradictions: Subsequent reality has shown how some countries, the weak limbs, detach themselves from the imperialist tree, a phenomenon foreseen by Lenin. In those countries, capitalism has developed sufficiently to make its effects felt on the people in one way or another, but it is not its own inner contradictions that explode the system after exhausting all of its possibilities. The struggle for liberation against an external oppressor, the misery that has its origin in foreign causes such as war, whose consequences make the privileged classes fall upon the exploited, the liberation movements aimed at overthrowing neocolonial regimes, are the customary factors in this process. Conscious action does the rest.

In these countries, there still has not been achieved a complete education for the work of society, and wealth is far from being within the reach of the masses through the simple process of appropriation. Underdevelopment and the customary flight of capital to "civilized" countries make impossible a rapid change without sacrifices. There still remains a long stretch to be covered in the building of the economic base, and the temptation to follow the beaten paths of material interest as the lever of speedy development is very great.

There is a danger of not seeing the forest because of the trees. Pursuing the chimera of achieving socialism with the aid of the blunted weapons left to us by capitalism (the commodity as the economic cell, profitability, and individual material interest as levers, etc.), it is possible to come to a blind alley. And the arrival there comes about after covering a long distance where there are many crossroads and where it is difficult to realize just when the wrong turn was taken. Meanwhile, the adapted economic base has undermined the development of consciousness. To build communism, a new man must be created simultaneously with the material base.

That is why it is so important to choose correctly the instrument of mass mobilization. That instrument must be fundamentally of a moral character, without forgetting the correct use of material incentives, especially those of a social nature.

As I already said, in moments of extreme danger it is easy to activate moral incentives: To maintain their effectiveness, it is necessary to develop a consciousness in which values acquire new categories. Society as a whole must become a huge school.

The broad characteristics of the phenomenon are similar to the process of formation of capitalist consciousness in the system's first stage. Capitalism resorts to force, but it also educates people in the system. Direct propaganda is carried out by those who are entrusted with the task of explaining the inevitability of a class regime, whether it be of divine origin or due to the imposition of nature as a mechanical entity. This placates the masses, who see themselves oppressed by an evil against which it is not possible to struggle.

This is followed by hope, which differentiates capitalism from the previous caste regimes that offered no way out. For some, the caste formula continues in force: The obedient are rewarded by the post-mortem arrival in other wonderful worlds in which the good are requited, and the old tradition is continued. For others, innovation: The division in classes is a matter of fate, but individuals can leave the class to which they belong through work, initiative, etc. This process, and that of self-education for success, must be deeply hypocritical: It is the interested demonstration that a lie is true.

In our case, direct education acquires much greater importance. Explanations are convenient because they are genuine; subterfuges are not needed. It is carried out through the State's educational apparatus, in the form of general, technical, and ideological culture, by means of bodies such as the Ministry of Education and the party's information apparatus. Education takes among the masses, and the new attitude that is praised tends to become habit; the mass gradually takes it over and exerts pressure on those who have still not become educated. This is the indirect way of educating the masses, as powerful as the other, structured, one.

But the process is a conscious one: The individual receives the impact of the new social power and perceives that he is not completely adequate to it. Under the influence of the pressure implied in indirect education, he tries to adjust to a situation that he feels to be just and whose lack of development has kept him from doing so thus far. He is educating himself.

We can see the new man who begins to emerge in this period of the building of socialism. His image is as yet unfinished. In fact, it will never be finished, since the process advances parallel to the development of new economic forms. Discounting those whose lack of education makes them tend toward the solitary road, toward the satisfaction of their ambitions, there are others who, even within this new picture of overall advances, tend to march in isolation from the accompanying mass. What is important is that people become more aware every day of the need to incorporate themselves into society and of their own importance as motors of that society.

They no longer march in complete solitude along lost roads toward far-off longings. They follow their vanguard, composed of the party, of the most advanced workers, of the advanced men who move along bound to the masses and in close communion with them. The vanguards have their eyes on the future and its recompenses, but the latter are not envisioned as something individual; the reward is the new society in which human beings will have different characteristics: the society of communist man.

The road is long and full of difficulties. At times the route strays off course, and it is necessary to retreat; at times a too rapid pace separates us from the masses; and on occasion the pace is slow, and we feel on our necks the breath of those who follow at our heels. Our ambition as revolutionaries makes us try to move forward as far as possible, opening up the way before us, but we know that must be reinforced by the mass, while the mass will be able to advance more rapidly if we encourage it by our example.

In spite of the importance given to moral incentives, the existence of two principal groups (excluding, of course, the minority fraction of those who do not participate for one reason or another in the building of socialism) is an indication of the relative lack of development of social consciousness. The vanguard group is ideologically more advanced than the mass; the latter is acquainted with the new values, but insufficiently. While in the former a qualitative change takes place that permits them to make sacrifices as a function of their vanguard character, the latter sees only by halves and must be subjected to incentives and pressures of some intensity; it is the dictatorship of the proletariat being exercised not only on the defeated class but also individually on the victorious class.

To achieve total success, all of this involves the necessity of a series of mechanisms, the revolutionary institutions. The concept of institutionalization fits in with the images of the multitudes marching toward the future as that of a harmonic unit of canals, steps, and well-oiled apparatuses that make the march possible, that permit the natural selection of those who are destined to march in the vanguard and who dispense rewards and punishments to those who fulfill their duty or act against the society under construction.

The institutionality of the Revolution has still not been achieved. We are seeking something new that will allow a perfect identification between the government and the community as a whole, adapted to the special conditions of the building of socialism and avoiding to the utmost the commonplaces of bourgeois democracy transplanted to the society in formation (such as legislative houses, for example). Some experiments have been carried out with the aim of gradually creating the institutionalization of the Revolution, but without too much hurry. We have been greatly restrained by the fear that any formal aspect might make us lose sight of the ultimate and most important revolutionary aspiration: to see man freed from alienation.

Notwithstanding the lack of institutions, which must be overcome gradually, the masses now make history as a conscious aggregate of individuals who struggle for the same cause. In spite of the apparent standardization of man in socialism, he is more complete; his possibilities for expressing himself and making himself heard in the social apparatus are infinitely greater in spite of the lack of a perfect mechanism to do so.

It is still necessary to accentuate his conscious—individual and collective—participation in all the mechanisms of direction and production, and associate it with the idea of the need for technical and ideological education so that the individual will realize that these processes are closely interdependent and their advances are parallel. He will thus achieve total awareness of his social being, which is equivalent to his full realization as a human being, having broken the chains of alienation.

This will be translated concretely into the reappropriation of his nature through freed work and the expression of his own human condition in culture and art.

In order for it to develop in culture, work must acquire a new condition; man as commodity ceases to exist, and a system is established that grants a quota for the fulfillment of social duty. The means of production belong to society, and the machine is only the front line where duty is performed. Man begins to free his thought from the bothersome fact that presupposed the need to satisfy his animal needs by working. He begins to see himself portrayed in his work and to understand its human magnitude through the created object, through the work carried out. This no longer involves leaving a part of his being in the form of labor power sold, which no longer belongs to him; rather it signifies an emanation from himself, a contribution to the life of society in which he is reflected, the fulfillment of his social duty.

We are doing everything possible to give work this new category of social duty and to join it to the development of technology, on the one hand, which will provide the conditions for greater freedom, and to voluntary work on the other, based on the Marxist concept that man truly achieves his full human condition when he produces without being compelled by the physical necessity of selling himself as a commodity.

It is clear that work still has coercive aspects even when it is voluntary: Man has still not transformed all the coercion surrounding him into conditioned reflexes of a social nature, and in many cases he still produces under the pressure of the environment. (Fidel calls this moral compulsion.) He is still to achieve complete spiritual recreation in the presence of his own work—without the direct pressure of the social environment but bound to it by new habits. That will be communism.

The change in consciousness does not come about automatically, just as it does not come about automatically in the economy. The variations are slow and not rhythmic; there are periods of acceleration, others are measured, and some even involve a retreat.

We must also consider, as we have pointed out previously, that we are not before a pure transition period such as that envisioned by Marx in the *Critique of the Gotha Program* but rather a new phase not foreseen by him: the first period in the transition to communism or in the building of socialism.

Elements of capitalism are present within this process, which takes place in the midst of violent class struggle. These elements obscure the complete understanding of the essence of the process.

If to this be added the scholasticism that has held back the development of Marxist philosophy and impeded the systematic treatment of the period, whose political economy has still not been developed, we must agree that we are still in diapers. We must study all the primordial features of the period before elaborating a more far-reaching economic and political theory.

The resulting theory will necessarily give pre-eminence to the two pillars of socialist construction: the formation of the new human being and the development of technology. We still have a great deal to accomplish in both aspects, but the delay is less justifiable as far as the conception of technology as the basis is concerned: Here, it is not a matter of advancing blindly but of following for a sizable stretch the road opened up by the most advanced countries of the world. This is why Fidel harps so insistently on the necessity of the technological and scientific formation of all of our people and especially of the vanguard.

In the field of ideas that lead to nonproductive activities, it is easier to see the division between material and spiritual needs. For a long time, man has been trying to free himself from alienation through culture and art. He dies daily in the eight and more hours during which he performs as a commodity to resuscitate in his spiritual creation. But this remedy itself bears the germs of the same disease: He is a solitary being who seeks communion with nature. He defends his environment-oppressed individuality and reacts to aesthetic ideas as a unique being whose aspiration is to remain immaculate.

It is only an attempt at flight. The law of value is no longer a mere reflection of production relations; the monopoly capitalists have surrounded it with a complicated scaffolding that makes of it a docile servant, even when the methods used are purely empirical. The artist must be educated in the kind of art imposed by the superstructure. The rebels are overcome by the apparatus, and only exceptional talents are able to create their own work. The others become shame-faced wage-workers, or they are crushed.

Artistic experimentation is invented and taken as the definition of freedom, but this "experimentation" has limits that are imperceptible until they are clashed with, that is, when the real problems of man and his alienated condition are dealt with. Senseless anguish or vulgar pastimes are comfortable safety valves for human uneasiness; the idea of making art a weapon of denunciation and accusation is combated.

If the rules of the game are respected, all honors are obtained —the honors that might be granted to a pirouetting monkey. The condition is not attempting to escape from the invisible cage.

When the Revolution took power, the exodus of the totally domesticated took place; others, revolutionaries or not, saw a new road. Artistic experimentation took on new force. However, the routes were more or less traced, and the concept of flight was the hidden meaning behind the word freedom. This attitude, a reflection in consciousness of bourgeois idealism, was frequently maintained in the revolutionaries themselves.

In countries that have gone through a similar process, endeavors were made to combat these tendencies with an exaggerated dogmatism. General culture became something like a taboo, and a formally exact representation of nature was proclaimed as the height of cultural aspirtion. This later became a mechanical representation of social reality created by wishful thinking: the ideal society, almost without conflict or contradictions, that man was seeking to create.

Socialism is young and makes mistakes. We revolutionaries often lack the knowledge and the intellectual audacity to face the task of the development of the new human being by the methods different from the conventional society that created them (once again the topic of the relation between form and content appears). Disorientation is great, and the problems of material construction absorb us. There are no artists of great authority who also have great revolutionary authority.

The men of the party must take this task upon themselves and seek the achievement of the principal aim: to educate the people.

What is then sought is simplification, what everyone understands, that is, what the functionaries understand. True artistic experimentation is obliterated, and the problem of general culture is reduced to the assimilation of the socialist present and the dead (and therefore not dangerous) past. Socialist realism is thus born of the foundation of the art of the last century.

But the realistic art of the nineteenth century is also class art, perhaps more purely capitalist than the decadent art of the twentieth century in which the anguish of alienated man shows through. In culture, capitalism has given all that it had to give, and all that remains of it is the foretaste of a bad-smelling corpse—in art, its present decadence. But why endeavor to seek in the frozen forms of socialist realism the only valid recipe? "Freedom" cannot be set against socialist realism, because the former does not yet exist: It will not come into being until the complete development of the new society. But let us not attempt to condemn all post-midnineteenth-century art forms from the ponitfical throne of "realism at all costs." That would mean committing the Proudhonian error of the return to the past, and straitjacketing the artistic expression of the man who is born and being formed today.

An ideological and cultural mechanism must be developed that will permit experimentation and clear out the weeds that shoot up so easily in the fertilized soil of state subsidization.

The error of mechanical realism has not appeared (in Cuba), rather the contrary. This is so because of the lack of understanding of the need to create a new human being who will represent neither nineteenth-century ideas nor those of our decadent and morbid century. It is the twenty-first century man whom we must create, although this is still a subjective and unsystematic aspiration. This is precisely one of the basic points of our studies and work; to the extent that we make concrete achievements on a theoretical base or vice-versa, that we come to broad theoretical conclusions on the basis of our concrete studies, we will have made a valuable contribution to Marxism-Leninism, to the cause of mankind.

The reaction against nineteenth-century man has brought a recurrence of twentieth-century decadence. It is not a very serious error, but we must overcome it so as not to leave the doors open to revisionism.

The large multitudes of people are developing themselves, the new ideas are acquiring an adequate impetus within society, the material possibilities of the integral development of each and every one of its members make the task ever more fruitful. The present is one of struggle; the future is ours.

To sum up, the fault of many of our intellectuals and artists is to be found in their "original sin": They are not authentically revolutionary. We can attempt to graft elm trees so they bear pears, but at the same time we must plant pear trees. The new generations will arrive free of "original sin." The likelihood that exceptional artists will arise will be that much greater because of the enlargement of the cultural field and the possibilities for expression. Our job is to keep the present generation, maladjusted by its conflicts, from becoming perverted and perverting the new generations. We do not want to create salaried workers docile to official thinking or "fellows," who live under the wing of the budget, exercising freedom in quotation marks. Revolutionaries will come to sing the song of the new man with the authentic voice of the people. It is a process that requires time.

In our society, the youth and the party play a big role. The former is particularly important because it is the malleable clay with which the new man, without any of the previous defects, can be formed.

Youth receives treatment in consonance with our aspirations. Education is increasingly integral, and we do not neglect the incorporation of the students into work from the very beginning. Our scholarship students do physical work during vacation or together with their studies. In some cases, work is a prize, while in others it is an educational tool; it is never a punishment. A new generation is being born.

The Party is a vanguard organization. The best workers are proposed by their comrades for membership. The Party is a minority, but the quality of its cadres gives it great authority. Our aspiration is that the Party become a mass one, but only when the masses reach the level of development of the vanguard, that is, when they are educated for communism. Our work is aimed at providing that education. The party is the living example; its cadres must be full professors of assiduity and sacrifice; with their acts, they must lead the masses to the end of the revolutionary task, which means years of struggle against the difficulties of construction, the class enemies, the defects of the past, imperialism.

I should now like to explain the role played by the personality, the man as the individual who leads the masses that make history. This is our experience and not a recipe.

Fidel gave impulse to the Revolution in its first years. He has always given it leadership and set the tone, but there is a good group of revolutionaries developing in the same direction as Fidel and a large mass that follows its leaders because it has faith in them. It has faith in them because these leaders have known how to interpret the longings of the masses.

It is not a question of how many kilograms of meat are eaten or how many pretty imported things can be bought with present wages. It is rather that the individual feels greater fulfillment, that he has greater inner wealth and many more responsibilities. In our country, the individual knows that the glorious period in which it has fallen to him to live is one of sacrifice; he is familiar with sacrifice.

The first came to know it in the Sierra Maestra and wherever there was fighting; later we have known it in all Cuba. Cuba is the vanguard of America and must make sacrifices because it occupies the advance position, because it points out to the Latin American masses the road to full freedom.

Within the country, the leaders have to fulfill their vanguard role; and it must be said with complete sincerity that in a true revolution, to which you give yourself completely without any thought for material retribution, the task of the vanguard revolutionary is both magnificent and anguishing.

Let me say, with the risk of appearing ridiculous, that the true revolutionary is guided by strong feelings of love. It is impossible to think of an authentic revolutionary without this quality. This is perhaps one of the great dramas of a leader; he must combine an impassioned spirit with a cold mind and make painful decisions without flinching. Our vanguard revolutionaries must idealize their love for the people, for the most hallowed causes, and make it one and indivisible. They cannot descend, with small doses of daily affection, to the terrain where ordinary men put their love into practice.

The leaders of the Revolution have children who do not learn to call their father with their first faltering words; they have wives who must be part of the general sacrifice of their lives to carry the Revolution to its destination; their friends are strictly limited to their comrades in revolution. There is no life outside the Revolution.

In these conditions the revolutionary leaders must have a large dose of humanity, a large dose of a sense of justice and truth, to avoid falling into dogmatic extremes, into cold scholasticism, into isolation from the masses. They must struggle every day so that their love of living humanity is transformed into concrete deeds, into acts that will serve as an example, as a mobilizing factor.

The revolutionary, ideological motor of the Revolution within his party, is consumed by this uninterrupted activity that ends only with death, unless construction be achieved on a world-wide scale. If his revolutionary eagerness becomes dulled when the most urgent tasks are carried on a local scale, and if he forgets about proletarian internationalism, the revolution that he leads ceases to be a driving force and it sinks into a comfortable drowsiness that is taken advantage of by imperialism, our irreconcilable enemy, to gain ground. Proletarian internationalism is a duty, but it is also a revolutionary need. This is how we educate our people.

It is evident that there are dangers in the present circumstances—not only that of dogmatism, not only that of the freezing up of relations with the masses in the midst of the great task; there also exists the danger of weaknesses in which it is possible to incur. If a man thinks that in order to devote his entire life to the Revolution he cannot be distracted by the worry that one of his children lacks a certain article, that the children's shoes are in poor condition, that his family lacks some necessary item—with this reasoning, the seeds of future corruption are allowed to filter through.

In our case, we have maintained that our children must have, or lack, what the children of the ordinary citizen have or lack; our family must understand this and struggle for it. The Revolution is made by man, but man must forge his revolutionary spirit from day to day.

Thus we go forward. Fidel is at the head of the immense column—we are neither ashamed nor afraid to say so—followed by the best party cadres, and right after them, so close that their great strength is felt, come the people as a whole, a solid bulk of individualities moving toward a common aim—individuals who have achieved the awareness of what must be done; men who struggle to leave the domain of necessity and enter that of freedom.

That immense multitude is ordering itself; its order responds to an awareness of the need for order; it is no longer a dispersed force, divisible in thousands of fractions shot into space like the fragments of a grenade, trying by any and all means, in a fierce struggle with their equals, to achieve a position that would give them support in the face of an uncertain future.

We know that we have sacrifices ahead of us and that we must pay a price for the heroic fact of constituting a vanguard as a nation. We, the leaders, know that we must pay a price for having the right to say that we are at the head of the people that is at the head of America.

Each and every one of us punctually pays his share of sacrifice, aware of being rewarded by the satisfaction of fulfilling our duty, aware of advancing with everyone toward the new human being who is to be glimpsed on the horizon.

Allow me to attempt to come to some conclusions:

We socialists are more free because we are more fulfilled. We are more fulfilled because we are more free.

The skeleton of our complete freedom is formed, but it lacks the protean substance and the draperies. We will create them.

Our freedom and its daily sustenance are the color of blood and swollen with sacrifice.

EPILOGUE

To Create Wealth with Social Conscience

FIDEL CASTRO

Guests:
Citizens of Las Villas:
Workers:

This year the time of this rally has been changed. Previously it was held at five in the afternoon. But we said to ourselves, this is the month of July, a very hot month; these huge rallies are attended by persons from all over the province, many of whom must travel great distances to get here. And we have observed that on many occasions tens of thousands of persons waited all day for the rally to begin, putting up with the oppressive heat. And we noticed that there were always cases of people fainting from the heat.

It would seem that not many persons have fainted today from the heat. Perhaps it's because the comrades of the Youth Centennial Column are in good training and none of them has fainted.

This commemoration rally has been scheduled for an early hour, for nine in the morning—daylight saving time—which would be eight o'clock standard time. Fine, there hasn't been much heat, but most of the people here have not had any sleep.

Translation of this transcript made by the Revolutionary government's department of stenographic transcriptions.

I don't think anyone here has slept, neither you nor us. But perhaps someone will fall asleep during this rally.

But I recall that fifteen years ago—on July 26, 1953—no one slept all day. Well, that day the soldiers in the garrison were asleep! But the revolutionaries didn't sleep that day. That was more or less the way—after hours of fatigue, hours without rest—we met at dawn on that July 26.

The people of Santa Clara, or Las Villas—as you prefer to call it—have, as always, on this July 26 come to this ceremony in vast numbers. We probably would not be far from the truth if we said that this rally is even larger than the one held here three years ago, in 1965, even though everything possible was done to persuade comrades from other provinces to refrain from organizing excursions to the province of Las Villas, from planning trips here. For it is true that in the provinces of Havana, Matanzas, Pinar del Rio, and Oriente there is always a great deal of enthusiasm for mobilizing for these rallies.

But it must be pointed out that these rallies are enormous in size. It must be pointed out that those who take part in these rallies have to make very great efforts. There are a great many vehicles and other means of transportation involved. There are often many accidents. Although, fortunately, this July 26—according to the reports from the comrades of the Party in this province—there was only one accident, in which one person was slightly injured. This is the only accident that has occurred, and let us hope that when you all return to your respective homes you will do so in as orderly a manner and as carefully as you came, so that we will not have to regret that lives were lost during this commemoration or that other misfortunes occurred. We have often thought about the significance of these gatherings. We have frequently asked ourselves why such large rallies should be held. Generally these huge rallies—although it must be stressed that this time the discipline of the crowds has been truly exemplary—are not the best places for reasoning things out. Often in a smaller gathering it is possible to converse, to discuss, to reason more clearly than in these large rallies, where it is sometimes very hard to do so. We have frequently wondered if it is proper for the Revolution to hold so many huge rallies.

Of course, we always have a great many guests from all over the world present for these celebrations. It is possible that for them a huge popular rally of our people is a demonstration of the force of the Revolution, although actually the Revolution does not need to demonstrate its force, and all those who have enough sensitivity to understand the phenomenon of a revolution have no need of such proof. Needless to say, our people do not need it, either.

OUR PEOPLE ARE VERY AWARE OF THEIR OWN STRENGTH

The fact is that our people are very aware of their own strength. However, the tradition of holding rallies on January 1st, on May Day, and on the 26th of July has gone on through the years.

On the way to Las Villas we spoke with Party comrades in the province of Matanzas. They told us they had a problem. The anniversary of the Federation of Cuban Women was coming up soon, at the same time that the anniversary of the Young Communist League was coming up. And at about the same time there was the rally for the Committees for the Defense of the Revolution, in the month of April. And, in addition, we are going to celebrate the Centennial, which in my opinion, is undoubtedly our nation's most important rally of the year. They felt they were going to have to dedicate a great deal of time to this and that they were going to have a lot of work. So what can be done about this? How can the number of rallies be reduced? And naturally each sector and each organization has made every effort to make those meetings as brilliant as possible.

You may wonder why I have brought all this up. And I say this because I am really proposing that in the future we not have so many rallies each year, that in the future we have one or two, or at first two and later one. We shall always have to have at least one. It is the same as with the military parades. You will recall that in the first days of the Revolution, when our first military units were organized, when our militia was organized, we had a parade on January 1st, a parade on May Day, a parade on the 26th of July, and so we had constant parades. Afterwards they were limited to January 1st. But these parades required the expending of a great deal of time, and the tanks damaged the streets, and so we reached the wise conclusion that the best thing was to have a parade every three years, or very five years, or if possible at even longer intervals.

Next January 1st marks the tenth anniversary of the triumph of the rebellion—not the triumph of the Revolution, but the triumph of the rebellion of our people—and logically, this January 1st we shall possibly have to hold a military parade.

Today we commemorate a fifteenth anniversary. As a rule, a fifteenth anniversary is always commemorated: traditionally, our girls celebrate their fifteenth birthdays; fifth, tenth anniversaries, etc., are always specially commemorated. On this occasion, the Revolution also commemorates the fifteenth anniversary of the attack on the Moncada Garrison.

Fifteen years have elapsed, and now we ask ourselves: "Is this a long time? A short time? . . ." What do you think? Fifteen years of revolution, 15 years of struggle? Certainly, it is a short time.

Well, then: the changes that have taken place during these few years, are they many or few? Many changes!

Does our country, by chance, resemble at all the country we had 15 years ago?

You say no, but many of you are only seventeen years old—those who are here in the front row—or sixteen, and I have no doubt that some of you among the members of the Centennial Column are fifteen, and perhaps some of you were not born yet on the 26th of July 1953. Then why do you say there is a great difference? Oh, because you have read it! And to have read it and to have experienced it, is it the same thing? Possibly your parents know it better because they experienced it.

Anyway, it is not always necessary to have experienced a thing in order to know it. But those of you who were old enough to register anything will surely remember many things about which at the time you, young people, did not have the slightest inkling, and, above all, you will recall what our country was like, what our people were like, a humble man or woman of the people, what a worker represented, what a student represented, and who were students.

Of course, things existed in the past that we have not experienced, either. But sometimes, touring the countryside in many places—in Matanzas Province, for example—we have come upon dark and sinister ruins where the slaves who did the work during the last century lived in chains. Those ruins give us an idea of how man lived in those times, and give us an idea of the extent to which man was capable of exploiting and enslaving man, of the extent to which man—in his selfishness, in his privileges and in his class interests—was capable of inhuman acts and was capable of treating his fellow men like beasts and sometimes worse than beasts.

A FORM OF VIRTUAL SLAVERY WITH INVISIBLE CHAINS, WHICH AT TIMES WERE WORSE THAN THOSE WORN BY THE EARLY SLAVES

When slavery disappeared—and it began to disappear precisely on that historic day of October 10th when those who initiated the armed struggle decreed the freedom of the slaves, slaves who made up a very important part of our army of liberation and struggled for our independence for 30 years—that form of slavery was replaced by another which was not based on the form of slavery in which a man was enchained, but nevertheless constituted a form of virtual slavery with invisible chains, which at times were worse than those worn by the early slaves.

And we still have left in our country many, many vestiges of that past, of that shameful past, of that past of injustices, of that past of abuses, of that past of exploitation, of that past of crime, from which we inherited so much ignorance, from which we inherited so much poverty, so much misery, which left us an underdeveloped and poor country, which left us—as the comrade who spoke here in the name of the students recalled—a million illiterates, which left us an inheritance of 700,000 unemployed; those painful days in which men had to stand in endless lines to get a 10-day job, or to work 20 days or a month; those times in which, in order to find a common laborer's job in road construction, a worker had to have piles of references, he had to bring a letter from a political boss, a ward boss, and he had to pledge part of the money he was going to earn in order to have a right to work there, to make a living.

What a difference between those times and these, in which all the people, intensively at work, find that their hands are not sufficient, that the hands of men and women, of young and old, of students, are not enough for the huge tasks we have to carry out, and that we need machines, we need airplanes, we need chemistry, in order to carry out the tasks that will permit our country to eradicate poverty and the backwardness of centuries inherited by our people at the triumph of the rebellion.

We must say with profound satisfaction that few things can give us—all of us who have gone through this process—more satisfaction than that statement, that declaration containing the thought of our students, containing the thought of our youth; because certainly our youth has had much to do with this revolutionary process; the students had much to do with our revolutionary process.

And the fact that the students in our country, all the students in the centers of learning—in the technological institutes, in the junior high schools, in the high schools and in the universities—have discussed and approved these points and have given a magnificent expression to this statement indicates that this Revolution has already begun to reap the fruit, the most lasting fruit, which is the fruit developing from the conscience of a people, from the conscience of our youth.

Because the Revolution . . . the great task of the Revolution is basically the task of forming the new man of whom we spoke here, the new man of whom Che spoke, the man of a truly revolutionary conscience, the man of a truly socialist conscience, the man of a truly communist conscience.

And when we reach the point where our young people are capable of such deep thought, when our young people are capable of expressing themselves correctly on all these questions, when our young people are capable of such profound meditation and analysis, and when they reach these conclusions and in these conclusions categorically express their conscience of young people who really want to live in a communist society, it is then that we can be completely sure of the fact that the effort in favor of liberation which began one hundred years ago and which marked a milestone 15 years ago, on that morning of July 26, 1953, when many young men like them gave their lives for the future of their country, gave their lives for the Revolution.

THERE IS NO PERSON OR THING ON EARTH THAT CAN MAKE THIS REVOLUTIONARY PROCESS RETREAT!

And we can certainly say, with complete assurance, that there is no person or thing on earth that can make this revolutionary process retreat! There will be nothing and no one that can hold back this revolutionary process! Because its strength stems not just from the number of men and women who defend it, from the mass of people who support it, from the formidable weapons which we have to fight with in a war, but basically from the degree to which it has taken root in the people's conscience, from the very high degree to which it has become the conscience of the people. And when a whole people takes up a cause, an idea, there is no force in the world capable of destroying it.

It is not the attitude of a nation of fanatics, it is not the attitude of a people accustomed to blindly taking orders, of people who do things because they are told to, because they are ordered to or because it is demanded of them. This is the attitude of people who really do things because they understand them, because they grasp them, because they want to do them.

And this morning our youth have expressed the essence, the core of Cuban revolutionary thought. There have been many revolutions throughout history, but the socialist revolutions are the most profound.

Every people, every nation, has its way of making its revolution; every people, every nation, has its way of interpreting revolutionary ideas. We do not pretend to be the most perfect revolutionaries. We do not pretend to be the most perfect interpreters of Marxist-Leninist ideas, but we do have our way of interpreting these ideas; we have our way of interpreting socialism, our way of interpreting Marxism-Leninism, our way of interpreting communism.

No human society has yet reached communism. The ways along which a superior form of society is reached are very difficult. A communist society means that man will have reached the highest degree of social awareness ever achieved; a communist society means that the human being will have been able to achieve the degree of understanding and brotherhood which man has sometimes achieved within the close circle of his family. To live in a communist society is to live in a real society of brothers; to live in a communist society is to live without selfishness, to live among the people and with the people, as if every one of our fellow citizens were really our brother.

Man comes from capitalism full of selfishness; man is educated under capitalism amidst the most vicious selfishness, as an enemy of other men, as a wolf to other men.

The students here expressed the idea that communism and socialism will be built simultaneously, and that idea and the expression of that idea have led to the situation where Cuban revolutionaries have been described as wishful thinkers; have led some people to say that these are petty bourgeois ideas; have led some people to say that this is an erroneous interpretation of Marxist-Leninist ideas, that it is not possible to build communism if socialism is not achieved first and that in order to build socialism it is necessary to develop the material base of socialism. We do not deny this last point.

In the very essence of Marxist thought, socialist society and communist society must be based on a thorough mastery of technology, on the complete development of the productive forces, so that man may be able to create material goods in such quantities that everyone may be able to satisfy his needs.

It is unquestionable that the Middle Ages society, with its minimal development of the productive forces, could not have aspired to live under communism; it is very clear that the old society, with even more backward and poor productive forces, could have aspired even less to live under communism; and communism arises as a possibility of man's control: a full command of nature, a full command of the processes of material-goods production.

A PERSON ASPIRING TO LIVE UNDER COMMUNISM MUST DO WHAT WE ARE DOING

And of course a people aspiring to live under communism must do what we are doing. It must emerge from underdevelopment. It must develop its productive forces. It must have a command of technology in order to be able to turn man's efforts and man's sweat into the miracle of producing practically unlimited quantities of material goods.

If we do not acquire a complete command of technology, if we do not develop our productive forces, we will deserve to be called dreamers for aspiring to live in a communist society.

The question from our point of view, is that communist awareness must be developed at the same rate as the productive forces; an advance in the conscientiousness of revolutionaries; in the conscientiousness of the people, must accompany every step forward in the development of the productive forces.

Communism is often defined by the simple formula: from each according to his ability, and to each according to his needs.

A good part of our people, an ever-growing part. . . . For example, our students. It was said here that there are already over 200,000 young people with full and partial scholarships. These 200,000 young people receive—free of charge—room, board, clothing, medical care, recreation, and books—that is, each person receives what he or she needs. And, if they do not receive more, it is because there is no more to give; if they receive two shirts a year, it is because there are only two shirts to give; if they get two pairs of shoes, it's because there are only two pairs; if there is only one, they get only one, which is what we have. Today they get one, but tomorrow they will get three, and in the future they will get four or five, as many as they need.

We deeply regret that the amount of dry goods available to our country is not sufficient to give the students, for example, and all of our people, the number of square meters of cloth which we know they need, that the materials available to our country are not sufficient to distribute the number of pairs of shoes that we know they need. The Revolution cannot give what it doesn't have, but what it does have, it distributes in the fairest way. For example, we give our students what we are able to give. We cannot give the students more shirts, because we would have to take them away from a worker, we would have to take them away from other people. But the fact of the matter is that, whatever we have, our students receive it in an egalitarian manner.

Some of our students are in very modern schools, while others live in very poor student lodgings. Why? Because we do not have enough dormitories. But there is no doubt that some day there won't be a single student in this country who is not housed in a dormitory and who does not attend a school with the best possible hygienic conditions and, in general, with the very best facilities for carrying out all his activities.

Be that as it may, the fact remains that hundreds of thousands of young people for all intents and purposes live in a communist way in our society.

Our day nurseries care for tens of thousands of children. And these day nurseries are a service that is rendered without charge and where the children receive all that our country has to give them. Without doubt, the children are living there in a communist way.

THE REVOLUTION WILL NEVER SPARE ANY EXPENSE IN SAVING A LIFE!

In our country medical care is free. The Revolution has built dozens of hospitals, and when any citizen requires this service, he does not have to pay, no matter who he is and no matter what the service may cost. The Revolution will never spare any expense in saving a life, the Revolution will never spare any expense in providing any person who has an on-the-job accident or any other kind of accident with the facilities for recovering his physical capacity. That is, society as a whole is responsible for the health of its citizens.

We know of many cases, of many people who have required very costly services in our hospitals, and they have felt calm and secure in the knowledge that they were in the best hospitals, getting the best care, the best treatment, and being cared for by the best doctors; this gives all our citizens a great feeling of security. That security did not exist before. Before, the patient had to pay; he had to pay a monthly payment to belong to an association; he had to lay out large sums of money. And the few public health services that existed in our country were very poor in quality; they were scandalously deficient. That is capitalism. That is capitalist society.

However, in a communist society health is conceived of as a sacred right of all citizens, a right which society—with all its resources—must make a reality.

Before, it was the same with education. No worker's son at a sugar mill, on a sugarcane latifundium, in a small town or even in a big town was able to study. Most children, if they went to school at all, went to school for one or two grades. If they were supposed to go on to higher education, they were unable to do so, because they had to pay for the schooling itself or go to live in a boarding house, and, naturally, 90 percent of the country's families could not afford such expenses.

However, the Revolution feels that every child has the right to study—not only the right but also the duty. And the right and duty to study not only two or three years, but six years. And now we are already thinking of the right and the duty to study up to thirteen years in school, with military training included in our study programs. These young people don't have to be rich or the sons of rich people. It doesn't matter how much their parents earn. All of society offers them that precious opportunity, that extraordinary possibility. And that is communism! Communism exists when society, considered as a whole, with all its resources, makes itself responsible for the education of each citizen, makes itself responsible for the health of each citizen, for the well-being of each citizen, and all of society—classes having disappeared, inequality having disappeared—works for each and all of its citizens.

In the past, the capitalists slandered revolutionary ideas, reviled communism. Nevertheless, that society, that way of life—in which no young person had a chance, in which even the sick were forsaken, in which each man was an alienated, desperate being, left to shift for himself in the midst of a society of wolves—can in no way be compared to what a communist society really means in the realm of human relations, social relations. We aspire to achieving that communist society in absolutely all ways some day. Our aspiration is that, just as books are distributed now to those who need them, just as medicines and medical services are distributed to those who need them, education to those who need it, so we shall progressively reach the day when food will be distributed in the necessary amounts to those who need it, clothing and shoes will be distributed in the necessary amounts to those who need them. We certainly aspire to a way of life—apparently utopian for many—in which man will not need money to satisfy his needs for food, clothing and recreation, just as today no one needs money for medical attention or for his education. Because nobody takes money to a hospital; nobody takes money to a senior high school; nobody takes money to a scholarship school; nobody takes money to a sports event.

Before, we had to take money to go to a baseball game. Since sports events have been made free to the public, nobody has needed to take a dime to go to a baseball game or to go to any sports event, and the world has not come to an end because of this. All this was made easier; all this was made simpler. Society has eliminated the need for many ticket-takers, many accountants, many administrators who did nothing but count money, receive money, make change, and give out tickets. Who benefited when payment for sports events was eliminated? The people benefited; everyone benefited!

Unfortunately, all this cannot be done in a day; this cannot be done with everything at once.

This is a long road. We can advance along that road to the extent that we develop our productive forces, to the extent that we develop our productivity, to the extent that we develop our productive processes.

THE DAY WILL COME WHEN IT WILL NOT BE NECESSARY TO PAY FARE TO TRAVEL FROM ONE PLACE TO ANOTHER

The day will come when it will not be necessary to pay fare to travel from one place to another. We have another interesting example in the case of bus fares. There was a conductor on every bus in this country; thousands of men were devoted to collecting fares. A system was set up, a system that could only be set up by a revolution, in which each passenger, fully aware of his obligation, deposits his own fare. The country recovered for its productive force thousands of workers who, like the box-office attendants at sports events, had been utilized only for making change, giving out tickets and engaging in other such activities.

Logically, there are still many cases—and will be for many years, for a long time—in which it will not be possible to dispense with money, but it will have a different meaning: that of a simple instrument of distribution. For a long time our country will have to use this symbol that is money: money as a means of distribution, money as a measure of the amount of products or specified services that are to be received. But our Revolution's aspiration—and certainly it is not utopian—is to do more than merely change the role of money. Because the role of money in a capitalist society is that of an instrument of exploitation, an instrument for exploiting the work of others, an instrument for accumulating wealth. Naturally, money does not have nor can it have that meaning in our country. Since even the smallest street vendors' stands disappeared and private businesses were ended with the revolutionary offensive, money cannot be utilized as a means of individual enrichment by someone who sets up a street stand and buys twenty pesos' worth of bread and other things in the stores or on the black market to sell fifty, sixty or seventy pesos' worth of merchandise. Certainly when the Revolution suppressed private enterprise, it took an extraordinary step forward. There is now no one who can earn thirty times as much as a hard-working worker does. There is now no one who can earn, without sweating his shirt, thirty times as much as the one who sweats his shirt.

Why must money still exist to such a great extent? Why are there still so many prices that are high? Many times some people ask: "Why is this so high?" "Why is this service so high?" Let's say a restaurant. This question has been asked many times; this problem has been raised many times. If everybody earned the same amount, then a given price could be set and everyone would have the same chance to go to a restaurant; everyone would have the same chance to acquire many things. The fact is that in our country there are many inequalities of income, some of them quite considerable. Many people have an income which is much greater than that of others. There are some people who ask: "Why aren't wages equalized?" And we say it can't be done, because if the Revolution took this measure it would not achieve its objectives. The Revolution cannot equalize incomes overnight. The Revolution's aspiration is to arrive at equal incomes starting from the bottom up, not from the top down. It would be incorrect for the Revolution to do it the other way.

There are many people who are accustomed to a certain income, to certain activities, and, if the Revolution sought to equalize incomes from the top down, we are sure that the Revolution would run into many obstacles. By what method will the Revolution achieve equality of income? By increasing production and by gradually increasing the incomes of those who receive less money.

THE FIRST THING THE REVOLUTION WILL DO IS TO INCREASE THE OLD-AGE PENSIONS AND SURVIVORS' BENEFITS

A few days ago we said that the first thing the Revolution will do is to increase the old-age pensions and survivors' benefits until they reach the level of today's lowest wages. Likewise, once these levels are reached and our economy grows, the wages of those who earn less will be gradually increased. Thus, the Revolution will establish equality in incomes gradually, from the bottom up, keeping pace with the progress of our production.

That is, the Revolution aspires—as one of the steps toward communism—to equalize incomes, from the bottom up, for all workers, regardless of the type of work they do. This means this principle will surely be given a name by "learned," "experienced" economists—because we must say that the field of economic doctrines is quite full of "brainy," "learned" economists—who will claim this goes against Marxist-Leninist principles and against the laws of economics. The question is "which" economics: capitalist economics or socialist economics, the truly Marxist-Leninist economics or a mercantilist economics.

To these economists, an assertion of this type sounds like sheer heresy, and they say that the Revolution is headed for defeat. But it so happens that in this field there are two special branches. One is the branch of the "pure" economist, be he capitalist or socialist. In short, just a plain economist. But there is another science, a deeper science which is a truly revolutionary science. It is the science of revolutionary awareness; it is the science of faith in mankind; it is the science of confidence in human beings.

If we agreed that man is an incorrigible individual, that man can only make progress through egoism, through selfishness; if we agreed that man is incapable of learning; if we agreed that man is incapable of developing his conscience—then we would have to say that the "brainy" economists were right, that the Revolution would be headed for defeat and that it would be fighting the laws of economics.

But the actual fact is that the history of this Revolution has furnished us with many examples, repeated examples of the fact that those who were in error were those who did not believe in man, that those who made the mistake and failed were those who had no confidence in the peoples, who had no confidence in man's ability to attain and develop a revolutionary awareness.

In the past, those of us who proclaimed the revolutionary struggle, who proclaimed the need for a revolution, were told the same thing: that we were mistaken, that we were a bunch of dreamers and that we would fail.

This was what the politicians, the "savants" of politics, the "professors" of politics, the "brains" of politics, the leaders of the traditional, bourgeois parties, had to say. They did not believe in the people; they underestimated the people. They thought the people incapable of accomplishing anything. They thought of the people as an ignorant herd to be manipulated at their will. Those of you who are here today—especially those who are here as guests—and can take a good look at this enormous congregation of people which is the living expression of our Revolution's power, should not forget that only 15 years ago we were a small group of youngsters whom many considered dreamers, who had been told they would fail because it was impossible to make a revolution in a country only 90 miles from the United States, that it was impossible to make a revolution in a country of illiterate, ignorant people.

And yet, what is it that we see today? What has been the result of the effort begun 15 years ago by a small group of youngsters at that stage of our revolutionary history? How much has been accomplished by this people? How much has this unarmed people accomplished? How much has this people that they called ignorant, that they underestimated, that they considered lacking in every virtue, accomplished?

This was an unarmed people faced by an army equipped by the Yankee imperialists. This army was 50,000 strong, counting soldiers and police. They had all the weapons, while the people did not have any weapons. And yet, this people, the people the "savants" of politics scorned, this uneducated people, this people of illiterates, this people without weapons, took up the struggle, continued the struggle, defeated that army and disarmed that army; and it is this people that today has an army, a true army of the people, because it is the people in arms, and this army is ten, twenty times more powerful than that other army!

THE PEOPLE THEY SCORNED, THAT PEOPLE OF ILLITERATES, MADE A PROFOUND REVOLUTION, A DEEP REVOLUTION NEVER BEFORE MADE BY ANY COUNTRY IN AMERICA

And those of us who at that time spoke of this possibility were called failures, dreamers and wishful thinkers. But that is not all. The people they scorned, that people of illiterates, made a profound Revolution, a deep Revolution never before made by any country in America. And it made it right under the very nose of Yankee imperialism, the most powerful, most aggressive exponent of world reaction!

The imperialists, who also underestimated the peoples, were used to defeating revolutions; they were used to buying off revolutionary leaders with a few miserable dollars; they were used to crushing revolutions through the use of counterrevolutionary gangs or through invasions, using mercenary troops.

So what happened? What can we say today? That this people that only 15 years ago had no weapons, this people of illiterates, has waged one of the greatest revolutionary and political battles of modern times by uniting, developing its revolutionary awareness and building up its forces. And it has successfully resisted 10 years of aggressions, 10 years of economic blockade. And all the tricks, obstacles, maneuvers and resources of the imperialists have been unable to force this people into submission, to weaken this people, to crush the Revolution!

It is true that we were a people of one million illiterates, that we had few engineers, few doctors and few technicians. In their effort to make us fail, the imperialists did their best to leave us without doctors, without engineers and without technicians. They were not satisfied with having forced our people to remain ignorant; they tried to take away many of the few who had had an opportunity to attend our universities—and in many cases succeeded.

The imperialists have used every weapon against our country to keep our people from making any headway, to make our people fail, to make our economy fail. And what have they achieved? All their weapons and their resources have failed against our people.

And all the "experts," all the political brains, all those who thought this Revolution was impossible, what must they be thinking now? What do they have to say now? It must be very hard for them to accept that all of this is possible!

But, while these victorious struggles carried forward by our people were hard and difficult, the struggles they are carrying forward today, the struggle to win the battle against underdevelopment, this fight in the midst of the blockade, is—if possible—even harder and more difficult. The struggle to arrive at a higher form of social relationship is among the most difficult of struggles, one of the most difficult courses that any people can take.

And the certitude that we felt yesterday is the same that we feel—stronger than ever—today when we assert that this people, that with its awareness, revolutionary spirit and firmness, has been able to win such difficult battles, will also win, and is already winning, the battle of the economy and will also win the battle to attain a higher form of society.

We have set forth some ideas, a few ideas, in order to describe many of the things that our Revolution is doing today that are practically communist. I also explained that today it is materially impossible to do everything in a communist way.

ONE OF THE FIRST BATTLES IN THE MARCH TOWARD COMMUNISM IS TO MOVE PROGRESSIVELY UPWARD, LESSENING INCOME INEQUALITIES, MOVING TOWARD INCOME EGALITARIANISM

The basic social services: education, health, housing, sports, all those services that contribute to the development of the people in all spheres—the Revolution provides them today in a communist manner; but most material goods are still not distributed in a communist way; there are still many inequalities.

And one of the first battles in the march toward communism is to move progressively upward—I repeat, lessening income inequalities, moving toward income egalitarianism, toward income egalitarianism! This still does not mean communist distribution, but it will be a big step in the direction of that form of communist distribution.

We made this explanation thinking of the words of the students, how they said that the problem of payment is no longer discussed among the students. At first the students acted as teachers; they taught classes, and they received some payment; and the students progressively have been acquiring awareness, above all because many of them were scholarship students who received everything, and it made no sense that they who had received everything free, all that they needed to develop, should demand payment for giving a little of their efforts and knowledge to others. They have said that material incentives do not matter to them, that what does matter is the awareness of their duty, and that their behavior is not motivated, nor will it be motivated, by money; their acts are motivated not by material incentives, but by their conscience and their sense of duty. Does this mean that they give up what they need? No, of course not. Give up food, clothing, all that they need? No! What they are giving up is the method, the procedure based on material incentives. With this they express their confidence in the future, their confidence in the possibility of a communist society, their confidence in a society where all work for all and all receive what they need. They said that they were not going to work by the clock, but that their workday would be dictated by their conscience. They stated very well that our country must emerge from underdevelopment: they expressed the idea that our people have to work very hard in these years—as much as they possibly can, give or take a few hours. Some day—and that day will not be far off—at a surprisingly rapid pace, with the aid of technology, with the aid of machines, with the aid of chemistry, many of the hard jobs done by our people today will become unnecessary. In the not-too-distant future no one will have to cut cane with a machete, no one will have to weed a field with a hoe; no one will have to do those hard jobs that we have to do today, while we don't have those machines, while we don't have that technology to win the battle of underdevelopment. Our students expressed here ideas of high moral worth by giving voice to those opinions, to those thoughts, by unfurling those banners: the idea that each person work according to his conscience, and that work is not an individual tool with which to earn one's living but is rather the tool of the whole of society, not the resources of an individual. An individual alone can do nothing, an individual alone is very little, but an individual integrated into the strength of society is everything!

They expressed the opinion that the Revolution will not use the tool of material incentives as the instrument for raising productivity, for raising the level of accomplishment. Of course this does not mean that in our society all citizens—not by any means—have reached these levels of conscience; there are many who have achieved this, but there are many who still have not done so.

What this means is that they express the conviction that every day the awareness of our people will become more developed in the direction of communist mentality and attitudes.

Many workers have given up overtime pay; the extraordinary thing here is that workers who don't have very high incomes have given up overtime pay. That is really a sacrifice for many of our workers. Now, what must be done? What must we do in keeping with this? Ah, workers give up their overtime pay; we are going to raise the pensions of all who receive low pensions, those who have worked all their lives and are now old. Many workers have given up overtime pay? Fine! Then we have to take a step in keeping with this. For example, what step? When the worker becomes ill he does not get his full pay, and that is contrary to the development of conscience; when a person gets sick, you can assume he needs his income more than ever.

THE FAIREST THING, IN ALL THE WORK CENTERS WHERE THE WORKERS HAVE HAD THAT ATTITUDE WHEN ONE OF

THOSE WORKERS GETS SICK, NO MATTER FOR HOW LONG A TIME, IS FOR HIM TO RECEIVE ONE HUNDRED PERCENT OF HIS PAY

However, what happened? Old concepts, old opinions from other times prevailed. In our opinion, the fairest thing, in all the work centers where the workers have had that attitude, when one of those workers gets sick, no matter for how long a time, is for him to receive one hundred percent of his pay.

Unfortunately, in one way or another, many workers have labor accidents, accidents which sometimes cost their lives or cause partial disability or incapacity to do the work they were doing, and at such a moment, at that bitter moment, part of the wages they received is affected. In the same way, it is equally just that, in all those work centers which have attained the high level of political awareness that is represented by the revolutionary workday and renunciation of extra pay for extra hours, the workers should receive, in case of accident or disability, the complete amount of the wages they had been earning. And the benefits should also be extended, in case of death, to their dependents.

This example shows us that without the development of political awareness we cannot act as Communists. If the old, selfish concept is maintained—the more I work, the more I earn—then, when such a man gets sick, society has to pay him less; when that man is disabled, society has to give him less; when that man retires, society has to give him less. And on the basis of these concepts, of these incentives, man depends exclusively on himself, and society can do very little for him. A collective sense, a communist conscience, is not instilled.

In the same way, we believe that, now that a review of pensions and increases in pensions is to be undertaken, those workers in these vanguard work centers who have that awareness should, at the time of their retirement, also receive one hundred percent of the wages they were earning.

Could anything be considered more just, more humane? And

from where do the necessary resources come? From the communist spirit of our workers. Those resources spring from that communist spirit. And here we find a contradiction: money plays, and for a long time will still play, an important role in distribution. We mentioned the services that are already provided free of charge. Money will have less and less significance when nobody pays rent any longer—and the majority of our people already do not pay rent—when all children are granted scholarships or are in day nurseries or in day boarding schools. Families have begun to realize that many of the payments they had to make before now no longer exist; they are beginning to find that the money they cherished before, because it meant the health of their child, the bread of their child, the medicine of their child, the recreation of their child, the education of their child, is losing its meaning. They worshiped that money because it was the instrument that made all of those things possible.

Money continues to be used for other things, but for these things it is becoming increasingly unnecessary. To enjoy oneself, to take a trip, to drink a beer, for any of those things, all right; and people value these, but they value more the health of their child, the education of their child, the bread of their child, the roof over the head of their child. In other words, all the essential things, the things they value most and for which they sacrificed recreation, beer and all the rest, are no longer obtained with money.

Money will have less and less meaning. But it still plays an important role; the majority of the individual needs of the workers are still satisfied through money, and, as long as money plays that role, it is fair that those work centers which have proved their political awareness, those work centers that gave up extra pay for extra hours, that adopted the revolutionary workday, should receive from the community, from society, those things and those resources they were receiving in payment for their work, when they get sick, or have an accident, or retire.

And these examples we have given, which you all understand perfectly well, are sufficiently clear and illustrative of the meaning of a communist spirit.

THE WAY TO DO THIS IS NOT BY CREATING POLITICAL AWARENESS WITH WEALTH, BUT BY CREATING WEALTH WITH POLITICAL AWARENESS

And we should not use money or wealth to create political awareness. We must use political awareness to create wealth. To offer a man more to do more than his duty is to buy his conscience with money. To give a man participation in more collective wealth because he does his duty and produces more and creates more for society is to turn political awareness into wealth.

As we said before, communism, certainly, cannot be established if we do not create abundant wealth. But the way to do this, in our opinion, is not by creating political awareness with money or with wealth, but by creating wealth with political awareness and more and more collective wealth with more collective political awareness.

The road is not easy. The task is difficult and many will criticize us. They will call us petty bourgeois, idealists; they will say we are dreamers; they will say we are bound to fail. And yet, facts will speak for us, realities will speak for us and our people will speak and act for us, because we know our people have the capacity to comprehend these roads and to follow these roads.

In the same way, some day we will all have to receive the same. Why? Some will ask: will a cane-cutter earn as much as an engineer? Yes. Does that mean that an engineer will receive less? No. But some day a cane-cutter—and I say cane-cutter symbolically, because in the future we won't have any cane-cutters—let us say, the driver of a harvest combine or a truck, will earn as much as an engineer today.

And why? The thing is clear, very logical. The Revolution has thousands of young students in the universities. The Revolution has thousands of young people studying abroad, dedicated to studying, to becoming engineers, chemists, specializing in different fields. Who pays for their expenses? The people.

If the Revolution needs to send many young people to study

in Europe and others in universities, all right; we ask them to study, and they do it in a disciplined way, but that doesn't mean they are privileged. It is important to the Revolution that they study, that they prepare themselves. But at the same time that thousands of our young people study abroad, thousands of others have to go into the fields to plant cane, to weed cane, to do very hard work. Within a few years there will be much more wealth in our country. The former will have finished three, five years of studies and will have become technicians, engineers; and the latter will have been working those years in the fields, and they will not become engineers, but they will develop our economy, they will be building the future of our country.

Under what concept and in what way would it be just for us to tell these young people after a few years, in a more prosperous country, in a country with much more wealth: you are earning one fourth of an engineer's wages? Would it be just, would it be basically just, that those whom the country called on not to go to the university but to work to win the battle of the economy, to make the effort which at this time we cannot make with chemistry or with the machines which we do not have, but must make with our hands, with our sweat—would it be just, whenever the nation is able to enjoy the riches which they are creating now, for us to treat them as fourth- or fifth-class citizens, entitled to receive from society an insignificant part of what in the future will be received by those who are in the universities, those who are studying abroad?

COMMUNIST CONSCIENCE MEANS THAT IN THE FUTURE THE WEALTH THAT WE CREATE THROUGH EVERYBODY'S EFFORT SHOULD BE EQUALLY SHARED BY ALL

No! not at all. Communist conscience means that in the future the wealth that we create through everybody's effort should be equally shared by all. That is communism; that is communist conscience! And there will not be a single honest citizen, there will not be a single head of a family, there will not be a single person in this country with human sensitivity who will not be able to understand how just this concept is which our people defend, which our Revolution proclaims and which our students have made their watchword.

And it is encouraging that it is precisely our students, our future engineers, our future doctors, our future professors, our future technicians, who put these things forward, the first ones to proclaim these things. Logically, it is because of this that we have to feel optimistic, that we have to feel enthusiastic, that we have to have faith in the bright future of our country. Classes will disappear in our country, and once classes have disappeared the struggle between the Revolution and the counter-revolution will disappear. Because, in the future, who will remember those who dared to defend the past? Who will forgive those who one day shed the workers' and farmers' blood to defend that past; who will defend that imperialist system; who will forgive that imperialist system, which shed the blood of our youth, of our workers and of our farmers to stop the just march toward the future, to uphold that repugnant, immoral, selfish, shameful past which our youth will not even be able to imagine?

And that is why I do believe that these young people who were here in the front row—who were three, or two, or one year old, or babies, or unborn at the time of the attack on the Moncada—are capable, through reasoning, sensitivity, education and awareness, to have an idea about that past, even though they did not live through it, and to reach this high level they have attained. Because that is sacrifice, real sacrifice; that is heroism, real heroism! There is the heroism of the battle at the moment of danger, of the young man who generously gives his life, and there is the heroism of the revolutionary, creative work of the young man who offers his sweat, his hands, his time, who is capable of going over there to wage that battle for the future of the country.

Fortunately, we understand what we are doing; we understand what we want, how we want it and why we want it. And that is why, as the conscience of the people develops, the march of the Revolution will be faster, the march of the Revolution will be more victorious. We will have a lot of things to do in this country. A lot! We could say that a good part of them are still to be done: tens of thousands of kilometers of roads, hundreds of dams, and, in the next ten years, thousands of buildings, thousands of shops, thousands of schools, hundreds of large factories, factories for everything.

A few days ago we were speaking of the accelerated growth in our rice production, of the fact that, by 1971, we will not need to import rice. But more mills than we now have will be needed to process all the rice the nation is going to produce in 1970, more installations and plants than we now have will be needed to process all the coffee the country is going to produce in 1970 and many more pasteurizing and bottling plants than we now have will be needed to process the milk which will be produced in 1970, just as our sugar industry has had to be considerably enlarged throughout these years to make it possible to reach 10 million tons of sugar. This increase in the capacity of our sugar industry will be more or less equal to the capacity of 90 sugar mills of the average size in Matanzas Province; the growth of the industrial capacity of our sugar industry by 1970 will be equal to that of 90 sugar mills of the average size in Matanzas Province. Ninety sugar mills! That is, there are sugar mills which are doubling their capacity, there are sugar mills which are practically being rebuilt, and there are sugar mills which are more than doubling their capacity.

Our people will have to work very hard in the next few years, and our resources will have to be given over to this purpose.

THIS COUNTRY IS WINNING THE BATTLE
AGAINST UNDERDEVELOPMENT; THIS
COUNTRY IS WINNING THE BATTLE OF
THE ECONOMY; AND, WHAT IS MORE
IMPORTANT, THIS COUNTRY IS WINNING
THE BATTLE OF REVOLUTIONARY CONSCIENCE!

And this is true in every field. . . . In this same province the Siguaney cement plant is being completed—let us hope we have enough fuel to put it into full production. An excellent industrial plant has been built—the machine-building plant of Santa Clara. The INPUD (home appliances) factory has been built. But, unfortunately, it is operating far below capacity, due to a shortage of raw materials. A very up-to-date fertilizer plant is under construction in Cilenfuegos, a plant which will have an annual production of almost half a million tons of fertilizer. A huge bulk-sugar shipping terminal is being built which will save the labor of thousands of workers—that overwhelming, exhausting labor of the stevedore who must load 250- or 325-pound sacks—because in the future that work will be done by cranes and other equipment. So, our country must make great efforts.

Irrigation works must be developed in this province. In this province alone, 50 dams must be built, 50 dams so as to make use of all the water in this province, so that our agriculture will have supplies of no less than three thousand million cubic meters of water for irrigation.

Those of you who live in Las Villas Province know what droughts are. Last year there was a very severe drought. This year not a drop of rain fell during the first months of the year. When it began to rain, it rained a great deal—actually, too much. For this is one of the provinces which have had the greatest amount of rainfall since the month of May. There are periods of heavy rain, and then five or six months without irrigation, without water, with the disastrous results which all this means for agriculture.

Thus, we are developing irrigation works throughout the country. And for some weeks the equipment needed for these projects has been arriving in this province so that all the farmland in this province will be irrigated.

You can well imagine what this means for the nation's economy, what it means for productivity, what it represents in the way of agricultural yields, how we will be able to plant the year round and not have to wait for rain in order to plant everything in a month, when the weeds are also coming up, and all those problems which you know about.

I only want to stress that the years that lie ahead will be years of great effort, of tremendous work.

But our country is winning the battle against underdevelopment. Our country, faced with the criminal imperialist blockade, with all the damage it has caused us, with the burden of the additional hundreds of millions of pesos it has forced us to spend to acquire goods on various markets, transport such goods greater distances, make purchases under difficult conditions—all of which has cost this country hundreds of millions of pesos—in spite of all this, this country is winning the battle against underdevelopment; this country is winning the battle of the economy; and, what is more important, this country is winning the battle of revolutionary conscience!

What a magnificently just homage, what a magnificently just homage to the one who best symbolizes these ideas, the strongest defender of man's conscience as an instrument of development in the Revolution, that comrade who one day, through his audacity, courage and intelligence, won the battle of Santa Clara, the eternally beloved Comrade Ernesto Guevara!

And this 26th of July, on which our students make these watchwords their own, on which our people make these watchwords their own, with true pride, and filled with confidence in the future, we can say: Che, we dedicate this 15th anniversary of our Revolution to you!

Patria o Muerte
Venceremos!

Bertram Silverman is Professor of Economics at Hofstra University, Hempstead, New York. He presently lives in New York City with his wife, Evelyn, and his two daughters, Julie and Devorah.